OW I WOULD
ITCH TO
BABE RUTH

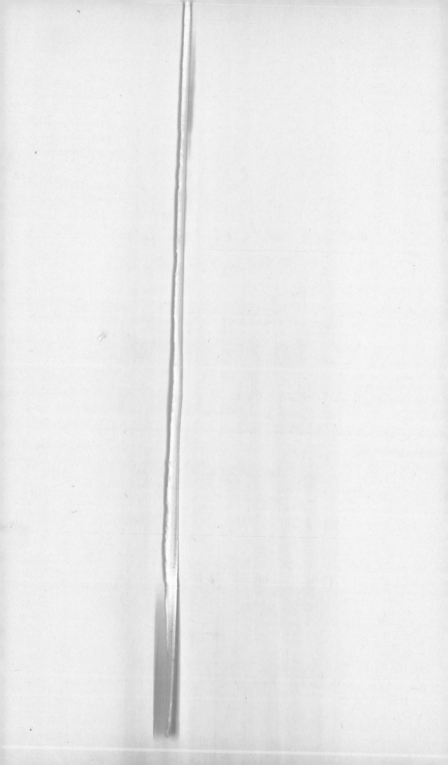

HOW I WOULD PITCH
TO BABE RUTH

HOW I WOULD PITCH TO BABE RUTH

Seaver vs. the Sluggers

written and edited by
TOM SEAVER

with *Norman Lewis Smith*

P✦P

A PLAYBOY PRESS BOOK

To the memory of Gil Hodges, the man who had the most influence on my professional career.

Contents

Preface

This is a book of great stories about great hitters. But not all the great hitters in baseball history are included. Jimmy Foxx, Mel Ott and Tris Speaker are three of the most obvious omissions. The reason you won't find them here is because we couldn't find good enough stories about them. Not all baseball stars were written about with as much talent as they deserved.

As a boy growing up in the '50s, I read as many magazine articles as any other young sports fanatic. But I wasn't very often impressed with what I read. It seemed that sports heroes were all leading the same lives: overcoming early hardships; being helped by understanding wives, managers and teammates; looking forward to bright futures. Except for the sport each played, it was hard to tell them apart.

You won't read that kind of story here. Neither will you read complete biographies of all the subjects. Some of the stories neglect to tell you much about the town where the player was born or what his minor-league batting averages were. Each selection in this book does, however, tell a story with an extra dimension about a great athlete.

Personal prejudice did enter into the selection, I confess. Someone else might have included a story on Duke Snider or Roy Campanella rather than one on Gil Hodges. All three were great hitters, but Gil was also my manager; so he's in the book.

Four of the players featured in the book are still active: Henry Aaron, Johnny Bench, Al Kaline and Frank Robinson. Four others—Ernie Banks, Roberto Clemente, Mickey Mantle and Willie Mays—I have played against. Too many contemporary players, some might object. I worry more that I haven't included enough. I hope Willie McCovey, Pete Rose, Willie Stargell and Billy Williams, all of whom I'll be facing regularly this season, don't think I'm downgrading their abilities by not having stories on them. I don't see American Leaguers very often, but I would hate to pitch to Dick Allen, Rod Carew, Harmon Killebrew, Tony Oliva or Carl Yastrzemski if they felt I had slighted them.

Tom Seaver

Acknowledgments

"The Babe" by Douglass Wallop. Reprinted from *Baseball, an Informal History* by permission of W. W. Norton and Company, Inc. Copyright © 1969 by Douglass Wallop.

"The Finest Hours of a Quiet Legend" by James Toback. Reprinted by permission of *Sport*. Copyright © 1970 by Macfadden-Bartell Corporation.

"The Last Days of Ernie Banks" by Paul Hemphill. Copyright © 1971 by Paul Hemphill. Reprinted from *Sport* by permission of The Sterling Lord Agency.

"I'm Going to Be the First $100,000 Catcher in Baseball History" by Ron Smith. Reprinted from *True* magazine. Copyright © 1970 by Fawcett Publications.

"The Man Who Fanned Casey" by "Sparkus." Reprinted from *The Annotated Casey at the Bat* by Martin Gardner. Copyright © 1967 by the author. Used by permission of Clarkson N. Potter Publishers, Inc.

" 'Nobody Does Anything Better Than Me in Baseball,' Says Roberto Clemente . . . Well, He's Right" by C. R. Ways. Copyright © 1972 by The New York Times Company. Reprinted by permission.

"Tyrus: The Greatest of 'Em All" by Ring W. Lardner. Reprinted from *The American* magazine, June 1915.

"The Longest Hitting Streak in History" by Dave Anderson. Copyright © 1961. Reprinted from *Sports Illustrated* by permission of the author.

"Winning Acceptance" from the chapter entitled "Gangsters, Bums and Heroes" reprinted from *Baseball* by Robert Smith. Copyright © by Robert Smith, 1969. Reprinted by permission of the Harold Matson Company.

"In Ruth's Shadow" from the chapter entitled "Yesterday" reprinted from *Times at Bat: A Half-Century of Baseball* by Arthur Daley. Copy-

A View From the Mound

Tom Seaver

When I throw a baseball, I want to see it arrive in the catcher's mitt untouched by a bat. The hitter facing me would rather see it sailing over the fence. Sometimes, though, I can understand the hitter's point of view.

If I were given the choice of pitching a no-hit game and batting 0-for-4, or pitching a one-hitter and winning the game with a home run, I'd take the one-hitter. I've never pitched a no-hitter in pro ball, but I have won two of my games with the Mets by hitting home runs. The first was in Montreal in 1970. The score was tied 1–1 in the top of the eighth when I came up to bat against Bill Stoneham. I hit a homer into the left-field bleachers, and we went on to win the game, 2–1.

The second time was two seasons ago in Cincinnati. Again the score was tied 1–1 when I came to the plate late in the game against Ross Grimsley. Willie Mays was on deck as I went to a 3–2 count. Grimsley threw me a fastball and, just as I hit it, I heard this high-pitched screech from the on-deck circle. I thought, there's a guy who has hit more than 600 of them, so if he's yelling, it's just got to be a home run. And by the time I got halfway to first base, I could see the ball going over the stands. When I came around to home plate, there was Willie, one of the greatest home-run hitters of all time, waiting to congratulate *me* for hitting one. We won that game by the margin of my homer, 2–1.

It gives me a lot of satisfaction to know that, for a pitcher, I'm a pretty good hitter. It means that my teammates know I'm giving them everything I can, even when I'm up there with a bat in my hands. (That's why I wouldn't like to see the National League adopt the designated-hitter rule. I would lose an important relationship with my teammates.) Unlike some of my colleagues, I try to keep my feelings about my own hitting abilities in reasonable perspective. Scratch the surface of many a pitcher, and you'll find a frustrated Babe Ruth.

You can see this in pitchers' batting practice. At Shea Stadium we're the first ones out on the field; the gates aren't even open so we have the park to ourselves. Even though pitchers are notoriously bad hitters in games, there are some great hitters in batting practice. And with every ball that's hit to the fence, someone's ego flies to the moon.

Take Jerry Koosman, one of the nicest guys you'd ever want to meet. There couldn't be a happier person in the world. Every day in the clubhouse, he has a smile, a laugh, a pat on the back for you. But he does have one problem. Much to the chagrin of every other pitcher on the staff, he thinks he's a good hitter. All of us pitchers have to put up with it; the hitters on the team won't waste their time talking with him about it. One day he came up to us and announced that if he were an every-day player, he'd hit .250. We told him he was losing his mind. No, he explained, he could do it by choking up on the bat and becoming a place-hitter. He wouldn't hit for power, but he'd get his one hit a game. He had himself so convinced that he decided to try it out. During batting practice, he'd choke up on the bat about six inches and show us his new place-hitting stroke.

He looked a little silly; he's six foot three and weighs about 210 but he was holding his bat like Bud Harrelson.

The next game he pitched, he used his new batting style —and got a single. Now there was no stopping him. He had us in a corner and was going to bring us to our knees. But the next game he pitched he didn't get a hit, nor the next, nor, thank God, the next. After that he showed up at batting practice with his hands right back on the end of the bat. "Heck with it," he said. "I'm not going to be a place-hitter anymore. I'm going for power again." Jerry has hit one home run in his six years with the Mets.

Jon Matlack is another Mets pitcher who is a pretty good hitter in batting practice. Two seasons ago I ended the year with three more hits than he had. So last year I bet Jon a dinner that I would get at least four more hits than he would over the season. He wound up with 10 hits, all singles; I had 15 hits, including a home run, a triple and two doubles—and a dinner. Now I'm hoping to bet him on total bases for the '74 season.

Of course, I know I'm not really a hitter. When I was younger, though, I was a fantastic hitter. One season I batted .543 with 10 home runs. But that was in the Little League. When I was 13, I graduated to the Babe Ruth League which had regulation-size diamonds, and I never hit well after that. By the time I was 16, I really did nothing but pitch. I wasn't a disgrace as a hitter, but I just wasn't good enough to play when I wasn't pitching.

Sometimes I have regretted not being able to play every day. But if I had to do it all over again, I would still want to be a pitcher. Nothing could be as satisfying to me as being in a one-to-one contest with every player on the opposing team.

That contest between a hitter and a pitcher isn't just a physical one. Each of us has to be aware of what can and can't be done in a given game situation. Each of us tries to outguess the other, to remember what pitches were thrown in similar situations and with what success. I've had to learn and remember a great deal in order to survive against all the great hitters in the league—and the not-so-great ones, too. Mostly I've learned by experience. I may know something about a hitter from coaches and other pitchers before I ever face him—whether he's a highball or lowball hitter, fastball or curveball hitter, etc. But much more significant is what I can learn by what happens with every pitch I throw him. A coach or manager can alert a pitcher about what to expect out there on the mound, but then the pitcher has to recognize each experience as it happens—and remember it and learn from it.

Harvey Haddix, the Mets' pitching coach in my first year, continually stressed, "Know yourself." One thing a pitcher has to find out is that he can't pitch to any hitter the same way another pitcher can because his abilities aren't exactly the same as any other pitcher's. Sometimes I have success pitching a particular batter high, while another pitcher might do better pitching him low. This kind of knowledge doesn't just come with time. You have to work at it, to study it.

The same goes for the hitter. He, too, has to learn by his experience and use his head as much as his body at the plate. Some hitters don't; they only see the ball out there and aren't aware of the pitcher and what he might be doing. If these batters have enough natural ability, they may get away with it. But I find them relatively easy to pitch to.

Much tougher are the hitters who stay mentally on top of the game, who continually think about what I'm trying to do out there on the mound. I don't think a hitter can be great without mental as well as physical abilities.

Pete Rose is an example of this kind of hitter. Not only does he have great batting reflexes, but he tries to guess what the pitcher is going to do and what pattern the pitcher is working in. He challenges the pitcher with his brain as well as his body.

On our team, Rusty Staub takes a very scientific attitude toward all aspects of the game. He studies pitchers and knows exactly what they can do and what they can't do, and what they've tried to do to him before. Cleon Jones also has a good philosophy about hitting. He has dissected it for himself like I've dissected pitching and has the ability to understand himself as a hitter.

The mental aspect of the game is so important because you can't rely on being in top physical form every day of the season. Some days when I go out to pitch, the chemistry is right, the rhythm is right, and the ball just explodes at home plate. Those are fascinating times, when the power's all there. But it's not something I can force, and it only happens for me six or eight times a year. Then there are the other days when everything isn't quite together and I have to win with my head. I may not be able to throw the ball hard enough to strike anyone out, so I have to work more on setting up batters. I take all the knowledge I have about a hitter and combine it with what abilities I have to work with that day. It's much more rewarding to win a duel against a great batter when I have to depend mostly on my wits.

That classic duel between a pitcher and a batter is what makes baseball so fascinating to me, not only as a participant but also as a fan. No other team sport has such a dramatic and vivid confrontation.

Some days, when I'm not pitching, I can be just as much a fan as the guy in the bleachers. I can sit on the bench and not try to analyze what's going on and just enjoy watching a pitcher throw to a batter. I'm not always prejudiced in favor of the pitcher, either. I can remember sitting in Dodger Stadium, when I was a teen-ager, and rooting for Henry Aaron to hit one off Sandy Koufax. The Milwaukee Braves were my team when I was growing up. I lived and died with them every day of the season, and Aaron was my hero. He still is, in many ways. Last season, the first thing I'd do in the morning was open the newspaper to see if Henry had hit a home run. Going into this season, I was looking forward to Henry hitting his 715th home run and breaking Ruth's record. But I was hoping he wouldn't hit it off me.

Records like Ruth's give baseball something else no other major sport has—a way of comparing players from entirely different eras. Baseball has far more history and continuity than football, basketball or hockey; in those sports, comparisons between now and 50 years ago are almost meaningless. But baseball fans can argue endlessly whether Mays was a greater center fielder than Tris Speaker, or how many home runs Roger Maris could have hit in 1927, or whether Nolan Ryan, Bob Feller or Walter Johnson was the fastest pitcher. And beyond arguing, fans can imagine confrontations between earlier and recent players. What would happen if Ty Cobb tried to steal second with Whitey Ford pitching and Yogi Berra catching? How would Babe Ruth do if *I* were on the mound?

Of course, the game has changed greatly over the decades. In 1923, the overall batting average for all players was .284. In 1973, it was .257, which was 20 points better than it had been in 1968. The biggest change in the game was the one Ruth himself caused. In 1919 when he set his first home-run record by hitting 29, the average number of home runs hit in a game was .39. In 1935, the year he retired, it had climbed to 1.07. Club owners had caught on to the fact that home runs drew fans into the ball park, so they agreed to make the ball livelier in 1920 and began searching for home-run hitters for their teams.

There have been other changes, too. Defensively, the game has become much more sophisticated. The gloves are bigger today, and artificial turf has almost eliminated bad hops.

Pitching is more scientific now. It used to be that a pitcher went out there and threw for a whole game and that was it. Increased reliance on relief pitching has caused great changes in pitching strategy. A starting pitcher now throws as strong as he can from the beginning of the game, because he knows he has a good pitcher coming in from the bullpen if he tires.

Some—mainly Ted Williams—say that the slider is a new pitch that began to be used only in recent decades; others claim it's just another name for the "nickle curve" used in the old days. I don't know. It's very difficult for me, a person who is 29 years old, to speculate on what pitches were used in 1930.

There's no question in my mind, though, that the players are generally better today—bigger, faster, stronger and more skillful. In sports with clear measurements of performance like track and field, and swimming, the records are constantly improving. And there's no reason to think the same wouldn't be true of baseball.

But I also think that the great players of earlier eras would be great players in this era. Cobb might not hit .400 today, but he would be fighting for batting championships. And Ruth might not have a .342 lifetime average if he played today, but he would probably hit just as many home runs. Even if he had to bat against Tom Seaver occasionally.

1

Babe Ruth

Babe Ruth is first in this book because, well, because he was the Babe, *the* great hitter.

It's almost impossible to imagine anyone else ever dominating the game—and changing it—as much as he did. When he set his first home-run record in 1919 by hitting 29 (also compiling a 9–5 record as a pitcher), the next highest total in the majors was 12. In 1920 he hit 54; no one else hit 20. And in 1921, when he hit 59, the second best home-run hitter had 24. He may not have invented the home run, but then Henry Ford didn't invent the automobile either.

The Babe's place in history can't be changed by his record being broken, because he was the first. More people know about Charles Lindbergh than know about John Glenn.

When I was a boy, I had a picture of Babe on my wall. It was a series of black silhouettes against a white background, showing the different stages of his home-run swing. I can see that picture even now, after eight years as a professional pitcher. And I can fantasize about what it would be like to pitch to Babe Ruth. . . .

It's a summer Sunday afternoon in Yankee Stadium—"The House That Ruth Built." A blue haze seems to drift beneath the shining facade of the new stadium. It's the bottom of the first and I'm on the mound. I've struck out the lead-off batter, Earle Combs, and the second batter, Mark Koenig, has flied to right. Now I watch Ruth walk to the plate and hear the tremendous roar from the capacity crowd of 65,000. Seeing Ruth take his practice swings, I have to remind myself that I'm a professional, not a kid, not a fan. I can't let myself be awed by him. I take a deep breath and stare at him; now he's an opponent, a very dangerous one, that I have to get out.

I've never faced Ruth before, so I don't know what would work best for me. I know only a few things about him. He is, of course, a left-handed hitter. This is trouble for me, a right-handed pitcher, because my curve breaks into him instead of away. Most home runs are hit off high pitches, but I know that Ruth, like many left-handed sluggers, can also golf low pitches into the stands. If I can keep him from pulling the ball, I have a much better chance to get him out. The home-run distance to right field is only 296 feet, while center field is 461.

I decide that my first pitch will be a sinking fastball, low on the outside corner of the plate. If he gets hold of it on the outside, he'll have to use his maximum strength to pull it down that right-field line. I wind up, pitch and . . .

I'll pitch him low and away again, now that I have him 0–1. Continue to keep the ball away from him . . .

He let the last pitch go by—too far outside. Ruth was a pitcher himself so he'll be guessing what I'm trying to do. If he guesses low and away again, he'll be compensating and he may clobber it. I'll keep him honest by throwing inside now. It'll be a slider that begins on the inside corner and breaks toward his protruding stomach . . .

I'm up on him 1–2; maybe he doesn't see many sliders.

But pitching him inside is very dangerous. If I don't have perfect control and let the ball come in over the plate, he'll murder it. I feel strong, so I'll throw him another fastball, low and away . . .

It's the fourth inning. I've allowed only two hits against the greatest hitting team in history. But now I've got a problem. Koenig has led off the inning with a double and Ruth is up again. The game is still scoreless and I'm worried about that runner on second. A single would score Koenig, and we'd have to play catch-up ball against the Murderer's Row Yankees. Ruth flied out to left-center in the first inning, but I don't want to let him hit any pitch now. He's a high-average hitter—.342 lifetime—and I don't want to risk him scoring that run with a single. The best way for a big hitter not to hurt you is to strike him out. Despite his tremendous swing though, he's not easy to strike out. He's never struck out 100 times in a season, as have many home-run hitters. But I feel strong enough to power-pitch him.

I'll challenge him with my best pitch, a rising fastball. A pitch that starts at the letters and goes up is tough to get hold of, though if he does hit it, it's got a good chance to be a home run. I may be fooling with death, but I think I can strike him out. . . .

The sixth inning and the score is tied, 1–1. I struck the Babe out last time, and now he's up there again. With a man on first and one out, I'll challenge him again, go for another strikeout. I don't feel tired. My rising fastball still seems good. Maybe not quite as fast as an inning or so ago, but still fast enough. I glance toward first, stretch, bring my left leg up, deliver . . .

I've seen movies of Ruth's pigeon-toed trot around the bases, but I was hoping not to see it today.

The next time I face the Babe, I'll make sure it's in my own era, at Shea Stadium, in a night game, just after the Yankees return from a road trip to the Coast with a bumpy plane ride and a three-hour layover in Chicago. Wait till Ruth sees what my fastball looks like then—especially after he has caroused in nightclubs, drinking pitchers of beer and wolfing down platters of pigs' knuckles, and shown up at the ball park without any sleep.

The Babe
●
Douglass Wallop

In baseball's hour of need came the big man with the mighty bat.

Whud-duh Babe dooduh day?

What the Babe usually had done that day was hit one out of the park, something he did 714 times from the day he joined the Red Sox as a youthful pitcher in 1914 until the day in 1935 when he played his last major-league baseball game, not as a member of the Yankees but so unfittingly as a member of a National League team, the Boston Braves.

Whud-duh....

In the 1920s, in season, it was a question asked each day all over America . . . in late afternoon in the dim light of a speakeasy . . . on a front-porch stoop in the cool of evening . . . on subways and trolleys and trains and from the tonneaus of Hupmobiles.

"He hit another one. . . ."

America, so it would seem, took unreasoning delight that a man, a rather fat man, a man who looked so out of condition that he seemed incapable of running the length of a city block or bending down to touch his toes, a rather ugly man with coarse pudgy features who wore a flapping camel-hair coat and a cap with a snap-button bill, who loved to eat and drink immoderately, who swore and murdered the English language—America took delight that such a man as this could stand up at the plate and day after day swing and send a baseball in a high arching parabola over a distant fence or into the distant stands, most often the right-field stands of Yankee Stadium, his stadium, built for him, built to accommodate his mighty swats, the House That Ruth Built. It was home, the most hospitable he had ever known and during the years of his glory as great, as hospitable a home as a man could ever ask. In it for long years he was the Babe, the Bambino, the Sultan of Swat, the king, his divine right challenged by his subjects only once and then by a man half his size, and then because he had gotten a king-sized belly-ache. But he got over the bellyache and patched up his troubles with the little man, Miller Huggins, and went on with his career, and for America life seemed good, because it had fought and helped win a war, because even though it was the time of Prohibition, a drink could be had and it was fun to sneak one under the old man Uncle Sam's nose and because Charles Lindbergh flew the Atlantic and because the Babe was hitting them out of the ball park and baseball in spite of the Black Sox was not dead.

"Sixty!"

He had come very close before, 54 and even 59—but 60 was magic. Sixty for the nation seemed to have a special significance, to bring a special thrill. It was an occasion for awe, for special rejoicing, the day in September 1927 when he faced Tom Zachary at New York and sent No. 60 into the right-field stands. The banner headlines on the late-afternoon papers would say simply: "The Babe: 60" and people would know what it meant and would marvel. In one and the same year, Lindbergh had flown the Atlantic —and Babe Ruth hit No. 60! A lucky nation, a nation of destiny, a marvelous time to be living. The reaction was as great as if, say, somebody had reached the moon.

"Who yuh think yuh are—Bay Bruth?"

The answer was yes. All over the United States, on its playgrounds, in its alleys, its city streets, its fields and its vacant lots, the kids were swinging from the heels and for a moment or two each day, yes, they were Babe Ruth. For America was the land of opportunity where even a poor boy could grow up to be Babe Ruth, who after all would earn more than the President of the United States, and Cal Coolidge, God knows, couldn't hit the broad side of a barn. All he could do was grunt. Cal Coolidge moved through life with careful sidesteps, smiling sour smiles. Babe Ruth laughed a mighty laugh, strode with the stride of a giant, slamming the door of his Stutz Bearcat and wading through the crowds, long camel-hair coat flapping near his ankles, big brown eyes shining, a long cigar stuck between the fat lips, and grinning as they all said, "Hiya, Babe," and yelling back, "Hiya, kid . . . sure, kid . . . attaboy, kid, keep swinging from the heels."

Ruth had been a special kid, raised in a Baltimore orphanage although he was not quite an orphan, but living in the orphanage was better, somebody decided, than living on the Baltimore waterfront where broken-down derelict ballplayers came to his father's saloon and where tough Chesapeake Bay oystermen came after a long icy winter on the bay, spending the money they had rightfully earned and some they would have had to pay in wages to deckhands they had knocked overboard to drown rather than pay—"paying off with the boom," it was called. So Ruth was raised in the orphanage, St. Mary's, a large, forbidding building of red brick looking very much like an orphanage might be expected to look—and he came out of the orphanage to earn more money than the President, to receive the awe of a flabbergasted nation, flabbergasted and delighted that in its midst there could be such a Charlemagne, such a Henry VIII as George Herman Ruth, who conquered like Charlemagne and dissipated like Henry; the Babe, who spent his energy as fast as it was renewed. The nation had Prohibition, a law it cheerfully flouted; it was in a mood for irreverence, and in a mood to admire this nonathlete who himself flouted all the no-tobacco, no-alcohol, early-to-bed, early-to-rise dicta that athletes were said to observe. For Ruth smoked and drank, he ate like a pig, was seldom early to bed, and rose only early enough to get out to the ball park for batting practice. Yet, hung-over from drink, from food, from long early-morning hours of card playing and carousing, he still had enough left the next day to swing from the heels and, more often than not, hit one into the stands and then move around the bases with the dainty steps he reserved for the aftermath of his home runs, and with his heavy upper body and his slim ankles looking always a little like a large pigeon, wearing a black baseball cap inscribed NY, circling the bases slowly and looking down at the steps he was taking.

He had two bad years, bad for him. In 1921 he defied the new czar, Kenesaw Mountain Landis, and took a team on a postseason barnstorming tour, whereupon Landis suspended him. Not until late May of 1922 did he get back into the game, and that year he didn't even win the home-run title. And then in 1925, a man who could dissipate even with hotdogs and ice cream, he flouted the training rules, got his big bellyache, ran afoul of his tiny manager, Miller Huggins, again lost the home-run title, and lost the Yankees the pennant. Finally Jacob Ruppert, a beer baron who owned Ruth legally if not in spirit and who marveled over him with all the rest, stepped in and made peace—and on through the '20s and into the '30s roared the Babe, and the Yankees roared with him.

In 1935 the sportwriters and the fans all said how strange it was to see Babe Ruth in the uniform of the Boston Braves, but he had started out in Boston and now he was finishing

in Boston, and after that year he was out of uniform forever
—bitter because baseball never gave him the managerial job
he said he wanted, and yet he probably would not have been
a good manager. He spent aimless days, he aged, he developed throat cancer, he paid a farewell visit to Yankee
Stadium and spoke a few words that were hard to make out
because by then the disease had him, and when the afternoon was over he returned to the hospital. There came the
day of August 16, 1948.

What the Babe did that day was die, and the flags in
Yankee Stadium flew at half staff.

But in 1921 Babe Ruth was alive and drunk in New York
City, if not on liquid joy then drunk with the glory of being
Babe Ruth in the third decade of the 20th Century, the
decade of Ruth, Dempsey, Tunney, Jimmy Walker, Charles
Lindbergh, Cal Coolidge, of the fringed miniskirt, the
charleston, the rumble seat and of the New York Yankees.

In the case of the Yankees it would be the first decade of
many, far too many, some would say, because the Yankees
dominated baseball on and off, but mostly on, for the better
part of 40 years, so that for better or worse the history of
professional baseball in the United States was for four decades often the history of the New York Yankees. There
were other teams and other players, good ones and even
great ones, and they too have a place in history because they
helped make it, but the Yankees made most of it. They were
the centrifugal force, the standard, the gauge, by which
other teams were measured and by which other teams measured themselves. To beat the Yankees in the World Series,
to beat them out for the pennant, to best them in a three-
game series, even to beat them in a single ball game—these
were the goals to which other teams aspired, and too often
they fell short.

It seems a matter of irony that as far back as October

1923 a national magazine should have asked: "Is New York Getting Too Many Pennants?" Little could it have known that in 1923 the Yankee dynasty had barely begun, little could it have known what was in store for baseball. From 1921 through 1964, a span of 44 seasons, the Yankees' proportionate share should have been five, at the most six, pennants. They won 29!

Yet even as far back as 1923 the point was well taken, for in that season, 1923, the Yankees had just won their third straight pennant—and the New York Giants of John McGraw had done likewise, trouncing the Yankees in the World Series the first two years and losing to them in 1923.

The article asked if it was money—the riches that came from representing the metropolis—that gave New York teams an advantage, and money of course helped, just as it would always help, but in the years ahead it would be proved that money alone could not topple the Yankees, no matter how much money a given club owner (Tom Yawkey of the Red Sox, for example) might be willing to spend. In the years ahead what the Yankees would have would be the most consistently productive farm system in baseball. What they had in the early '20s was a lot of good ballplayers and the home-run power of Babe Ruth, who upstaged the place-hit-and-slash-em tactics of Ty Cobb and made the country crazy over home runs. Home runs, as the *Literary Digest* said in 1921, were in season and they became an epidemic. In 1918 the major-league total was only 235, while in 1922 there were 1055, and even though that season, the season of his suspension, Ruth lost out to Ken Williams's 39, the year before he hit 59 and the year before that, 54.

"The home-run epidemic," the magazine said, "might better be called the Babe Ruth epidemic, for the habit began with the so-called and very much admired 'Bambino.'" It went on to quote a baseball critic of the day: "He has batted home runs at so dizzy a pace that he has fired the enthusiasm of the entire country. He has not only slugged his way to fame but he has got everybody else doing it. The home-run fever is in the air. It is infectious. . . . Babe has not only smashed all records, he has smashed the long-accepted system of things in the batting world, and on the ruins of that system he has erected another system, or rather lack of system, whose dominant quality is brute force.

"Most of us," the article continued, "plod along and seem to exert little influence on the scheme of things. But now and again a superman arises in the domain of politics or finance or science and plays havoc with kingdoms or fortunes or established theories. Such a superman in a narrow but nonetheless obvious field is Babe Ruth. He might not make much impression in the fine arts or classical literature. Doubtless Thomas Edison, applying his celebrated questionnaire test, would label Babe 'amazingly ignorant.' Nevertheless, in his own particular field, Babe is a true superman."

His fields were many. One was eating. Another was drinking. "He absorbed enough punishment off plates of food and out of bottles to have killed an ordinary man," wrote Ty Cobb, a Ruth watcher and Ruth baiter who infuriated the big man by calling him an egg on stilts, a beer keg on two straws. "I've never seen such an appetite. He would start shoveling down victuals in the morning and never stop. I've seen him at midnight, propped up in bed, order six huge club sandwiches and put them away along with a platter of pigs' knuckles and a pitcher of beer. And all the time he'd be smoking a big black cigar. Next day he'd hit two or three home runs and trot around the bases, complaining all the way of gas pains and bellyache."

The year of the big bellyache was 1925, while the Yankees were in Asheville, North Carolina, en route back north from spring training. An ambulance rushed the Babe to the hospital and newspaper headlines all over the country heralded the national crisis. Ruth was still sick when the season opened, and it was not until he got back into the lineup that his differences with Huggins reached the point of blowup. Huggins fined him $5000 for breaking training rules. Ruth, in a rage, directed owner Jake Ruppert to lift the fine but Ruppert stuck by Huggins. The Babe sulked and then, promising to be a good boy, picked up his big bat again but too late for a Yankee pennant that season.

2

Henry Aaron

I can fantasize about pitching to Babe Ruth, but I don't have to fantasize about the man who is toppling Ruth's career home-run record. I have faced Henry Aaron many times over the course of seven seasons in the majors, and I'm still not sure if I've gotten over my childhood hero-worship of him. I used to play that I was Henry Aaron in my back-yard when I was 12 years old, imitating his swing and his mannerisms.

Some might find it odd that a young white boy aspiring to be a pitcher should find his hero in a black batting star. But I didn't see a baseball player in terms of his race, or even his personality off the field. What mattered to me was Aaron's performance on the field, his home runs and his average and his grace swinging a bat or catching a line drive. To me he was the dedicated, complete professional athlete.

In 1967 in Atlanta, I faced Henry Aaron as a professional competitor for the first time. As he approached the plate, I knew so well what his every action would be—how he'd put on his batting helmet with both hands, how he'd carry his bat, how he'd walk, what the expression on his face would be—that I deliberately turned away from him and stared out to the outfield. When I turned around again, I was no longer a hero-worshipper, I was a professional. I got him to hit into a double play with an inside fastball. The next time he came up, I threw him another inside fastball. He hit it for a home run and I learned that hitters can remember pitches too.

Some pitchers were talking last year about "grooving" a pitch to Aaron to let him hit his 715th home run. I felt that any pitcher who'd do that would be doing Henry a disservice. He worked to hit all of his other homers, and I knew he wanted to hit the one that broke the record the same way he hit all the others. Besides, the pitcher giving up the record-breaking homer is insignificant. The whole meaning of the event is right there at home plate.

I'm writing this before the opening of the '74 season, so Aaron might just hit his 715th off me. (He has hit four homers against me, with a .211 batting average.) I admit that I'd have very mixed feelings. Let's say it was a game in which he beat us with the home run. For a few moments I'd be upset and angry for losing a ball game; the professional side of me would be infuriated. But then I'm sure the fan side of me would take over, the side I had to snuff out in order to pitch to him that first time in my rookie year. As I watched Henry circling the bases, I'd feel caught up in one of the great emotional moments in baseball history— and in the life of a man I idolized growing up. I'm afraid I might even cheer.

It pleases me that Henry is finally getting the kind of recognition from the sports press that he has long deserved. The following article was written in the days, just four years ago, when Henry was the superstar who didn't get much press—only a fraction of what Mays and Mantle had gotten all through their careers. But to me, that was never significant. Just because he didn't get his picture on the front pages as often as Mantle or Mays didn't mean he hadn't gotten the recognition all along. Recognition isn't shaving-cream endorsements or newspaper coverage. It's in the heart of the baseball fan. I know, because I recognized him with every practice swing of a bat I took all alone in my backyard.

The Finest Hours of a Quiet Legend
•

James Toback

It was late in May. Less than a week earlier, Henry Aaron, born 36 years ago in Alabama, quiet hero since 1954 of the Milwaukee-Atlanta Braves, had recorded the 3000th base hit of his major-league career and thus became the first player in the history of the game to achieve both 500 home runs and 3000 hits. Such a unique accomplishment suggests superiority of unsurpassed dimension, a niche high on, if not at the top of, the roster of all-time baseball stars. It confirms his existence as a living, playing legend, to be followed, watched, cherished by all with any kind of serious claim to taste or feeling for the sport. And yet, general admiration from fans, the respect of his peers and a $125,000 salary notwithstanding, Henry Aaron, like sunset, music and summer, is taken for granted. With the added interest of his being a black athlete in the Deep South, the case becomes one of the most intriguing in the game.

So I had come down to Atlanta to learn what it is that makes Aaron so remarkable in what he does, what kind of man in general and black man in particular he is, and why the public would consider DiMaggio, Mantle or Mays before they would consider him. I would be talking to him the next day, but now, as I sat behind the Atlanta dugout, I'd have a chance to watch him, first as the center of a celebration over his latest success, and then as a player in the game against the Astros.

The crowd was close to 25,000, racially balanced, many obviously there to pay tribute, a fact attested to by the shower of signs in all levels of the stands: "WE LOVE HENRY," "715 COMES NEXT," "HAMMERIN' HANK IS OUR HERO" and "KING HENRY." Bill Bartholomay, the president of the Braves, announced Aaron's name, and the throng—men, women and children, old and young, black and white, executive and laborer, Afro and Cracker—rose in unrestrained and tumultuous ovation. Henry ran from the dugout, stopped short at the microphone, turned gracefully, easily, removed his cap, nodded, half bowed and smiled broadly enough to radiate all the way downtown. The entire Astro bench was on its feet applauding, and Aaron acknowledged the consideration, grinning, waving. Bartholomay called out Milt Pappas who presented Aaron with a silver hammer. He was followed by Braves manager Luman Harris, who brought out a silver tray autographed by all of Aaron's teammates; next a fishing outfit; then a certificate promising gasoline for 3000 miles; a set of pewter ware; a year's supply of Coke; a French poodle (which Henry cuddled warmly in his arms) and a year's supply of dog food. Then Bartholomay declared that he and his colleagues in the front office imagined that Henry would want a vehicle for all that gasoline, so here it was, his demonstration of gratitude (a Cougar? a Charger? a Cadillac? a Mercedes? a Rolls?)—a, let's hear it, *personalized golf cart* with a "44" painted right on it! Henry shifted in place, shuffled, smiled wryly, feeling what—gratitude, amusement, or resignation?

Paul Richards, Braves' vice-president, stepped in and blurted that it was beyond him why Henry wasn't named athlete of the decade, No. 1 on the all-time All-Star team.

And then Henry edged in shyly, quietly, with his thank you, how wonderful it's been playing in Atlanta, thank you very much. And Bartholomay replied: "Henry, thank *you* for the *privilege* of having been able to watch *you*. Let me just mention in closing that among the many telegrams that came for you today was one from *Satchel Paige* which, as we can all understand, was *particularly appropriate*, I thought." I looked around, but no one seemed to have noticed. Had *Henry*?

The game began, and Aaron glided—not ran, trotted, walked—*glided* for the, what, 2000th time out to right field to await the national anthem and the first pitch. As the lead-off man, Jesus Alou, took his crack at Jim Nash, the first clue to understanding the traditionally unhysterical, unexcited attitude toward Aaron appeared. He was relaxed to the point of apparent unconcern. Mike Lum, the center fielder, was tight, intense, coiled in concentration; Aaron was easy, loose. His hands were on his hips as Nash, a deliberate worker, moved into his motion, and it was only as the ball headed toward home that Aaron bent, dropped his hands below his knees, closed his stance and looked anything close to prepared for a ball that might be hit in his direction. No pounding of the glove, no bouncing on the toes, no glaring in at the plate. Between pitches he paced, seemingly aimless, back and forth. It was only gradually, as the inning progressed, that I began to discern the subtle method, the cunning, the calculating intelligence in Aaron's relaxed pose. For not only was he, in fact, eminently ready to pursue any fly ball or line drive hit within reach, but also, between pitches, he'd move ever so slightly, to the left, to the right, backward or forward, depending on the situation, intuiting that on a given count Nash would most likely be throwing a curveball, a fastball or a change of pace and that a particular batter would be swinging late or early on it, getting around or failing to, pulling or punching.

A 400-foot home run by Norm Miller gave Houston a 3–0 lead, but when Aaron came to the plate in the bottom of the first, Felix Millan was on third with one out and the Braves had a chance to get back. His helmet obviously a nuisance to him, to be used rather than valued, Aaron carried it with him, putting it on only at the last moment, as he stepped into the box. He moved up close, high on the plate, hungry for the pitch, confident, waiting to jump on it, as though the extra second for final judgment cherished by so many hitters who habitually erase the back chalk line with their foot was absurdly unnecessary for him. One practice half-swing, a deep breath for looseness, another practice swing and the bat was cocked at a 145-degree angle behind the ear, shaken in hard, quick, short jolts. As the pitch came in, a low curveball from Larry Dierker, the crowd was rumbling in anticipation—anticipation fulfilled, as Aaron, hard, thick, muscular forearms and whiplash wrists, thrust the bat down, across, through the ball, around, a bullet single to center. As he *glided* to first base and took his turn, I realized the naturalness, the sheer inevitability of this feat of gratitude toward the fans who had come to do him honor. No way in the world he would not have delivered in this situation this first time. In its turn the crowd also was appreciative, its roar for Aaron pitching in a crescendo. But I had seen clearly now how his abilities have gone unemphasized, if not unnoticed, around the league, around the nation through the years. For there had been no flash in the execution of this loaded moment, no lost cap, no circles of dust kicked up by a sudden stop, no vehement swing responsible for this success; simply a graceful, rhythmic realization of possibility.

In the top of the second Joe Pepitone hit a foul home run to right field, but the ball bounced back down near Aaron. He reached down, picked it up and without looking behind him or up, flicked it back into the stands, a crowd-pleasing gesture performed so unobtrusively as to draw notice only from the handful of fans who had a shot at reaping its benefits.

The Braves tied it at three and in the bottom of the fifth had a chance to go ahead. Millan singled and with one out Aaron came up again. Ahead 2–1 on the count, he edged forward as Dierker went into his windup and then swiped at a vicious fastball, low and outside, and missed badly. Suddenly, for a brief moment, I sensed how it will be when Aaron begins to slide, when his timing begins to fail him, when his average starts to drop, when his career starts to fade. But I was reassured by the knowledge that when the time does come, Aaron, like DiMaggio before him, will quit before a serious dent in the respect of others and in his own pride is made. On 2–2 Millan was going, but Aaron missed the same low outside pitch, swung a full foot over it and watched the doubleplay completed at second base. He did not, however, throw his helmet in disgust, nor did he hurl his bat, as say Mantle in a similar situation could be expected to do. Rather, Aaron dropped them, quietly, gracefully, going out now the way he will go out when he goes out for good.

In the top of the sixth the Astros threatened to break the game open. Nash was wild, didn't seem to have much more on the ball than the cover. With runners on first and second and two men out, Denis Menke, a former Brave and a .300 hitter, hit a high line drive to the opposite field into the corner. Aaron, drifting, loping over as though synchronized not with Menke's, not the game's but his own time and beat, reached out with his glove, interrupting the ball's path to the wall and, without ever breaking stride, headed toward the dugout and disappeared into it. There were cheers but they were controlled. And yet it was a catch than Ron Swoboda, if he made it, would have done tumbling at the risk of a broken collarbone, and it was a catch most right fielders would not have been expected to make and would not have made at all.

It was Bob Tillman who won the game for the Braves with a two-run homer, but he described himself later on in the clubhouse as a "reluctant" hero, for it was, he said, as usual, Aaron's night.

Waiting for Aaron in the Braves' locker room the next afternoon I talked to Mark Gladulich, who has been the club's equipment manager for four years. Steve Friedman, a local nightclub owner, lawyer and Brave fanatic, had suggested Gladulich as the most uninhibited observer of the Atlanta players in those moments when their guard is down. I began by asking if he would call Aaron the leader of the team.

"The verbal leader, the guy who stirs the team with his talk, his backslapping and his energy is Cha-Cha [Orlando Cepeda]. But Henry is the real head because he's the one that the whole team has the real great respect for. It's just that he's so quiet and so modest that unless you watch him over a long period of time you don't realize what a strong, deep influence he has.

"Take the young players, for example. They will always be watching Henry from the bench, looking to see how he swings, how he reacts to different pitchers, how he moves. And they soon know from experience that Henry is never too busy to answer their questions about hitting, fielding, base running, or any personal problems they might have. He's always there when you need him.

"He's a real good listener, too. He'll laugh at their jokes, make them feel wanted, like they're an important part of the team. He creates a whole kind of family mood that's especially valuable when things aren't going so well. He's a take-charge guy with deeds rather than words, a leader by example. He's always neat and clean, not flashy but a kind of credit to baseball and to manhood, the sort of fellow everyone can look up to, everyone can feel proud of. I'll be honest with you: I've been with a lot of teams and I've seen a lot of players come and go over a long period of time but nobody that I know of has such a consistently high standard of conduct on the field and off the field. I can't ever remember seeing Henry do anything or say anything that he or anyone else would be ashamed of—and how many people do you know that you can say that of?"

Aaron came in wearing black pants, a black sweater with thin white stripes. It was early afternoon, hours before game time, but as always Henry was among the first to dress. Introductions made, I asked him about his subtle defensive changes.

"An intelligent player is always thinking on the field," he answered. "On a three–two pitch, for example, I'll probably assume that a guy like Nash is going to try to slip a fastball by a hitter like Doug Radar. So I'll edge over to the line a bit guessing that Doug will go with the pitch late to right field."

I thought of Bill Russell's observation that he had never known a superior athlete who did not possess a superior intelligence. No matter how richly endowed with strength or speed, the few transcendent figures in every sport—West, Russell, Robertson; Brown, Sayers, Tittle; Aaron, Seaver, Williams—are of necessity men who have studied, learned, analyzed, improvised the game that is their life. It is a continuing educative process, and ultimately one which will shift the athlete into the role of teacher, the conveyor of the lessons he has learned over long years to younger players— the role, finally, of manager or coach.

I asked Aaron if that kind of thinking out in right field isn't really what a manager is paid to do.

"Sure, but a player's got to help him out and help himself out too. A manager is valuable not only for strategic intelligence and knowledge of the game but also for his ability to understand his players, to get along with them, to create an easy situation, and to lead them in a kind of spiritual way. Take a guy like Bobby Bragan. I'm all for him, I learned from him and I think he's a great guy, but he never really made it as a manager because he couldn't relate to his players as individuals. Each guy needs to be treated on his own terms in his own way if you're going to get the most out of him and create a winning team."

Aaron should know. By experience. On his own team no fewer than three of its stars were at one time "problem" players. Felix Millan is capable of being brought to tears by open, public criticism from a manager, rendered impotent to demonstrate his broad range of skills. Cepeda, who had begun to fade as a Cardinal where he felt he was unappreciated by the management (on the field and off), showed as soon as he moved to Atlanta that more sensitive handling was the only element needed for a total rejuvenation of his powers. And Rico Carty, who, several years ago, at the low point of his morale, engaged in a well-publicized airplane fight with Aaron himself, attributes a large share of his current phenomenal success to the emphatic attitude of Luman Harris. In fact, one need only recall the case of Alvin Dark for crystallization of the whole question. The exhibitor of a first-class baseball mind throughout his long career, Dark rendered himself useless, even destructive, as the San Francisco field general by callously denigrating the cerebral powers of his black and Puerto Rican players.

I asked Aaron if he thought he would make a good manager some day.

"I think so," Aaron said. "I think I know enough about the game and about how to get along with a whole team to produce a winner. And I'd say the same about Ernie Banks and Willie Mays. Unfortunately, no owner has had the guts up to this point to hire a black manager. In fact, I wouldn't even call it guts; I'd call it common sense. Because it's already been proved in other sports, like basketball, that a Negro—a black man—can both produce a winner and bring in sellout crowds. Hell, there's a whole nucleus of black people around Atlanta and Chicago and San Francisco that would come to every game faithfully if Ernie or Willie or I were managing the club. They'd have a real personal stake in the game and in the team and feel that their people had finally been given credit for some brains and organizational talent.

"It burns me up a little that there's this kind of—what would you call it?—managerial club, whereby the owners seem to have gotten together and decided that certain men, white men, should be hired and rehired no matter what kind of failures they have been. Take guys like Gene Mauch or Harry Walker. They've both had real good teams at one time or another but have never produced a winner, and yet as soon as they're fired by one owner, another owner picks them up and gives them a new chance. A second chance is one thing, but third and fourth chances when you've been lousy time and again with first-rate material seems ridiculous —especially when you've got guys like Ernie and Willie available in the wings.

"Now a guy like Walt Alston or Gil Hodges *should* be hired and rehired again and again, because each of them has proved that he can work well with players, that he knows the game, and that he can get the most from the team. But there aren't all that many guys like that around."

The statement revealed much about the growth of the man. Ten years ago, even five, Aaron's constitutional reticence would have precluded such strong, open criticism, such thinly veiled rage directed at the baseball establishment. He was a star, verging on recognition as a superstar, and seemed content, as the jargon has it, to do his talking on the field. But he is getting older now, and no matter what geriatric miracles he may seem to be working, he must be grow-

ing increasingly aware, increasingly apprehensive, about the
directions and possibilities his life will take when, finally, he
feels compelled to retire. So will he attack, in a quiet voice,
but attack nonetheless, the conspiratorial establishment and,
by implication, his own gift-bearing president, Bill Bartholomay.

Moreover, there is a corresponding release of submerged,
and entirely justified, resentment on racial lines. Again, this
is not a field in which Aaron was at all vociferous until recently. But he had grown weary of watching baseball lag,
flaccidly, behind other sports in this area. And, in his own
tempered, moderate fashion (too moderate? too tempered?)
Aaron had obviously decided it was time to apply the needle.

I reminded Aaron of the statement he made about Stan
Musial and his 3000 hits, that it was not the former Cardinal
star's batting record that he coveted but his front office job.
He nodded.

"The same thing applies there. It's just a question of one
owner showing enough courage or decency to break the ice.
I can't understand why it hasn't happened already. Surely
no one thinks at this point that white fans are going to boy-
cott a team because it has a Negro in a front office or managerial position. So why not just do it?"

I asked him whether he felt that Atlanta, the only southern city in the major leagues, might not constitute an exception and whether he felt a kind of bitterness about the
political and racial attitudes that a large number of his white
Braves fans undoubtedly hold and live by when they're not
at the ball park.

"Not at all. As a matter of fact, I get a better feeling here
than I did up north in Milwaukee. There are some bigots
here, some rednecks, but there are bigots in Chicago, Milwaukee, New York and everywhere else. It's not worth it
to waste time or energy feeling anger toward them. Anyway, I'm convinced that the great majority of people who

come out to a ball park and pay to get in are paying to see good, winning baseball and that if you're good, they'll cheer you and appreciate you and like you whether you're black or white, and that if you mess up, they'll boo you and get on your back—and that's the way it should be.

"On the question of Atlanta, it's really only since I got here that I've begun to get a lot of attention. In Milwaukee I was playing in the shadow of a lot of more experienced stars like Spahn and Burdette and Mathews. Not that I resented that in the least, but now I get a little more in the way of endorsements, which means more money, and that's sure not bad."

Not bad at all, which quite naturally raised the question of why Aaron with his matchless record has existed behind the first rank of major-leaguers in the popular imagination.

"Well," he said, "being overshadowed by those great stars obviously had something to do with it, and then there's the question of the media. You simply can't get the kind of attention or recognition outside of New York that you can get in it. There's something about the fans there, their intensity, their enthusiasm, even their rage, that lights up a special kind of fuse that might be a prerequisite for real stardom in any sport. And, finally, there's the matter of style. It's just not my way to be flashy or flamboyant the way, say, Willie is. I have my own even rhythm and I guess it just doesn't attract the kind of attention that a more colorful style does.

"But really, it doesn't bother me a bit. And I'll tell you why. First off, who knows how successful I would have been with a lot of added attention and pressure? Look at Roger Maris. He was almost driven nuts by the fame he achieved when he was on his home-run spree. And secondly, the attention that any one ballplayer gets doesn't mean much in the end; the only thing that's important is whether or not you win. It may seem like a cliché, but I'm concerned with the outcome of a game, the score, not with my personal statistics in it. I don't care who gets the winning hit—Cha-Cha, Rico or Clete—as long as we win. And last year, even though my statistics were good and even though we won the Western Division, I felt miserable at the end of the season because we didn't win the pennant and I knew we should have.

"Three or four years ago there were a lot of losers on the Braves. There were a lot of guys who only thought about their own performance and couldn't have cared less whether or not the team finished on top. But now Luman has weeded them all out and the attitude is great. We should be able to go all the way."

And there, perhaps, in its essence, is the key to the quiet greatness of Henry Aaron. No truly outstanding athlete buys the hopeless, old loser's dictum that "it's not whether you win or lose, it's how you play the game." Rather with champions, it would run: "It's not only that you win, but how you *win* the game." Winning is the precondition, the given.

A winner, but a quiet one. It is a necessary part of his personality. Aaron must seek out his own best way, his most effective means of contribution, and when he finds that this way is likely to diminish, rather than augment, public fascination, he must nonetheless hold fast to this mode.

Such singlemindedness of intention, informed with such modesty, results not only in individual confidence, but also in the kind of team confidence that is indispensable to winning. The idea always that, as a unit, "We should go all the way."

All the way with Henry the A. Which reminded me to ask how it was that a man in his athletic senescence should, incredibly, in the last two or three years, have been getting *better* rather than worse? Was it related to Jim Brown's observation that Elgin Baylor's outstanding 1970 playoff performance was the result of his realization that everybody expects the athlete in his middle-30s to fold at any moment and that as a result the aging star will push with extra force the closer he comes to the end of his career?

"I would say so," said Aaron. "I don't know whether it's a conscious thing, but it's definitely somewhere in the back of your mind. You know that one bad year, even a bad month or a bad week will have everyone speculating about your crumbling abilities." Aaron paused in thought, then said emphatically: "So you do put out extra, not only for their sake but even more for your own. You just hate not to do justice to a talent you have taken pride in and dedicated yourself to your whole life."

An artist and a winner. The two are indistinguishable in his mind. The fulfillment of his own possibilities related integrally to the potential of the whole, he will always look to work *with*, rather than apart from. If his movements, his rhythm, his style and the forms in which his achievements are recorded are unspectacular, even frequently unnoticed, it does not matter to Henry Aaron. What does count is that somehow that style be suited, complementary, to the group with which he is playing. For if it is, then not only will he win against himself but they will all win against others. And his quietness, his gentleness of pace and mood, his muted tone, will have achieved a kind of ultimate justification. A justification, moreover, that will serve notice to Bill Bartholomay, to other owners all around the league, and to America, that Henry Aaron had better be given new fields on which to play his lovely and winning game when his time is up in this one, or else we will all see the sport slowly drained of the juices that keep it alive.

3

Ernie Banks

Ernie Banks was one of the greatest players I've ever faced. He hit 512 home runs in his career, to tie him for ninth on the all-time home-run list. He drove in 1636 runs; only Aaron, Mays, Musial, Frank Robinson and Ted Williams had more RBIs in the last quarter-century. He tied a major-league record by hitting five grand-slam home runs in one season (1955). He established a number of fielding records at shortstop, where he played for the first half of his career. He was named the National League's Most Valuable Player two years in a row (1958, 1959), an especially impressive honor when you consider that he played for the Cubs, a second division team in those years.

But Ernie was also one of the great personalities in the game. You'd take the field in Wrigley Stadium and there Ernie would be, chattering away. "Yes sir-r-r, gonna play all day. Great day for baseball here in Wrigley Field. Yes sir-r-r. Love this game." At first it hit you like a ton of bricks. It couldn't be real. Nobody was like that. But after you'd see him over the course of a few seasons, you knew that it was real. Ernie Banks just sincerely loved the game of baseball. It meant everything to him. He loved being in uniform, he loved being on the field, he loved being a Chicago Cub. Most players lose a little of their enthusiasm after a few years, but Ernie never lost any of his joy in the game.

One of his joys was hitting a baseball over the fence. He had extremely strong wrists that could whip a bat around with great force at the last instant. When I faced him, he was a very good breaking-ball hitter and a good lowball hitter. Usually I would throw him hard stuff upstairs and go for the strikeout. Sometimes I'd throw him low and away or jam him with an inside pitch, trying to make him hit it on the ground, because he wasn't a fast runner in his later years; shortstop, a tough position on a player's legs, had taken its toll.

These techniques didn't always work. I remember one time in Wrigley Field when I had him no balls to two strikes. I threw him a curve about six inches off the ground, and he golfed it over the left-field screen. All the way around the bases, he chattered and chuckled: "Yes sir-r-r, a home run, in Wrigley Field, yes sir-r-r." He was 38 years old but he just couldn't contain his enthusiasm. I don't like giving up home runs, but that time I couldn't help but smile—just a little.

The Last Days of Ernie Banks
•

Paul Hemphill

There is something infinitely sad about the closing days of a baseball season, a melancholia not unlike that accompanying the last dance or the end of an affair, and it was no different on this the final weekend of September in Chicago. The Cubs and the Phillies were headed nowhere except home for the winter. The upper deck of Wrigley Field had been closed due to lack of interest on Friday, when the smallest crowd of the season stopped by to see if the Phils' Barry Lersch could avoid losing his 12th straight decision. The next day it had rained right up to game time, and the players had managed to finish the game in less than two hours; their anxiety to get in out of the cold was so acute that they seldom bothered to throw the ball around the infield after a putout. And now, on a slightly overcast fall Sunday morning, the end was at hand. Somebody had a portable television in the press box so they could watch the Bears's football game from Minneapolis. The names of recently recalled rookies dotted both lineups. The few veterans ticketed to start were playing for themselves, working on next year's salaries. Vendors were desperately touting their remaining souvenir caps and bats and Cubs pennants. A brisk wind snapped in from Lake Michigan. But perhaps the surest sign that it was about to end for another summer was found on Phil Wrigley's brick outfield walls where the ivy, that ivy which has been there for more than three decades, was turning a distinct brown.

It was fitting that the place didn't come to life until the door to the clubhouse in the left-field corner eased open and Ernie Banks stepped into the hazy sunlight to begin the long walk to the batting cage. It would probably be the last time he would make that walk as a player, a fact broadly trumpeted in the Chicago papers in advance of this season-ending home series, and that is why about a thousand of the faithful were on hand more than two hours early. Blinking at the harsh light, carrying two bats and a glove in his right hand, he paused there for a few seconds and took it all in one more time and then began striding through the blue-green grass along the foul line. That was the signal for them to begin.

"Ernie, Ernie, come over here," one of them yelled. "I'm your best fan, Ernie. Honest, Ernie. Hey, *Ernie*." Ernie was smiling like a little boy, waving to them and even calling some of the kids by their first names, now and then doing a little jive step and winking and circling his index finger and thumb into the "O.K." sign. By the time he reached the cage they were near hysteria. "Ernie, you still got my lipstick on your cheek? . . . Ernie, Ernie, *please, Ernie. . . .*"

Loosening up near the cage, he spied one of the Phillies. "Hey," he said, "are you inspired?"

"Now I *know* you're crazy, Banks," the player said.

"*Inspired.* You *must* be *inspired.*"

"It's too damned cold to be inspired."

"Ah, but you must remember those who have to work for a living. You must put it in the proper perspective."

The Phillie shrugged and went back to warming up. "Isn't it a beautiful day?" Banks yelled to nobody in particular, breaking into song. "*On a clear day, you can see forever. . . .* The Cubs of Chicago versus the Phillies of Philadelphia, in beautiful, historic Wrigley Field," he said, grabbing a bat and jumping into the batting cage. "Let's go, let's go. It's Sunday in America."

Sunday in America, indeed. Witnessing a weekend of baseball at Wrigley Field may be one of the last recurring opportunities we have for seeing an America that used to be, an America pregnant with memories of handlebar mustaches and sudsy beer mugs and promenades in the park. The Cubs have been playing their games at Wrigley Field since 1916, and what is so amazing in this age of artificial grass and domed stadiums and scoreboard fireworks is how little has changed there since the glorious days of Rogers Hornsby and Grover Alexander and Hack Wilson.

Primarily responsible for this hold on tradition in Chicago is, of course, Philip K. Wrigley, perhaps the last of the truly benevolent clubowners. The Cubs still wear the same basic uniform and play in a park that has remained startlingly constant for half a century: Ivy-draped walls, no billboards, wonderful close-in seating, organ music and no lighting system. (Wrigley may soon install lights, but only for the purpose of completing long doubleheaders.) Pat Pieper, at 85, is still handling the public address system as he did 55 years ago. In Chicago the fans still actually *sing* the National Anthem, and stand to applaud the Cubs before and after a game as though it were a concert, and scornfully throw back opposition home-run balls hit into the left-field seats. A good Cubbie fan cares not so much whether his lads are winning or losing, but what time they play the game, and this season over 1.6 million showed up to see a club that finished in a distant tie for third place.

Of all the heroes in the 96-year history of the Cubs, none has been bigger than Ernie Banks. Not only because of his excellence afield during 19 seasons—he holds nine of the 15 Cub career records available to a nonpitcher—but because of his general demeanor, he has become known in recent years as "Mr. Cub." That is no mystery, because Ernie Banks is the epitome of what the Wrigley family always intended Cub baseball to be: Pure of heart, exuberant in spirit, a living symbol of the way things used to be.

"I put my glasses on him one day during the National Anthem," says Chicago sportswriter Jim Enright, Banks's collaborator on a fast-selling book called *Mr. Cub*, "and he was singing and crying at the same time." The only time Banks ever showed a temper on the field was a few years ago when the Giants's Jack Sanford nailed him in the back with a fastball. "We could use the same mug shot of him in the press book that we used in 1954, and nobody would know the difference because he simply hasn't changed," says Cub publicist Chuck Shriver. "If he's got any problems, he's hiding them behind the thickest veneer known to man," marvels another Chicago journalist. Uncomplaining, forever happy, totally predictable, Banks enjoys a rapport with Cub fans that borders on the ridiculous. "He don't cuss, he don't bitch and he don't smoke," said an elephantine lady fan bundled up in the box seats. "I guess you could call him a saint."

Whether we shall have to bid farewell to Ernie Banks as an active player may have to wait until the Cubs report to spring training in March in Scottsdale, Arizona. He turns 41 on the last day of January, and arthritic knees have kept him on the bench for most of the past two seasons. He is only a shadow of the 28-year-old who, in 1959, batted .304, hit 45 homers and drove in 143 runs while setting a major-league record for shortstops with a .985 fielding percentage. It has been rumored that he would replace Leo Durocher, thereby becoming the first black manager in big-league history, or else continue as a coach (having been designated a player-coach since 1967). "He's got a lot of options," says Enright, who probably knows Banks more intimately than any other writer. "Manager, coach, up in the broadcast booth, maybe in the front office, maybe even in politics or public service. By playing or coaching one more year, he can get his 20-year pension. I personally think he'll be the Cubs's manager some day." Banks himself remains noncommittal. "Whatever he decides to do, he'll have to announce it himself," says a Cub official, with some exasperation and a lot of understanding of Banks's popularity in Chicago. "You don't retire an Ernie Banks in this town."

Whenever an official announcement comes of Banks's intention to retire as a player, it is certain to spark visions of a purer and more stable period in the history of American sports. Has it really been that long? Born into a large family in Dallas during the depression ("I never invited friends home for lunch because there just wasn't enough food," he says in *Mr. Cub*), he escaped poverty by excelling in sports. "I'd seen so many people in my neighborhood get stuck on bad installment payments, I'd made up my mind I was going to be a Philadelphia lawyer." He was luckier than most black athletes at that time, of course, because just as he was graduating from high school Jackie Robinson was breaking the color line in the majors. Just the same, he was nearly 23 years old before he got his chance in organized baseball. Late in the 1953 season, the Cubs bought his contract from the Kansas City Monarchs of the old Negro American League for $10,000 (his salary was to be $800 a month) and called up Gene Baker to play beside him at second base. Banks and Baker thus became the first blacks to play for the Cubs.

Pennantless since 1945, the Cubs didn't have many heroes back then. Phil Cavarretta was the manager in '53, and Hank Sauer and Ralph Kiner were almost finished. So Banks quickly became the darling of Wrigley Field. In only his second full season he hit .295 with 44 homers and played superbly at shortstop. He didn't have the greatest range in the world, or the strongest arm, but he had fine quick hands and the fluid moves of a Marty Marion. At bat he was deceptive: willowy-looking at six foot one, 185, with delicate slender hands and average shoulders but a smooth swing right out of a Lew Fonseca training film. Between 1957 and 1960 he had home-run productions of 43, 47, 45 and 41, and was named the National League's Most Valuable Player in '58 and in '59. When it appeared he was slowing down a bit at shortstop he was tried late in the 1961 season at first base, where he has starred ever since. (During the Cubs's futile pennant push of two years ago he set a league fielding record of .997.) The type who never had to worry about getting back in shape for another season, Banks was a beautiful physical specimen who never spent a moment on the disabled list until 1970.

When Leo Durocher took over as manager of the Cubs for the '66 season, insiders predicted trouble; Banks, 35, was past his prime for one thing, and for another it was impossible to envision a happy marriage between him and the man who once noted that nice guys finish last. But trouble never came, or at least never came to the surface. "Leo tried to 'retire' Ernie all during spring training that year, trying out about four other guys at first base," says one Cub writer, "but when they got back to Wrigley there he was in the lineup." One reason for his survival is that Banks is the kind of man who has the capacity to put the blinders on when trouble is imminent, skirting danger by minding his own business. Durocher has very wisely taken to joking about how he "tried to retire Ernie, but he wasn't ready for it." In '69, at the age of 38, Banks hit 23 homers and drove in 106 runs and was named "Chicagoan of the Year."

Much sadder than watching a baseball season come to an end is observing the painful last attempts of a great star like Banks, and it has not been a pretty thing, over the past two seasons, to see him try to make his body work for him as it had during the good years. With rumors starting up again that he was through, he went on the disabled list in the middle of the '70 season with the arthritic knee, only to come back and hit .326 in the last month and take false hope that he could make it again in '71. This time, though, there was to be no comeback in the dry heat of Scottsdale, Arizona. Gene Baker had long since given up the ghost and taken to scouting for the Pirates. Hank Aaron was on the verge of a tremendous year and Willie Mays was still in there, but most of the others of the early '50s had departed: Richie Ashburn, Bobby Thomson, Stan Musial, Ted Williams, Minnie Minoso, *et al.* The Cubs had their bright moments, but they also had their bad ones, and it was obviously time to start bringing in some fresh young faces.

If, as many feel, Ernie Banks epitomized a certain definable period in the history of American sports, then Banks's decline also marked the end of that period. Baseball in the '50s was marked by a *joie de vivre*, a free-wheeling independence that was a leftover from the postwar years of the old Dodgers and Cardinals and Red Sox; of the traditional two eight-team leagues; of nurtured images and huge minor-league systems and an almost boyish purity. In the '60s drastic changes came to almost all aspects of baseball.

And lost in all of it was an old-fashioned Ernie Banks. "One reason they come out for day baseball here is because of the atmosphere in the cities at night," says a Cubs official. When Ernie Banks started, it wasn't that much of an issue. "I can't remember Ernie ever saying anything negative about the [Cubs] organization," says another. When he started, nobody dared question the baseball establishment or even acknowledge that there was one. "Most of the young blacks regard him as an Uncle Tom," says a writer. When he joined the Cubs it wasn't a question of "black power," but a question of whether he could find a place to eat a decent meal. So what you did last summer, in perhaps his last season, was close your eyes to the cold figures—entering the last homestand, Banks had managed only 13 hits in 72 at-bats for a .181 average—and try to conjure up images of how it used to be, not only for Ernie Banks, but also for the game of baseball.

Durocher himself ("I can tell you there's no love lost between Leo and Ernie," says one observer) had made the announcement on a post-game show Thursday that Banks would start all three games of the Cubs's home finale against Philadelphia. "We want him to play in the event he *does* announce something later," was the official explanation. He had gone all the way in only seven games that season. On Friday he went hitless in four trips, and when a ground ball shot through his legs in the seventh inning, the scorer mercifully called it a hit. On Saturday, as brutally cold and wet as it was, he had a good day: Two hits in four trips, one for a double, and four outstanding plays in the field. Now it was Sunday, the last day, and while the Phillies finished batting practice he sat in the Cubs's dugout along the third-base line being photographed and interviewed.

"Hey, Vukovich," he yelled to a young Phillie working at third base, "you love this game?" John Vukovich looked at Banks incredulously for a moment, before spitting and nodding toward the dugout. "Yeah," said Banks, "everybody's going to be happy today."

"Feel anything special today, Ernie?" a reporter asked.

"Special? Special? Sure, it's the last Sunday of the season," he laughed.

"Naw, I mean, you know. . . ."

"Nostalgia? That how you say it?"

"Right." Banks's first game had been against the Phils. "I mean, like, do you remember what kind of day it was?"

"Beautiful day. Inspiring day."

"What about today? In comparison."

"Beautiful day. Inspiring day."

"Jesus, Ernie"—the crowd in the dugout had broken up laughing—"aren't you gonna say something controversial for us?"

Banks pondered it and then said, "You inspired?" Nobody expected anything else from him, and while he hunkered down to sign a dozen or so copies of *Mr. Cub* brought over from the box seats by a guard, I tried to remember some of the things he had said the day before, well before the game, under the grandstand in a dank private corridor near the umpires' dressing room; tried to piece them together and make some sense of this man who has managed to show not a sliver of his inner self in nearly two decades of being in the spotlight. He knew they called him an Uncle Tom, he said, but black power was "silly." Had he ever worried about anything? "I have problems, like everybody else, but it doesn't do any good to go around spreading bad news." What about the "new athlete?" "These today have been to college and have something to fall back on if they don't make it. Baseball isn't the most important thing in their lives. I'm not so sure that's good for baseball." Did he plan to retire soon? "It depends on my knee, and whether there's a place for me on the club." What's been your attitude toward other people? "I always looked at everybody as if they had an invisible sign on their back saying, 'Please Handle With Care.' "

It would be nice to say that Ernie Banks, in what may have been his last game as a player at Wrigley Field, hit a home run to move out of an eighth-place tie with Eddie Mathews for career homers. It would be nice to be able to say that immediately after the game there was a press conference announcing him as the first black manager in major-league baseball history. Neither of those things happened, of course, because he managed a dubious infield hit in three trips and after the game raced to the parking lot for the hour drive home to his beautiful wife and three kids. But what actually did happen during that last long day at Wrigley Field, the place he has been identified with for so long, was quite enough. It was just before the game when Pat Pieper came over the public address system with an announcement. "Your attention, ladies and gentlemen, your attention, please," he said, his heavy voice booming off the graying concrete stands and the thick brick walls. The crowd of more than 18,000 obediently turned the volume down. "Today marks the end of a distinguished career in baseball." Now there was a deathly quiet from the stands. "Today is the last day in uniform at Wrigley Field"—*No, not Ernie, he isn't going to do it, is he?*—"for umpire Al Barlick, who has spent 31 years as an umpire in the. . . ." The applause began behind home plate and spread all the way out to the left-field bleachers, and if it was not thunderous it was most definitely not for Al Barlick, decent man though he may be. It was for what Ernie Banks had not yet chosen to do.

4

Johnny Bench

Note the title of this article on Johnny Bench: "I'm Going to Be the First $100,000 Catcher in Baseball History." That was his goal when the article was first published in the spring of 1970. Since then he has won two Most Valuable Player awards and now makes about $150,000 a year—and not because of inflation. It won't be long before he's up to $200,000.

A few current players rank with Bench as great power hitters, but nobody's more of a force in the game today. He not only hits with power but hits in the clutch, and he's a team leader. And he's a great catcher.

When I started the All-Star Game of 1970, he was behind the plate. In the second inning Frank Howard came up to bat, all six feet seven and 260 pounds of him. He looked as if he were waving one of those Wiffle bats kids play with rather than a Louisville Slugger. I glanced over at my third baseman, Tony Perez, and he was playing so far back toward the left-field wall it seemed silly to call him an infielder. I couldn't blame him. A line drive by Howard could behead someone.

Then I looked at John and he was signaling for a changeup. And with me only 60 feet, six inches away from that mammoth of a hitter. I could see that John was giggling behind his mask, though, so I called time and called him out to meet me. "What're you trying to do—kill me?" I demanded, trying to keep from laughing. "Just wanted to see if you'd really throw it," he said, and trotted back behind the plate. I threw Howard fastballs—pitches he'd either hit eight miles or miss, but not line back up the middle—and I struck him out.

John likes to keep pitchers on their toes. A good catcher has to be able to adjust to his pitchers' personalities, and John can do that. Some he chews on, but others he handles gently. He seems to know just how to handle each one.

Great as he is as a catcher, though, I wouldn't be surprised if he winds up playing another position eventually. Bench is a very strong man, but catching wears a player out. I think the Reds will want to keep his power in the lineup for as many years as possible. And he could utilize that superpowerful arm of his at third base or right field.

Not that I'm anxious to help him conserve his strength. He's already given me enough trouble. He beat me in the first game of the playoffs last season by hitting a home run in the bottom of the ninth. When I started the fifth and final game at Shea Stadium, I had that home run clearly in mind. I didn't have real good stuff that day, and by the time Tony Perez came up in the first inning with Bench to follow, there were men on second and third, with one out. Since first base was open, I could have walked Perez and tried to get Bench to hit into a double play. But I knew John is an intelligent hitter and would be going for at least a sacrifice fly. So I decided to work on striking Perez out, then walk Bench, and work on the next hitter, Ken Griffey, for the final out. Probably only a handful of people at the park that day knew I had already decided to walk Bench before I pitched to

Perez. But the strategy worked: I struck out Perez, put Bench on first, and got Griffey for the third out. And we went on to win, 7–2. That's one way to handle a great hitter: Walk him.

"I'm Going to Be the First $100,000 Catcher in Baseball History"

•

Ron Smith

Jarry Park is a tiny, tottering stadium that is home to the Montreal Expos, and one night in 1969 in a game against the Cincinnati Reds, base-stealing Maury Wills, then with Montreal, was inching farther and farther from first. Up in the stands the crowd started hollering in French. Down on the field the Reds did not need a translator to tell them what was happening. Everybody in Canada knew Wills would be running on the next pitch.

Wills got his usual jackrabbit jump. Behind home plate the Cincinnati catcher gathered in the pitch. Straightening up, he reached into his mitt for the ball but found it tangled in the webbing. He jerked at it a second time, and at this stage in the proceedings nearly any catcher you can name would have forgotten about the whole thing. But not this catcher. Out came the ball. Down went the throw. Wills, sliding smoothly, was out. The shortstop, astraddle the bag, had been waiting for Wills with the ball in his glove and a smile on his face.

In the Expos's dugout startled players clapped themselves on the forehead and whistled through their teeth. "What the hell was that?" someone wanted to know. "That," said Gene Mauch, the Montreal manager, and a man noted for his ability to size up talent on the hoof, "was baseball's first $200,000 player."

That—as National League rivals have come to know and agonize over—was Johnny Bench. He is only 22 years old and has played but two full seasons in the majors, yet he stands today as the hottest piece of merchandise in the game. Baseball people snap, crackle and pop at the mention of his name, for here is the rarest of all perishable commodities. Here is a catcher who can hit and think and throw.

In the major-league marketplace, diluted by expansion, nothing is in greater demand or shorter supply than a good catcher. The front offices of team after team are practically having conniptions because they cannot find one. Detroit has Bill Freehan, Philadelphia has Tim McCarver and Chicago has Randy Hundley. But a great many clubs have nothing. Some are trying to get by behind the plate with people who do little more than throw the ball back to the pitcher, or stop it from hitting the umpire. Bench is so good he has graduated out of normal conversation and into a special frame of reference. He is being called not only the best young catcher ever, but a player who someday is going to ask the Cincinnati Reds for $200,000 a season, and the Cincinnati Reds are going to ask him does he want cash or a check.

Consider Luman Harris, who is manager of the catcherless Atlanta Braves. One day somebody asked him what kind of a catcher was Johnny Bench. Harris could not answer for a long time. Instead he gazed longingly across the diamond. "Well, I'll tell you," he finally intoned, "the other day he misjudged a windblown pop-up and it fell for a three-foot single. But, God, he looked magnificent even while losing the ball." Bench does look magnificent. He is six foot one and 195 pounds of iron, with thighs that seem about to burst through his flannel knickers. His shoulders are wide and a guy with a back as strong as his should be out working. He has thick wrists, a round face and a warm, lopsided grin. He is one-eighth Choctaw Indian on his father's side and was reared in Binger, Oklahoma, which is 600 people and two blocks of downtown.

Last year Bench batted .293, walloped 26 homers, drove in 90 runs and scored 83 himself. At the plate or behind it, no other receiver was close to him. He was a landslide pick for the All-Star team. In 1968 he was Rookie of the Year (first catcher ever so honored) and was voted the Gold Glove award for his defensive play (first rookie to win it). He also was 1967 Minor League Player of the Year. Before that he entered the Carolina League a mere mortal but when he left the management decided there would never be another like him, and promptly retired his uniform.

Once, against the St. Louis Cardinals, Bench slammed a homer with two on in the first, doubled home another run in the fifth and homered again in the ninth. He threw out three base runners, made a driving, tumbling catch of a foul ball, and called a flawless game. Afterward the reporters marched into the clubhouse. Johnny already had showered, dressed and left. "Where'd Bench go?" the press wanted to know. Alex Johnson, the outfielder, did not hesitate. "To a higher league," he said.

As it happens, there has never been a $100,000 catcher let alone a $200,000 player. "Yeah, well, there's going to be one now," says Bench, who fully expects to be both.

If such observations make Bench appear to be very high on himself, it is only because he is. He is not, mind you, one of those "I-can't-tell-you-how-lucky-I-am" dullards. Mostly he is a bright, big-talking combination of breezy egotism and cold self-analysis. He has no inhibitions about discussing himself. With too many players a few grunts, a couple of muttered obscenities and a turned back constitute a conversation. Bench, on the other hand, welcomes few things more than a chance to sit down and talk with as many people as possible about how good he is.

"Sometimes when people first meet me they think I'm conceited," Bench will allow, striving to be fair. "Maybe they can't tell conceit from pride. I do have a lot of pride. I also have a lot of confidence. I have to have it because a catcher has got to be a leader. If I move a fielder a few feet to the left or right because I'm going to call a certain pitch, he has to believe I know what I'm doing. Hell, I'm not pumped up. I just know what I can do."

What he can do is quite a lot. He takes charge of a game—any game—whether it is baseball on the field or cards in the clubhouse. He is an excellent bridge player, a poised after-dinner speaker, and was valedictorian of his high-school class. As a needler his face should go on the Post Office wall as one of the Ten Most Wanted. He once broke up a close game with a home run and the losing pitcher, still fuming, told a writer that Bench was nothing but a lucky bastard because, "I got that pitch where I wanted it." Bench heard about this. "I got it where I wanted it, too," he said, "—in the seats."

Perhaps the most astonishing thing about Bench is his arm. To begin with, it is about the size of a cannon and just about as powerful. It even awes pitchers. More than a few of them have said they wished they had his arm. They would even settle for his hand. Bench's hand is so big it can, by his own calculation, hold six baseballs at once. His fingers are extremely long and he grasps the ball far out on the end of them so that he can get plenty of whip.

Most of the time during a game, when a catcher throws to second base between innings, he performs the act matter-of-factly. He rises up and heaves it down and thinks no more of it than a mechanic would think of reaching for a wrench. Not Johnny. For him this is a time to zing one; a time for what is known in throwing circles as "serious heat"—that is, throwing the ball so hard it warms the infielder's hand.

No one does this better than Bench. When he pegs to

second the ball does not tail off at the end. Nor does it gain
any noticeable loft. "You see the ball coming in low," said
Woody Woodward, the shortstop, "and you are certain you
are going to have to one-hop it. But it keeps right on coming.
It explodes on you." Said Wayne Granger, the reliever,
"When Johnny hums one down, the pitcher better get the
hell out of the way. Johnny's liable to hit you right between
the eyes."

One day last spring in a preseason game against the Baltimore Orioles, Bench was warming up the pitcher and in the
Baltimore dugout some of the Birds—those who had played
against John in Puerto Rico in winter-league ball—were
standing on the top of the dugout steps and hollering. "Oh,
oh, look who's catching today. Oh, we are going to run
those bases today. We are going to steal everything that isn't
nailed down."

Of course, they did not even try. Brooks Robinson, the
incomparable Baltimore third baseman, will make a mistake
about as often as a manager will admit one. But he was
standing a few inches farther away from first base than
Bench thought he should be after singling to open an inning.
He did not stand there very long. Bench's throw arrived on
the wrong side of the bag. It got there so quickly, though,
that Lee May, the first baseman, had time to tag Robinson
before he could scramble back.

Later Robinson was sitting in the locker room, still visibly
impressed. "I don't get picked off very often," he was saying. "I have never seen a better arm."

Among other things, a catcher has to guard home plate
as though it were about to be burglarized. There are two
ways this can be done. One is force and the other fine art.
Bench does it either way and does it well. For instance,
against the Chicago Cubs he took a high throw from the
outfield. He made a quick, graceful little movement and

swept his glove across the sliding runner's spikes. He looked like Nureyev in shin guards. "I still have trouble believing what I saw," said Leo Durocher. "I have never seen that play executed so precisely."

Another time, against Philadelphia, Bench was hunched at home awaiting a throw while Deron Johnson, the Phillies's rugged, muscle-up slugger, rounded third base and set sail for the plate. Johnson was a football fullback in California and when he realized he was going to be out, he lowered his head and plunged forward like it was third down and two. Johnson neither scored a run nor gained a first down. He bounced off Bench and landed like a pile of rubble in the dust. In the dressing room a teammate asked him where he hurt and Johnson said, "Everywhere but the roof of my mouth."

Bench does so many things so well that the cumulative effect tends to irritate the opposition. Rivals take one look at his caveman physique and know he can be physical. But they also are finding out he is very good at gamesmanship.

Bill Singer is a rough, tough, six-foot-four fastballing righthander for the Los Angeles Dodgers and he has found out a lot about this. He is called The Singer Throwing Machine by his teammates, but the people who have to hit against him call him other names. One day at Dodger Stadium, Tony Perez caught hold of a Singer fastball and hammered it to the general neighborhood of Hawaii. Bench was the next batter and he knew what was coming. He was going to be dusted.

This is one of those traditional baseball tactics that batters accept as an occupational hazard. Anybody hits a home run off a tough pitcher, the next man up had better be looking for an inside, eye-level pitch that is supposed to intimidate him. Fans call it a brush-back pitch. Managers call it a "purpose pitch." The purpose, of course, is to make the batter get the hell out of the way.

Singer threw and Bench got the hell out of the way. The next pitch he could not get out of the way fast enough. The ball slammed into his shoulder. Bench did not like it. He trotted to first base, all the while glowering at Singer. The Reds figured any moment he was going to charge the mound. They figured wrong. John spent the rest of the game studying Singer. And he found what he was looking for. He is very observant of little things in a pitcher that will tell him whether a fastball or curve is coming next. Jimmy Stewart, the Reds's outfielder, is a lot like that too. Stewart and Bench compared notes and two weeks later in Cincinnati Singer was pitching again. Johnny crunched a curveball ("Of course it helps to know when the hook is on the way," said Johnny) and it did not stop flying until long after it had left the playing field in dead center field. Johnny rounded the bases triumphantly.

Johnny Lee Bench was born December 7, 1947, the son of a man who himself was an athlete and a good one. Ted Bench could run faster, throw harder and hit better than anyone in Caddo County. But one night at a big high-school basketball game a new coach decided to start somebody else and the next day Ted Bench walked out of the high-school building and never went back.

He might have made it to the majors himself as a catcher, but World War II got in the way and by the time Ted was out of the army, he was too old to interest the scouts. Instead he knocked about from job to job before starting his own little business, which was selling natural gas. As it turned out, he was better at baseball than business. The family had very little money and by the time Johnny was nine, he already was out working. He was running errands, unloading boxes at the grocery store, and he was digging peanuts out of the ground and shucking them. ("Binger is the peanut capital of the world in that area," says John.)

He also was learning to play baseball. Ted Bench could see that here was a boy with a chance to make it big. So when Johnny was 10 and ready for Little League, Ted did not let the fact that Binger had no Little League team stop him. He organized his own. Saturday mornings Ted's pickup truck would go jouncing down Route 152 with the team in the back and Johnny Lee in the front, listening to his father tell him how they were going to whip Carnegie and Clinton and the other teams they played.

Usually they did. Johnny pitched and batted fourth. Later he pitched for Binger's nine-man state championship team, and for a neighboring town's American Legion team. He also was an honorable mention high-school All-America as a basketball guard.

"But I was always known as a catcher," said John. "My dad kept telling me catching was the quickest way to the majors because that's what they needed. And I'd been planning on being in the majors since the first grade."

Cincinnati's scouts did not have to be hit over the head to see that for themselves. Bench went one-for-eight in two Legion games, but the bird dogs beamed. They liked the way he moved and threw and handled a bat. The Reds drafted him and John signed the contract. Next day he was on an airplane headed for Tampa of the Florida State League.

The plane landed at nine o'clock that night, and Johnny went straight to the ball park. It was the ninth inning and the manager did not even bother to shake his hand. "All right, stud," he grumped, "get the gear on." Johnny got the gear on. He caught the ninth inning of his first pro game and afterward the manager told him from now on he was the regular catcher. The manager also told him he was the only catcher they had.

"I remember I woke up the next morning and I was scared," John recalls. "I said to myself, 'What the hell am I doing here?' I was 17 and a country boy. All I had in my suitcase were Levi's and old shoes. I looked around at the ball park and saw guys 24 or 25 who had given it their best shot and they knew they weren't going anywhere. I was one damn sad little country boy."

He said this one night not long ago from the vantage point of a modern, expensive, fifth-story apartment whose sliding glass doors overlook the city of Cincinnati. It is called The Forum and there are lots of singles, especially girls, who live there. Bachelor Bench, since that ninth inning in Tampa, has caught on fast—off the field as well as on. He wears Edwardian suits now, and alligator shoes, and his long brown sideburns are trimmed at Gentleman's Choice. Three years ago he was showing up for the teen hops in the Binger high-school gym. Now he pops up at a place in Cincinnati called The Inner Circle, and at discotheques around the league, and he dances the funky Broadway, the tighten up and the horse.

Being an Oklahoman, Bench now and then finds himself regarded as Mickey Mantle in a facemask. But similarities between them are purely superficial. They both are strong and come from Oklahoma and that is where the sameness ends. Mantle, for most of his career, was shy, suspicious, ill-educated, and talked the way you would expect Li'l Abner to sound. Bench is witty, warm and articulate. In the off-season he makes two or three speaking appearances. He tells the civic clubs of the tri-state area (Ohio, Kentucky and Indiana) that Binger is "two-and-a-half miles beyond Resume Speed" and that the way to deal with Lou Brock, the St. Louis speedster, when he breaks for second, is to "throw to third and head him off." The tri-state civic clubs cannot get enough of him.

"John will come up to you for the first time," said Bob Howsam, the Reds's general manager, "and give you that boyish grin and stick out that big paw, and it's like you have known him all your life. He's a real asset to the organization."

Typically, Bench could not agree more. He considered

himself such an asset to the Reds that the first time he signed a big-league contract he held out and got $25,000. Last winter he practically had Howsam turning purple before Howsam agreed to pay him $52,000 for the coming year's labors. Howsam had better get used to that color. With so many seasons ahead of him, barring injury or disaster, Bench seems certain to make a $100,000 paycheck look like loose change.

Not that he is shylock-hungry for money. "Johnny knows that a catcher's plentiful years are short," said Hy Ullner, who is Bench's newly acquired financial adviser. "He wants to be comfortable when he gets out. Some guys make big money for years and in the end you have to rip the damn uniforms off their backs to make them stop playing. They can't afford to quit, and they have no idea where the money went. Johnny doesn't want that happening to him."

Ullner is a self-made entrepreneur who hit it big in the discount-store business. He has steered Pete Rose into several successful ventures. ("You look in the *Wall Street Journal*," says Bench, "and any stock going up—Pete has it.") One day at Johnny's behest, Rose asked Ullner if he would be interested in taking on another client. The result is Pete Rose-Johnny Bench Enterprises, Inc., and the first step of the fledging firm was the down payment on an automobile dealership in nearby Dayton.

Dave Bristol, the Cincinnati manager when Bench hit the big leagues, went bananas over Johnny the first time he saw him. Bench didn't exactly start off like a house afire. His batting average was less than his weight as late as June in his first year, 1968. But Bristol stayed with him.

In August Bench hit well over .300 and in September he began to stroke home runs. He started out batting seventh in the Reds's lineup. He moved to sixth, to fifth, and finally, near the end of the year, he was batting cleanup on the top hitting team in the majors. Teammates began to like as well as respect him. They took to calling him Corkhead—a name

Bench hates—because of the size of his head. They meant it kindly, for to be truthful, Johnny's head is rather large even for a man of muscle.

Dave Bristol was thinking along similar lines last summer. He was thinking that Johnny's head was too big.

Between chaws on a mountain of gum and furious tugs at the bill of his cap, Bristol is a baseball traditionalist. He can spout the longest stream of vintage bromides in the game. ("A win in April is as good as a win in September," etc.) With the Reds he conducted more team meetings than anybody (an example, said critics, of overmanaging). "You got to communicate," proclaimed Bristol. "Some people don't like it, but I don't care. I got to tell it like it is." Last summer he and Johnny conducted their own small version of a cold war because of something Bristol said. What he said was that John Bench could do everything but listen.

He said this in a column written by Bill Connors of the Tulsa *Tribune*. "Bench has a great chance to be a superstar," Connors quoted Bristol. "But it irks me that so much is being made of him. I hate it. Every day everywhere I go it's Johnny Bench, Johnny Bench, Johnny Bench. He's not super yet. A super player can do anything. Bench still has some problems. But he doesn't like to be told about them. He does not want to hear about his shortcomings."

Understandably Johnny was wounded when he read Bristol's remarks, which were picked up and put on the national wire by the Associated Press. "If there is one thing I am not," he insists passionately, "I am not a know-it-all." Bristol insisted just as passionately that not all of his remarks were picked up by the press service—particularly the part where he said, "Bench is so intelligent, so far above average, and so conscientious that it hurts him when I tell him that he has done something wrong. But I tell him because I want him to be the greatest player in baseball."

The damage was done, however, and the result was

that Bench and Bristol did not speak to each other very much in the waning days of the pennant race that autumn.

It was not a good time for a player and his manager to be mad at each other. Five teams in the National League's wild, wild West Division were scrambling for the pennant, and the Reds were one of them. They came to Dodger Stadium for a key series and someone pinned a newspaper story on the wall of the dressing room. It said a computer picked the Dodgers to win the title. Jimmy Stewart wrote over the story with a pencil, "Do not fold, staple or mutilate."

The Reds swept the Dodgers out of the race, winning four out of four. But in the end it was they who were mutilated. On the last weekend of the season, the Reds lost to Houston and were erased from contention. Ten days later Bristol was fired.

So now George (Sparky) Anderson is the manager. He is up from the minors and he knows he has inherited a team that is as enigmatic as a Kremlin caper. The history of the Reds is that they always seem to start out on target but lose sight of the bull's-eye along the way. Yet experts say this year Cincinnati is primed for a pennant run. [*Ed. The Big Red Machine did, of course, win the pennant in 1970.*] . . .

One thing for certain . . . Bench provides the team not only with hitting, but superiority at perhaps the most important position on the field.

Bristol, telling it like it was, was right about something, however. Bench does have problems, albeit the rest of the managers in the game would like to have a guy with his woes. He has a catcher's usual trouble handling the low, inside pitch. (He led the league in passed balls with 18 as a rookie, but cut the figure nearly in half last year.) He has a habit of snatching at outside pitches. To be sure, such misdemeanors can be easily corrected. But because of this, there are some baseball men who are inclined to wait and see before hailing Bench as the new Bill Dickey.

Rube Walker, the New York Mets's coach, feels differ-ently. "So what's to see?" snorted Walker, himself a former big-league catcher. "This boy can do it all now. For his age there never has been one like him. Not Dickey or Yogi Berra or Mickey Cochrane. How often does a guy like this come along? How often do you see this kind of an arm and that kind of intelligence? Hell, here's a kid who is going to be the biggest thing in baseball. He is going to be worth a fortune."

In Binger one day not long ago there were at least 5000 people who agreed. These were the home folks who turned out from all parts of the county for Johnny Bench Day. In Oklahoma, of course, sports are an ideological crusade. The natives will brag all night about their chili, beautiful women and the university football team's manifest destiny. Now there is Bench to brag about, too. Everybody was pumping his hand and whomping him on the back. They poked cameras in his face and asked him to smile. Johnny just kept smiling and smiling.

Chances are he will keep on smiling—if not all the way to the Hall of Fame, then certainly to the bank.

5

Casey

Casey was a mighty batter, as every baseball fan knows. A fearsome fellow at the plate.

> *There was ease in Casey's manner as he stepped into his place;*
> *There was pride in Casey's bearing and a smile on Casey's face.*

Obviously a tough man for a pitcher to face in a clutch situation. But in the bottom of the ninth, with two men on and the winning run at the plate and the Mudville fans screaming for Casey to belt one, that pitcher—Fireball seems to be his name—didn't choke.

It's about time he was given some credit—and he is in this obscure ballad written by someone known only as "Sparkus."

Of course, you must remember that Fireball's strategy, though appropriate in the year the game was played—1888 —would *never* be used today.

The Man Who Fanned Casey

•

"Sparkus"

I'm just an ordinary fan, and I don't count for much,
But I'm for writing history with a true and honest touch.
It isn't often that I knock—I'll put you next to that—
But I must interpose a word on *Casey at the Bat*.

Oh, yes, I must admit it; the poem is a beaut.
Been runnin' through my thinker since our team got on the
    chute.
I heard an actor fan recite it thirteen years ago;
He sort of introduced it in the progress of the show.

It made a hit from gallery, down to the parquet floor;
But now I've got to thinking, and that poem makes me sore.
I'd like to know why any fan should be so off his nut
About the Mighty Casey who proved himself a mutt.

The score, we're told, stood four to two, one inning left to
    play.
The Frogtown twirler thought he had things pretty much
    his way,
So in the ninth, with two men down, he loosened up a bit;
And Flynn scratched out a single, Blake let loose a two-base
    hit.

Then from the stand and bleachers there arose a mighty
    roar.
They wanted just that little hit they knew would tie the
    score.
And there at bat was Casey, Mighty Casey, Mudville's
    pride;
But was the Frogtown pitcher sent balloonin', terrified?

Now in the ninth, with two men down and Casey at the
      bat,
Most pitchers would have let him walk—we all are sure of
      that.
But Fireball was a hero, he was made of sterner stuff;
It's *his* kind get the medals and the long newspaper puff.

He knew the time had come for him to play a winning role.
He heard the fans a-yelling; it was music to his soul.
He saw the gleam of confidence in Mighty Casey's eye.
"I'll strike him out!" Fireball resolved. "I'll do it or I'll die!"

He stood alone and friendless in that wild and frenzied
      throng.
There wasn't even one kind word to boost his game along.
But back in Frogtown where they got plays by special wire,
The fans stood ready, if he won, to set the town on fire.

Now Fireball twirls his body on the truest corkscrew plan,
And hurls a swift inshoot that cuts the corner of the pan.
But Casey thought the first ball pitched would surely be a
      ball,
And didn't try to strike it, to the great disgust of all.

Again the Frogtown twirler figures dope on Mudville's
      pride;
And Casey thinks the next will be an outshoot breaking
      wide.
But Fireball shot a straight one down the middle of the plate,
And Casey waited for a curve until it was too late.

And now the mighty slugger is a-hangin' on the string.
If another good one comes along, it's up to him to swing.
The jaunty smile, Fireball observed, has faded from his face,
And a look of straining agony is there to take its place.

One moment Fireball pauses, hides the ball behind his glove,

And then he drives it from him with a sweeping long arm
    shove.

And now the air is shattered, and the ball's in Thatcher's
    mitt,

For Casey, Mighty Casey, hadn't figured on the spit!

6

Roberto Clemente

I can remember seeing Roberto Clemente play once when I was in college. I was sitting in my uncle's box seats behind third base at Dodger Stadium, and Clemente hit a long line drive to right field, good for extra bases. He was exceptionally fast, but he ran in a very unorthodox style, and as he rounded second, it looked as if his arms and legs were flying in every direction. He slid into third for a triple. The expression on his face hadn't changed from the time he walked up to the plate until he was brushing himself off as he stood on third. I was thinking about playing professionally then, and Clemente helped confirm my idea of a true superstar—one who gives 100 percent at all times. You could see just by the way he ran that triple that there was nothing more he could give.

I talked with Pittsburgh pitcher Dave Giusti after Clemente died. We were discussing how Roberto was so often criticized for sitting out games when he didn't feel well enough to play. Dave explained that, for Clemente, it was a matter of honor. If he couldn't go out and give the fans the real Roberto Clemente, he just didn't want to perform in front of them; he wanted to give what Roberto Clemente was capable of giving and nothing less. He was that proud.

He was a phenomenal hitter: exactly 3000 hits in his career, four batting championships, five times over .340 for a season, .317 lifetime average. He was slow in gaining superstar recognition, though, mainly because he wasn't a home-run hitter. He did have great power—twice he hit three home runs in a game—but for most of his career he played in Forbes Field, which had a left field the size of an apple orchard. So instead of trying to pull the ball for home runs to left, he made himself into a line-drive hitter and adopted a style that gave him power to right. Once in a while, just to keep the pitcher honest, he would pull the ball hard to left, but most of his hits were line drives to right.

In his prime, Clemente could handle almost any pitch. The only exception was a fastball or a slider on the extreme low outside corner of the strike zone. You could imagine a box in that corner just big enough to hold a baseball, and if you were good enough to get the ball into that box three times in a row, Clemente would walk away from the plate. He knew the strike zone and his capabilities as a hitter so well that he would not swing at a pitch in exactly that spot, the only one where he couldn't hit the ball solidly. He'd give that tiny spot to the pitcher. But if you got the ball anywhere else in the strike zone, he'd hit a line drive just about every time.

"Nobody Does Anything Better Than Me in Baseball," Says Roberto Clemente . . . Well, He's Right

●

C. R. Ways

Like novelists' and Presidents', baseball stars' reputations fluctuate, and Roberto Clemente's is currently, finally, pretty close to what Clemente thinks it ought to be.

The Pittsburgh Pirates's Puerto Rican right fielder is coming into the 1972 season from a great World Series. Last October, when the Pirates upset the Baltimore Orioles four games to three, Clemente batted .414, hit two home runs and missed another by three inches, made two notable running catches, intimidated runners with his throws and was named Most Valuable Player of the Series.

Now, that would be a fine consummation of anyone's 17th season in the major leagues, but in the case of Clemente it was especially right and timely. Like an 0-for-4 slugger who is said to be "due" for a hit, Clemente was due to lead a team to glory. He is after all the only active member of the Pirates who will unquestionably be elected to baseball's Hall of Fame, and yet until the '71 Series he had never been established as the man who *made the difference*.

This is a delicate matter. The man who makes the difference is the team leader, the *macher*, the tough out in the last inning, the man who comes up with the big play when it counts. The other active players who are Hall of Fame cinches—Willie Mays, Hank Aaron, Bob Gibson, Frank and Brooks Robinson—are all solid make-the-difference figures. Of these only Mays and Aaron can be said to be as gifted as Clemente; as Clemente said defensively but defensibly early on in last year's Series, "Nobody does anything better than me in baseball."

Clemente, however, had not proved himself as a kingpin. Yes, a thrilling performer on a given play; yes, an astoundingly consistent high-average hitter (four batting championships, .318 lifetime and climbing), but also a man who is in and out of the line up, who complains about myriad ills, and who, most tellingly, had never been identified with the winning of a pennant or a Series.

In 1960, when the Pirates were world champions, Clemente hit safely in every Series game for a .312 average, but he figured in only two memorable moments. One, he ran into Bill Virdon after Virdon made an important leaping catch. Two, he reached first on a dribbly grounder in the seventh game and therefore was on base when Hal Smith hit a big eight-inning home run. The two things that will be remembered longest about that Series are the ground ball that hit then Yankee second baseman, Tony Kubek, in the Adam's apple and the ninth-inning home run by Pirate second baseman Bill Mazeroski that won the seventh game and the Series. Clemente, the team's leading hitter during the regular season, was virtually ignored in post-Series coverage —until it transpired that he had rushed away from the dressing room and back toward Puerto Rico after the final game, before the team's beer-sloshing celebration began. Then, when word came that teammates Dick Groat and Don Hoak had finished one-two in the voting for Most Valuable Player in the National League and Clemente had come in eighth, Clemente sent up a cry of outrage.

This was embarrassing. It inhibited the development of a proper make-the-difference mystique about Clemente. In the 1961 All-Star game in San Francisco's Candlestick Park, Clemente tripled, drove in a run with a sacrifice fly and knocked in the winning run in the 10th. The papers gave more space to the wind blowing pitcher Stu Miller off the mound.

Then, in 1966, when Clemente was voted the league's Most Valuable Player, the Pirates failed to win the pennant. In 1970, when they finished first in their division, Clemente hit .352, but played in only 108 of 162 games. In 1971 he hit .341 for the regular season, but he missed 30 games with assorted injuries, and the big man in the batting order was prepotent Willie Stargell, whose number was written on his bats and shower shoes in Roman numerals, and whose home runs, sheer presence and run production, all achieved in spite of agonized knees, overshadowed Clemente's contribution.

But in the Series Stargell didn't hit. Clemente did. He hit and hit and hit and hit, as TV looked on more intimately—in close-ups from several angles—than ever before. He got at least one hit in every game (so that he has never gone hitless in a Series game, a nice item for myth-making), he produced runs, and his second home run put the Pirates ahead to stay in the final game. You could feel throughout the media a great rush of relieved commemoration. Clemente, the great talent, was finally, after all these years, a winner, a heavy dude.

All of which has to be rethought. As it stands, it is Casey-at-the-Bat thinking, which ignores the true distinction of Clemente. Plenty of ballplayers have starred in a World Series, but only Clemente ever said, "When I wake up in the morning, I pray I am still asleep." Only Clemente ever explained that he scored all the way from first on a single to beat the Dodgers because "I had a sore foot. I wanted to rest it."

Baseball is a team competition and not an art form, so the value ascribed to Getting the Job Done (Winning), as opposed to expressing oneself intensely and with style, is apt enough. But baseball is not really a sport that gives rise to figures like basketball's Bill Russell and Willis Reed, who at their best could be relied upon to dominate a game and deliver victory. In baseball a hitter can bat only four or five times a game—he can't just grab the ball or station himself under the basket and take over—and a pitcher can start a game only once every four or five days. Also, baseball is too chancy. Casey could hit the ball on the nose and still be an easy out, or he could get just a little piece of it and get a game-winning single or even a cheap home run. Casey might never come up with men on base, and in the field he might never have a difficult chance. Luck aside, not even the best hitters can reasonably be expected to come through more often than once every three times at bat. But the fans want them to. When the big hitter grounds out in the clutch, after perhaps getting two hits on nearly identical ground balls earlier, they feel betrayed. When veteran Detroit star Al Kaline came up in a do-or-die spot in the 1968 Series and hit an intrinsically dinky single, it was received by fans as a great and almost necessary confirmation. They want to be assured that the star is *there*, that he has a probability-defying integrity that comes through when it is crucial that he do so.

But Clemente has other, inimitable ways of showing he is *there*. It is expected of ballplayers that they discuss their injuries and ailments, even minor ones, in grim understatements prefaced by "I'm not making any excuses." Clemente is utterly up front, not to say confessional about anything that is bothering him—even if it is something minor, even if it is something uncanny. This can be more interesting than a propitious hit.

In his time, Clemente has been bothered not only by the usual pulled muscles, but also by tension headaches, nervous stomach, a tendon rubbing against the bone in his left heel, malaria, a strained instep, bone chips in his elbow, a curved spine, countless bruises, one leg heavier than the other (according to a chiropractor), hematoma of the thigh incurred in a lawnmowing accident, wayward disks in his neck and back, a systemic paratyphoid infection from the hogs on a small farm he owns, severe food poisoning and insomnia. And he has always been very open about these things, with teammates and managers, who have not always been sympathetic, and with writers, who have sometimes been gleeful. Writers report that Clemente has to "boop" his back and neck into place every morning before getting out of bed. Or they quote him as saying, "My wrist is still swollen but all the bad blood left it. I felt a pain in my stomach, like poison there, you know? I think that was the blood running down out of my wrist."

Then Clemente is incensed. He claims that he has been made out a hypochondriac. When you ask him how he feels, he responds not like a hero and not whiningly either, but ingenuously—earnestly expressing a natural resentment against having to suffer.

"It hurts *sooo bad*," he will say. Now, Clemente grew up as the youngest child in a large, happy, hard-working but comfortable family, his father the foreman on a sugar-cane plantation, and he often gives heartfelt thanks to his parents for taking such good care of him. He talks about his hurts as a favorite son might in all honorable candor to his mother.

This does not always look well in print, especially to Clemente, who is not only very sensitive to his body's signals, but also very proud. Sometimes he is innocently proud, as when he says, "If I am going good I don't need batting practice, but sometimes I take it so the other players can see me hit." Sometimes he is proud in self-defense.

"Lots of times I have the feeling people want to take advantage of me, especially writers," he says. "They talk to me, but maybe they don't like me, so they write about me the way they want to write."

Maybe he is spoiled by the adulation he gets in the off-season in Puerto Rico where he lives palatially in the hills outside San Juan with his beautiful wife (whom he met in a drugstore while buying medication for a bad leg) and two children. In Puerto Rico he is constantly giving talks and appearing at ceremonies. He was recently named an honorary doctor of education by the Catholic University of Puerto Rico. He plans to retire to Puerto Rico in two or three years to start a chiropractic clinic and a utopian boys' sports camp.

Or maybe Clemente wants to be accorded the simple gee-whiz deference with which Mays and Aaron have generally been written up in recent years. But Clemente is not like other great players. Even aside from his forthrightness about pain, he has more to say than other great players. Mays and Aaron do not go around saying aggrievedly that they are the best and should get more recognition. But then again, Mays and Aaron do not go around protesting baseball's reserve clause, which keeps a player from changing jobs on his own accord and therefore, as Clemente has pointed out, deprives ballplayers of one of the freedoms of a plumber. Mays and Aaron do not protest that blacks and Latins get too few offers of outside money for product endorsements. Clemente has been complaining about the endorsement matter for so long that he now affects indifference—but vocal indifference. "I've had a couple of endorsements but they never came to nothing. I don't want to make any. I don't need them. If the people who give them out don't think Latins are good enough, I don't think *they* are good enough. The hell with them. I make endorsements in Spanish countries and give the money to charity."

When it comes time for formal gratitude, Mays and Aaron do not speak as feelingly as did Clemente when presented his Series MVP trophy. "I respect people. I respect my mother and father. This has given me the opportunity to know people, to hurt people once in a while, but mostly to love people."

Nor has either Mays or Aaron ever told as strange a story as Clemente told suddenly last August when he revealed that one night during the previous season as he was walking back to the Pirates's hotel in San Diego with a bag of fried chicken, he was kidnapped at gunpoint by four men and driven into the hills. There, he said, his abductors forced him to strip and took his wallet, his All-Star ring and $250, and were all set to shoot him—"They already had the pistol in my mouth"—when he managed belatedly to convince them of his identity. Whereupon they gave him back his clothes, wallet and ring and drove off. Then he heard them drive up again behind him. They rolled down the window of the car, said "Here," and handed him back his fried chicken.

That is the kind of thing, it might be said in all respect, that happens to a Latin ballplayer. Latins in the 20 years since they began to enter American baseball in numbers from Cuba, Mexico and South America, have added more color and unexpected personal drama to the game than any other ethnic group. Chico Ruiz, recently killed in an automobile accident, made a vivid reputation as a bench-warmer (with a special cushion and alligator shoes). It was Ruiz who once tied a feather on his head and chased Atlanta Braves mascot Chief Nok-a-Homa all the way to his teepee in the stands and pulled off his blanket. Then, last year, it was Ruiz who was goaded by his former close friend Alex Johnson into pulling a gun in the California Angels's clubhouse.

Rico Carty of the Braves, who calls himself "The Beeg Boy," and is the only active major-leaguer with a higher career batting average than Clemente, has suffered one calamity after another in the past three years, from tuberculosis to being beaten up by Atlanta police. On Rico Carty Appreciation Night last summer he stood tearfully at a microphone in Atlanta Stadium and complained that certain members of the Braves (by implication including Aaron, with whom he once traded blows in an airplane) did not like him. Juan Marichal of the Giants throws myriad pitches from myriad angles with a tremendous leg-kick and once hit then-Dodger John Roseboro on the head with a bat. Both César Tovar of Minnesota and Campy Campaneris of Oakland have played every position on the field, one inning each, in a single game, and Campaneris can pitch with either hand.

Zoilo Versalles was nagged and cajoled by Billy Martin, then a coach with the Twins, into becoming the American League's MVP in 1965, but that was his only good season. Clemente's teammate Manny Sanguillen is one of the three or four sunniest human beings and sincerest Christians in baseball, as well as the fastest-running catcher, but he complains that he has lost a good deal of his physique since switching from boxing to baseball. "I used to be *big*. But still, you don't see many guys that can do this!" He flexes one biceps with gigantic results and gives it a tweak with his fingers, causing an extra small muscle to spring up on top. "That's *moscle*," says Sanguillen. Wherever Clemente ranks among today's superstars, he is the best Spanish-speaking player ever, and that places him at the head of a rich tradition.

But it also entails a communication problem. By and large the baseball press has not been able to cope with the Latin influx. First-rate players like Minnesota's Tony Oliva, Cincinnati's Tony Perez and Baltimore's Mike Cuellar go virtually uninterviewed because they don't like to be quoted phonetically ("bayzebol," etc.) and because Tom Quinn, who covered the Senators for a while in long hair, a beard and a frock coat for the The Washington *Daily News*, but is now off to Colombia to write a book about a witch doctor, is the only regular baseball writer I know of who could interview in Spanish. (Myron Cope, however, when he did a portrait of Clemente for *Sports Illustrated* in 1966, took the trouble to consult a San Juan engineer and close friend of Clemente's named Libertario Aviles, who said "You have to understand that the Latin is touchy. If you say to me, 'Who is the best engineer in town?' I will say 'For me, I am the best.' It is a Spanish saying, an expression of self-respect.")

Clemente, who knew no conversational English when he left Puerto Rico in 1954 and had the usual problems of great loneliness and inability to order food, has not let language problems silence him. He still has a considerable accent, but he is the only Latin player to speak out in English (though several did to Quinn in Spanish) against the ethnocentrism of the American press. "If a Latin player is sick," Clemente said a few years back, "they said it is all in the head." Now, from his Series-hero eminence, he says, "There was never any problem about the people misunderstanding Latin players. But the writers, at first, they thought Latins were inferior to the American people. Now they know they can't be sarcastic about Latins. Which is something I have fought all my life."

There might have been something ethnocentric about the remark of a Pittsburgh coach: "These Latin hitters. They just see that little white thing coming up there and they *hit* it." But that observation seems a fair introduction, at least, to the essential Latin batting style. Once Sanguillen was asked why he kept on swinging at the first pitch, even though he knew it was a bad practice. "Because it makes me feel good!" he said happily.

Ted Williams, the former Red Sox slugger and current Texas Ranger manager and batting maven, has always maintained that a hitter should be moved only by pitches thrown to certain high-percentage-yield areas of the strike zone. The Latin hitter is more likely to go with his viscera after any pitch anywhere that looks sweet and challenging to him at the moment.

Clemente almost never goes for the first pitch, because he hates to end his time at bat too quickly, but he, like Tony

Oliva, has long been known as a bad-ball hitter who can line
a pitch off his ear into right field, which is the opposite direction from where a normal right-handed hitter would hit
such a pitch if he could hit it at all.

Along with the stomach spasms and the bad-blood rushes
and the peculiar neck-twitches he resorts to every couple of
minutes to relieve the pressure on his vertebrae, Clemente
gives the public many such astounding sleights of hand and
arm.

At five foot eleven, 180 pounds (or thereabouts, depending on how his stomach is), Clemente is almost exactly the
same size as Mays and Aaron, and they are all three right-
handed batters, but they all hit quite differently. Clemente
has hit balls as far as Mays and further than Aaron's best
bolts, but he has averaged fewer than 20 home runs a season.
Until mid-1970, the Pirates's home stadium was Forbes
Field, whose fences are so far back that the long ball was
less wise than the line drive. Partly no doubt by design or
instinctive adaptation, but largely by virtue of the inclina-
tion he has always shown toward free swinging, which
obviates a home run groove like Aaron's, Clemente has concentrated from the beginning on singles, doubles and triples.
This has cost him publicity . . . and is also the main reason
why he has produced far fewer runs than Mays or Aaron
(each of whom makes something between $35,000 and
$60,000 a year more than Clemente's current $140,000 salary) or Frank Robinson. But Clemente's more angular hits
spring from a stroke that deserves to be ranked with anyone's in terms of consistency, discipline and force.

The good hitter holds back late, to see how the pitch is
going to behave, and then somehow obtains enough sudden
leverage—enough elbow room to get around on the ball—to
avoid being "jammed" when it is full upon him. Aaron ac-
complishes this with fabled wrists, Stargell with sheer trunk-
and-arm strength. Mays "bails out," pulling away from the

plate with his front foot so that he can pull the ball to left field, while keeping his hands back so that he is not over-committed. Clemente's maneuver is almost the opposite of Mays's. He stands far back from the plate, waits very late and then, with his hands close in to his chest, shrugs the front of his body in on the ball so that he can reach way back and swipe it out of the catcher's mitt, virtually, and into right field.

This is known as "hitting from the inside out." It is not showy, in fact it looks rather constricted to the casual observer, but anyone who has dwelt at all upon the problem of hitting good pitching will appreciate the torsion and tensile stress involved in Clemente's solution. Such a wrench is enough to make anybody's body develop kinks. One of Clemente's chiropractors tells him, Clemente says, "that what I have wouldn't bother most men so much. But I am so strong, I strain my back so."

On the field he strains everything so, including credulity. Mays makes basket catches with his hands cupped at his waist, but Clemente makes them offhandedly way below his waist. Other outfielders make running or even diving catches, but Clemente makes sitting-down catches, sliding-on-one-hip catches and catches which provoke manager Harry Walker of Houston to say, "He took it full flight and hit the wall wide open. It was the best I've ever seen."

Once Clemente fielded a *bunt*. There were runners on first and second, and the Pirates's shortstop was covering third. The ball was bunted to where the shortstop would have been. Clemente, playing right field, the position farthest from shortstop, came running up, grabbed the ball on the ground and threw the runner coming from first base out at third. On more conventional throwing plays, Clemente exhibits the best outfield arm in baseball. And nobody quite combines a running catch, a whirl and throw the way Clemente does—so that he is occasionally photographed suspended sideways in the air, about four feet above the ground, releasing a lightning bolt.

But Clemente has always had these marvelous bodily functions. In the past, on the mainland, he has also had too few rewards to suit him. As recently as last spring he had boos from the Pittsburgh fans because he was sitting out so many games. And until recent years he tended to be on the outs with his managers and teammates.

The fans in 1972, however, will be cheering and indulging a new national institution. And today's Pirates have incorporated Clemente into one of the loosest and best integrated teams ever. When Clemente broke in with the Pirates in the mid-'50s, they had racial tensions that doubtless contributed to Clemente's moodiness, but last year they fielded (on occasion) the first all-black nine in big-league history, and for the last couple of years their dressing room has echoed with joyful racial slurs and exuberant interethnic grappling, such as Stargell seizing Sanguillen from behind, lifting him off the ground and declaring that he can't stand him.

Nobody grabs Clemente, but Sanguillen and pitcher Dock Ellis do open imitations of his limps and complaints, which no one would have dared to do or had enough affection to do, a few years back. And when asked about Clemente's qualities of leadership, Sanguillen says, seriously, "He is the inspiration."

Clements is still too enigmatic and misses too many games to be the rock on which the team is built, but there are so many stout personalities among the Pirates and so many fine young line-drive hitting outfielders to step in for him that nobody minds. Mazeroski once, years ago, reported to then-manager Danny Murtaugh that Clemente was well enough to play despite his literal belly-aching. Thus did Mazeroski help set off one of the two or three intense Murtaugh-Clemente confrontations over alleged goldbricking.

And in his years as a star Mazeroski used to play himself even when he was hurt or worn out because he had to hold the infield together. Now Mazeroski says about Clemente's games off in 1971, "I was glad to see him rest, because when he sat out a game it meant three or four when he would be at his best."

Clemente doesn't want to sit quietly by while something is making him feel bad, and he doesn't want to play with injuries when they might cause him to embarrass himself. No one else in baseball has managed to maintain such a posture and still claim the highest respect of peers and public. Now that he has last year's Series to his credit, Clemente can do it.

As a matter of fact, Steve Blass, an Anglo-Saxon nervous wreck who was spotty during the season but held firm to pitch two three-hitters over the Orioles, was arguably the player who swung last year's Series to the Pirates, since you figure Clemente is going to hit anyway, and since Clemente's seventh-game homer, as it happened, was the only one of his hits that figured in the crucial scoring. But if it takes an MVP trophy to certify Clemente in the public mind, then by all means he ought to have one, because he is more than a superstar, he is a man who not only hits but also talks and behaves from the inside out.

"It was not the best I could do," said Clemente after the Series, "but maybe the best anyone else could do. I have an injury." The dressing room was flowing with slung champagne. Pitcher Dave Giusti crept up behind Clemente with a fizzing bottle. "Don't spray me," Clemente cried. "I got a bad eye." Who else in baseball could get away with that?

7

Ty Cobb

No record is unbreakable. Ruth's 714 home runs once seemed to be, but now that has fallen. Ty Cobb's record of 96 stolen bases in a season was never going to be broken, the old-timers used to say; then Maury Wills came along and stole 104 in 1962.

But two of Cobb's records won't be broken until baseball undergoes another major change—his 4192 lifetime hits and his .367 lifetime average.

Cobb must have been a combination of Maury Wills and Pete Rose. Wills could steal bases almost every time he got on, and he was the type of player who would do everything in his power to beat you. Rose doesn't have Wills's speed, but, like Cobb, he's a great singles hitter with a burning desire to win.

This article by Ring Lardner, published in 1915, shows some of the ways Cobb could find to beat you, by combining baseball intelligence with fierce competitiveness.

There's a dividing line between competitiveness and viciousness. You respect the competitor, but not players who deliberately try to hurt others. I know Wills and Rose as hard-nosed competitors that I respect, not as dirty players. Some claim that Cobb filed his spikes to razor edges to slash at basemen in his way. If he did, he carried competitiveness too far, but the stories may well have been exaggerated.

If I were pitching to Cobb, I'd keep the ball low, trying to make him hit it on the ground rather than on a line drive to the outfield. Even the fastest runners today can't outrun the arm of a Buddy Harrelson if the ball is hit near him. And if Cobb bunted and I had to cover first base, I'd be very careful.

Tyrus: The Greatest of 'Em All

●

Ring W. Lardner

Sit down here a while, kid, and I'll give you the dope on this guy. You say you didn't see him do nothin' wonderful? But you only seen him in one serious. Wait till you been in the league more'n a week or two before you go judgin' ball-players. He may of been sick when you played agin him. Even when he's sick, though, he's got everybody I ever seen skun, and I've saw all the best of 'em.

Say, he ain't worth nothin' to that club; no, nothin'! I don't know what pay he's gettin', but whatever it is, it ain't enough. If they'd split the receipts 50–50 with that bird, they wouldn't be gettin' none the worst of it. That bunch could get along just as well without him as a train could without no engine.

He's twicet the ballplayer now that he was when he come up. He didn't seem to have no sense when he broke in; he run bases like a fool and was a mark for a good pitcher or catcher. They used to just lay for him when he got on. Sully used to tell the pitchers to do nothin' but waste balls when he was on first or second base. It was pretty near always good dope, too, because they'd generally nail him off one base or the other, or catch him tryin' to go to the next one. But Sully had to make perfect pegs to get him even when he knowed beforehand that he was goin'. Sully was the boy that could make them perfect pegs, too. Don't forget that.

Cobb seemed to think they was only one rule in the book, and that was a rule providin' that nobody could stay on one base more'n one second. They tell me that before he got into the South Atlantic League he was with a club down there in Georgia called the Royston Rompers. Maybe he thought he had to keep on rompin' up here.

Another thing was that he couldn't hit a left-hander very good. Doc W'ite used to make him look like a sucker. Doc was a fox to begin with, and he always give you just what you wasn't lookin' for. And then, his curveball was somethin' Ty hadn't never saw before and it certainly did fool him. He'd hand Cobb a couple o' curves and the baby'd miss 'em a foot. Then, when he was expectin' another one, Doc'd shoot his fast one right past his chin and make a monkey out of him.

That was when he first come up here. But Ty ain't the guy that's goin' to stay fooled all the time. When he wises up that somebody's got somethin' on him, he don't sleep nor do nothin' till he figures out a way to get even. It's a good thing Doc had his chancet to laugh when he did, because Cobb did most o' the laughin' after a couple o' seasons of it. He seen he couldn't hit the curve when it was breakin', so he stood way back in the box and waited till it'd broke. Then he nailed it. When Ty'd learned that trick, Doc got so's he was well pleased when the balls this guy hit off'n him stayed in the park.

It was the same way with every pitcher that had his number when he first busted in. He got to 'em in short order and, before long, nobody was foolin' him so's you could notice it. Right now he's as good agin left-handers as he is agin regular fellas. And if they's any pitcher in baseball that's got him fooled, he's keepin' the fact well concealed.

I was tellin' you what a wild base runner he was at first. Well, he's still takin' chances that nobody else takes, but he's usin' judgment with it. He don't run no more just for the sake o' runnin'. They was a time when the guy on the base ahead of him was afraid all the time that he'd get spiked in the heels. But no more o' that. They's no more danger of him causin' a rear end collision, providin' the guy ahead don't blockade the right o' way too long.

You may not believe it, but I'll bet most o' these here catchers would rather have somebody on second base when Ty's on first base than to have him on first base alone. They feel pretty safe when he can't steal without bumpin' into one of his own teammates. But when the track's all clear, look out! . . .

You know I ain't played no ball for the last few years, but I seen a lot of it played. And I don't overlook no chancet to watch this here Tyrus. I've saw him agin every club in the American League and I've saw him pull more stuff than any other guy ever dreamed of. Lots o' times, after seein' him get away with somethin', I've said to myself: "Gosh, he's a lucky stiff!" But right afterward, I've thought: "Yes, and why don't nobody else have that luck? Because they don't go out and get it."

I remember one time in Chi, a year or two ago. The Sox was two to the bad and it was the ninth innin'. They was two men down. Bodie was on second base and somebody hits a single to center field. Bodie tries to score. It wasn't good baseball to take the chancet, because that run wasn't goin' to do no good without another one to put with it. Cobb pegs to the plate and the umps calls Bodie out, though it looked to everybody like he was safe. Well, it was a bad play of Bodie's, wasn't it? Yes. Well then, it was a bad play o' Cobb's to make the throw. If Detroit hadn't of got the best o' that decision, the peg home would of let the man that hit the ball go to second and be planted there in a position to score the tyin' run on another base hit. Where if Ty had of played it safe, like almost anybody would, the batter'd of been held on first base where it would take two base hits or a good long wallop to score him. It was lucky for Ty that the umps happened to guess wrong. But say, I think that guy's pretty near smart enough to know when a umpire's goin' to make a rotten decision.

O' course you know that Ty gets to first base more'n anybody in the world. In the first place, he always manages to hit better'n anybody. And when he don't hit safe, but just bounds one to some infielder, the bettin's two-to-one that the ball will be booted or throwed wild. That's his luck, is it? No, sir. It's no such a thing. It's his speed. The infielder knows he ain't got no time to spare. He's got to make the play faster'n he would for anybody else, and the result is that he balls it all up. He tries to throw to first base before he's got the pill to throw, or else he hurries the throw so much that he don't have no time to aim. Some o' the ball-players 'round the league says that the scorers favor Ty and give him a base hit on almost anything. Well, I think they ought to. I don't believe in handin' a error to a fella when he's hurried and worried to death. If you tried to make the play like you do for other guys, Ty'd beat the ball to first base and then you'd get a hot call from the bench for loafin'.

If you'd saw him play as much baseball as I have, you wouldn't be claimin' he was overrated. I ain't goin' to come right out and say he's the best ever, because they was some old timers I never seen. (Comiskey, though, who's saw 'em all, slips it to him.) I just want to tell you some o' the things he's did, and if you can show me his equal, lead me to him and I'll take off my hat.

Detroit was playin' the Ath-a-letics oncet. You know

they ain't no club that the Tigers looks better agin than the Ath-a-letics, and Cobb's more of a devil in Philly than anywheres else. Well, this was when he was battin' fourth and Jim Delehanty was followin' him. Ty singles and Del slips him the hit-and-run sign on the first ball. The ball was pitched a little outside, and Del cuts it down past Harry Davis for a single to right field. Do you know what Cobb done? He scored; that's all. And they wasn't no boot made, neither. Danny Murphy picked the ball up clean and pegged it to Davis and Davis relays it straight home to Ira Thomas. Ty was there ahead of it. If I hadn't o' been watchin' close, I'd o' thought he forgot to touch two or three bases. But, no, sir. He didn't miss none of 'em. They may be other guys that could do that if they tried, but the diff'rence between them and Cobb is that he done it and they didn't. Oh, I guess other fellas has scored from first base on a long single in the hit and run, but not when the ball was handled perfectly clean like this one.

Well, here's another one: I forget the exact details, except that the game was between the White Sox and Detroit and that Tannehill was playin' third base at the time, and that the score was tied when Cobb pulled it. It was the eighth innin'. He was on first base. The next guy hits a single to left field. Ty, o'course, rounds second and starts for third. The left fielder makes a rotten peg and the pill comes rollin' in. Ty has the play beat a mile and they ain't no occasion for him to slide. But he slid, and do you know what he done? He took a healthy kick at that rollin' ball and sent it clear over to the grandstand. Then he jumped to his feet and kept on goin'. He was acrost the plate with the winnin' run before nobody'd realized what he'd did. It's agin the rules, o' course, to kick the ball a-purpose, but how could the umps prove that this wasn't a accident? Ty could of told him that he thought the play was goin' to be close and he'd better slide. I might o' thought it was a accident, too, if that had of been the only time I seen him do it. I can't tell you how many times he's pulled it, but it's grew to be a habit with him.

I've saw him score from second base on a fly ball, too; a fly ball that was catched. Others had did it, but not as regular as this guy. He come awful near gettin' away with it agin a little while ago, in Chi. They was also somebody on third when the ball was hit. The guy on third started home the minute Bodie catched the ball and Ping seen they was no chancet to get him. So he pegs toward Weaver, who's down near third base. Cobb's at third before the ball gets to the infield. He don't never hesitate. He keeps right on goin' for the plate. Now, if Weaver'd of been able to of intercepted the ball, Ty'd of been out 30 feet. But the throw goes clear through to the third baseman. Then it's relayed home. The gang sittin' with me all thought Ty was safe. I don't know about it, but anyway, he was called out. It just goes to show you what this guy's liable to do. You can't take no afternoon nap when he's around. They's lots of other fast guys, but while they're thinkin' about what they're goin' to do, he's did it. He's figurin' two or three bases ahead all the while. So, as I say, you don't get no sleep with him in the game.

Fielder Jones used to tell us: "When that bird's runnin', throw the ball somewheres just's soon as you get a-hold of it. I don't care where you throw it, but throw it somewheres. Don't hold onto it."

I seen where the papers says the other day that you outguessed him. I wasn't out to that game. I guess you got away with somethin' all right, but don't feel too good about it. You're worst off now than you was before you done it because he won't never rest till he shows you up. You stopped him oncet, and just for that he'll make you look like a rummy next time he plays agin you. And after he's did it oncet and got even, he'll do it agin. And then he'll do it

agin. They's a lot o' fellas 'round this league that's put over
a smart play on Tyrus and most of 'em has since wished
they hadn't. It's just like as if I'd go out and lick a policeman. I'd live to regret it.

We had a young fella oncet, a catcher, that nailed him
flat-footed off'n first base one day. It was in the first game
of a serious. Ty didn't get on no more that day, but he
walked the first time up the followin' afternoon. They was
two out. He takes a big lead and the young fella pegs for
him agin. But Tyrus was off like a streak when the ball was
throwed, and about the time the first baseman was catchin'
it, he was slidin' into second. Then he gets a big lead off'n
second and the young catcher takes a shot for him there.
But he throws clear to center field and Ty scores. The next
guy whiffs, so they wouldn't of been no run if the young
guy hadn't of got so chesty over the precedin' day's work.
I'm tellin' you this so's you won't feel too good.

They's times when a guy does try to pull something on
this Cobb, and is made to look like a sucker without de-
servin' it. I guess that's because the Lord is for them that
helps themselves and don't like to see nobody try to show
'em up.

I was sittin' up in the stand in Cleveland one day. Ty was
on second base when somebody hits a fly ball, way out, to
Birmingham. At that time, Joe had the best throwin' arm
you ever see. He could shoot like a rifle. Cobb knowed that,
o' course, and didn't feel like takin' no chancet, even though
Joe was pretty far out there. Ty waits till the ball's catched
and then makes a bluff to go to third, thinkin' Birmy'd
throw and that the ball might get away. Well, Joe knows
that Cobb knows what kind of arm he's got and figures
that the start from second is just a bluff; that he ain't really
got no intention o' goin'. So, instead o' peggin' to third, he
takes a quick shot for second, hopin' to nail Cobb before
he can get back. The throw's perfect and Cobb sees where

he's trapped. So he hikes for third. And the second sacker—
I don't think the big Frenchman was playin' that day—drops
the ball. If he'd of held it, he'd of had plenty of time to
relay to third and nail Ty by a block. But no. He drops the
ball. See? Birmy'd outguessed Ty, but all it done for him
was to make him look bad and make Ty look good. . . .

Sometimes I pretty near think they's nothin' he couldn't
do if he really set out to do it. . . .

One time, in 1912 I think it was, I happened to be goin'
East, lookin' for a job of umpirin', and I rode on the train
with the Tigers. I and Cobb et breakfast together. I had a
Sunday paper with me and was givin' the averages the oncet
over.

"Read 'em to me," says Ty.

"You don't want 'em all, do you?" I says.

"No, no. Just the first three of us," he says. "I know about
where I'm at, but not exactly."

So I read it to him:

"Jackson's first with .412. Speaker's second with .400.
You're third with .386."

"Well," says Ty, "I reckon the old boy'd better get busy.
Watch me this trip!"

I watched him, through the papers. In the next 21 times at
bat, he gets exactly 17 hits, and when the next averages was
printed, he was out in front. He stayed there, too.

So I don't know, but I believe that if Jackson and Speaker
and Collins and Lajoie and Crawford was to go crazy and
hit .999, this Cobb would come out on top with 1.000 even.

He's got a pretty good opinion of himself, but he ain't no
guy to really brag. He's just full o' the old confidence. He
thinks Cobb's a good ballplayer, and a guy's got to think
that way about himself if he wants to get anywheres. I know
a lot o' ballplayers that gets throwed out o' the league because they think the league's too fast for 'em. It's diff'rent

with Tyrus. If they was a league just three times as fast as the one he's in and if he was sold up there, he'd go believin' he could lead it in battin'. And he'd lead it too!

Yes, sir, he's full o' that old stuff, and the result is that lots o' people that don't know him think he's a swell-head, and don't like him. But I'm tellin' you that he's a pretty good guy now, and the rest o' the Tigers is strong for him, which is more'n they used to be. He busted in with a chip on his shoulder, and he soon become just as popular as the itch. Everybody played him for a busher and started takin' liberties with him. He was a busher, too, but he was one o' the kind that can't take a joke. You know how they's young fellas that won't stand for nothin'. Then they's them that stands for too much. Then they's the kind that's just about half way. You can go a little ways with 'em, but not too far. That's the kind that's popular.

Cobb wouldn't stand for nothin'. If somebody poured ketchup in his coffee, he was liable to pick up the cup and throw it at the guy nearest to him. If you'd stepped on his shine, he'd of probably took the other foot and aimed it at you like he does now at the ball when it's lyin' loose on the ground. If you'd called him some name on the field, he'd of walloped you with a bat, even if you was his pal. So they was all stuck on him, was they not?

He got trimmed a couple o' times, right on his own club, too. But when they seen what kind of a ballplayer he was goin' to be, they decided they'd better not kill him. It's just as well for 'em they didn't. I'd like to know where their club would of finished—in 1907 and 1908, for instance—if it hadn't of been for him. It was nobody but him that beat us out in 1908. I'll tell you about it later on.

I says to him one day not long ago, I says:

"You wasn't very strong with the boys when you first come up. What was the trouble?"

"Well," he says, "I didn't understand what was comin'

off. I guess they meant it all right, but nobody'd tipped me that a busher's supposed to be picked on. They were hazin' me; that's what they were doin', hazin' me. I argued with 'em because I didn't know better."

"You learned, though, didn't you?" I says.

"Oh, yes," says Ty, "I learned all right."

"Maybe you paid for your lessons, too," I says.

"Maybe I did," he says.

"Well," I says, "would you act just the same way if you had it to do over again?"

"I reckon so," he says.

And he would, too, because if he was a diff'rent kind o' guy, he wouldn't be the ballplayer he is.

Say, maybe you think I didn't hate him when I was playin' ball. I didn't know him very well, see? But I hated him on general principles. And I never hated him more'n I did in 1908. That was the year they beat us out o' the big dough the last day o' the season, and it come at a time when I needed that old dough, because I knowed darn well that I wasn't goin' to last no ten years more or nothin' like that.

You look over the records now, and you'll see that the Detroit club and us just about broke even on the year's serious agin each other. I don't know now if it was exactly even or not, or, if it wasn't, which club had the best of it. But I do know one thing, and that is that they beat us five games that we'd ought to of copped from 'em easy and they beat us them games for no other reason than that they had this here Georgia Peach.

The records don't show no stuff like that, but I can remember most o' them games as if they was played yesterday; that is, Cobb's part in 'em. In them days, they had Crawford hittin' third and Cobb fourth and Rossman fifth. Well, one day we had 'em licked by three runs in the seventh innin'. Old Nick was pitchin' for us and Sully was catchin'. Tannehill was at third base and Hahn was switched from right to left field because they was somethin' the matter with Dougherty. Well, this seventh innin' come, as I was sayin', and we was three runs to the good. Crawford gets on someway and Cobb singles. Jones thought Nick was slippin', so he hollered for Smitty. Smitty comes in and pitches to big Rossman and the big guy hits one back at him. Smitty had the easiest kind of a double play starin' him in the face—a force play on Crawford at third and then the rest of it on Rossman, who wasn't no speed marvel. But he makes a bad peg to Tannie and the ball gets by him. It didn't look like as if Crawford could score, and I guess he was goin' to stop at third.

But Tyrus didn't pay no attention to Crawford. He'd saw the wild peg and he was bound to keep right on comin'. So Crawford's got to start home to keep from gettin' run over. Hahn had come in to get the ball and when he seen Crawford startin' home, he cut loose a wild peg that went clean to the bench. Crawford and Cobb both scored, o' course, and what does Ty do but yell at Rossman to follow 'em in, though it looked like sure death. Sully has the ball by that time, but it's just our luck that he has to peg wild too. The ball sailed over Smitty, who'd came up to cover the plate. The score's tied and for no reason but that Tyrus had made everybody run. The next three was easy outs, but they went on and licked us in extra innin's.

Well, they was another game, in that same serious I think it was, when Big Ed had 'em stopped dead to rights. They hadn't no more business scorin' off'n him than a rabbit. I don't think they hit two balls hard all day. We wasn't the best hittin' club in the world, but we managed to get one run for the Big Moose in the first innin' and that had ought to of been a-plenty.

Up comes Cobb in the fourth and hits one that goes in two bounds to Davis or whoever was playin' short. If he could of took his time, they'd of been nothin' to it. But he has to hurry the play because it's Cobb runnin', and he pegs low. Izzy gets the ball off'n the ground all right, but juggles it, and then Ty's safe.

They was nobody out, so Rossman bunts. He's throwed out a mile at first base, but Ty goes all the way to third. Then the next guy hits a fly ball to Hahn that wouldn't of been worth a nickel if Cobb'd of went only to second on the sacrifice, like a human bein'. He's on third, though, and he scores on the fly ball. The next guy takes three swings and the side's out, but we're tied up.

Then we go along to the ninth innin' and it don't look like they'd score agin on Big Ed if they played till Easter. But Cobb's up in the ninth with one out. He gets the one real healthy hit that they'd made all day. He singled to right field. I say he singled, because a single's what anybody else would of been satisfied with on the ball he hit. But Ty didn't stop at first base. He lights out for second and whoever was in right field made a good peg. The ball's there waitin' for Ty, but he slides away from it. Jake thought he had him, but the umps called him safe. Well, Jake gets mad and starts to kick. They ain't no time called or nothin'. The umps turns away and Jake slams the ball on the ground and before anybody could get to it, Cobb's on third. We all hollered murder, but it done us no good. Rossman then hit a fly ball and the game's over.

The last game o' the season settled the race, you know. I can't say that Tyrus won that one for 'em. They all was due to hit and they sure did hit. Cobb and Crawford both murdered the ball in the first innin' and won the game right there, because Donovan was so good we didn't have no chancet. But if he hadn't of stole them other games off'n us, this last one wouldn't of did 'em no good. We could of let our young fellas play that one while we rested up for the world's serious.

I don't say our club had a license to be champions that

year. We was weak in spots. But we'd of got the big dough if it hadn't of been for Tyrus. You can bet your life on that.

You can easy see why I didn't have no love for him in them days. . . . It's all foolishness to hate a fella because he's a good ballplayer, though. I realize that now that I'm out of it. I can go and watch Tyrus and enjoy watchin' him, but in them days it was just like pullin' teeth whenever he come up to the plate or got on the bases. He was reachin' right down in my pocket and takin' my money. So it's no wonder I was sore on him.

If I'd of been on the same club with him, though, I wouldn't never of got sore at him no matter how fresh he was. I'd of been afraid that he might get so sore at me that he'd quit the club. He could of called me anything he wanted to and got away with it or he could have took me acrost his knee and spanked me 80 times a day, just so's he kept on puttin' money in my kick instead o' beatin' me out of it.

As I was sayin', I enjoy seein' him play now. If the game's rotten or not, it don't make no diff'rence, and it don't make a whole lot even if he's havin' a bad day. They's somethin' fascinatin' in just lookin' at the baby.

I ain't alone in thinkin' that, neither. I don't know how many people he draws to the ball parks in a year, but it's enough to start a big manufacturin' town and a few suburbs. . . .

They's a funny thing I've noticed about him and the crowds. The fans in the diff'rent towns hates him because he's beat their own team out o' so many games. They hiss him when he pulls off somethin' that looks like dirty ball to 'em. Sometimes they get so mad at him that you think they're goin' to tear him to pieces. They holler like a bunch of Indians when some pitcher's good enough or lucky enough to strike him out. And at the same time, right down in their hearts, they're disappointed because he did strike out.

How do I know that? Well, kid, I've felt it myself, even when I was pullin' agin Detroit. I've talked to other people and they've told me they felt the same way. When they come out to see him, they expect to see him do somethin'. They're glad if he does and glad if he don't. They're sore at him if he don't beat their team and they're sore if he does. It's a funny thing and I ain't goin' to sit here all night tryin' to explain it.

But, say, I wisht I was the ballplayer he is. They could throw pop bottles and these here bumbs at me, and I wouldn't kick. They could call me names from the stand, but I wouldn't care. If the whole population o' the United States hated me like they think they hate him, I wouldn't mind, so long's I could just get back in that old game and play the ball he plays. But if I could, kid, I wouldn't have no time to be talkin' to you.

The other day, I says to Callahan:

"What do you think of him?"

"Think of him!" says Cal. "What could anybody think of him? I think enough of him to wish he'd go and break a leg. And I'm not sore on him personally at that."

"Don't you like to see him play ball?" I says.

"I'd love to watch him," says Cal, "if I could just watch him when he was playin' Philadelphia or Washington or any club but mine."

"I guess you'd like to have him, wouldn't you?" I says.

"Me?" says Cal. "All I'd give for him is my right eye."

"But," I says, "he must keep a manager worried some, in one way and another; you'd always be afraid he was goin' to break his own neck or cut somebody else's legs off or jump to the Fed'rals or somethin'."

"I'd take my chances," says Cal. "I believe I could even stand the worry for a few days."

I seen in the papers where McGraw says Eddie Collins is the greatest ballplayer in the world. I ain't goin' to argue with him about it, because I got nothin' but admiration for Collins. He's a bear. But, kid, I wisht McGraw had to play 22 games a year agin this Royston Romper. No, I don't, neither. McGraw never done nothin' to me.

8

Joe DiMaggio

I never saw Joe DiMaggio play, but he must have been something to watch, both at bat and in the field. Someone once told me that when a ball was hit to center you could never glance from the batter to DiMaggio and see him starting after it. He was always in full flight toward the ball, no matter how quickly you looked.

He is certainly one of the most respected of former ballplayers. He still has a kind of mystique about him, an aura of mystery. He attracted such a dedicated following in the late '30s and '40s because of his grace, his bearing, the way he'd hit line drives from that beautiful wide stance and short stride.

DiMaggio's 56-game hitting streak strikes me as a record that will remain on the books for some time. One of the prime qualities a great ballplayer must have is consistency, and that record—hitting in every game for two months—is the very essence of consistency.

If I were pitching to him during that streak, I know I'd be doing my best to end it. It would be tough to face him in his last at-bat, with runners on second and third and first base open, and him having no hits. The usual game strategy would call for a deliberate base-on-balls. But I'd be reluctant to do that. I'd hate to make him lose an opportunity to continue his streak. So I'd pitch to him, with everything I had.

Unless the game were on the line. Then, much as I'd hate to, I might just walk him.

The Longest Hitting Streak in History
•

Dave Anderson

It was, in 1941, a strangely smoldering summer. President Roosevelt, sitting before four microphones in the East Room of the White House, spoke of a "national emergency" and warned of Hitler's plan "to extend his Nazi domination to the Western Hemisphere." Defense plants worked a seven-day week. Some people read a new bestseller: *Berlin Diary*. In the coastal cities people listened to a new sound: The ghostly wail of air-raid sirens signaling test blackouts. But Americans, as usual, had some other things on their minds, too. Many of them sang a silly tune that went, "Hut sut rawlson on the rillerah" and, nearly every day for a few weeks of that summer, they waited expectantly for Joe DiMaggio to get his hit.

From May 15 through July 16 the lean, graceful New York Yankee center fielder hit safely in 56 consecutive games. It is the most remarkable achievement in baseball history. In the 20 years that have elapsed, only three men have hit safely in 30 or more consecutive games—Tommy Holmes set the National League high of 37 in 1945, younger brother Dom DiMaggio had 34 in 1949 and Stan Musial had 30 in 1950. In *The Little Red Book of Baseball* there are more than 2000 records; Joe DiMaggio's game-by-game statistics stand, significantly, on the final page.

DiMaggio's streak, however, is more than a record. It was,

at the time, a sociological phenomenon. In 1927, when Babe Ruth hit his 60 homers, the drama was intermittent—there were homerless games in between. The Babe and the fans could pause for a deep breath. For DiMaggio there was no escape from the relentless day-by-day pressure of the last few weeks of the streak. For the fans there was no escape from the magnetic force that drew them to their radios to hear the news announcer report the grim but still dreamlike news of the war in Europe and then, at some point in the program, add, "and Joe DiMaggio got his hit today to extend . . ."

That summer, DiMaggio was everybody's ballplayer. In later years, the term "hero symbol" was applied to him. The hitting streak shaped that symbol. Even now, nearly 10 years after he told the Yankees to keep their $100,000 and retired at 36, DiMaggio lives on a pedestal.

He is still everybody's ballplayer. "When we go out to dinner," says George Solotaire, a Broadway ticket broker who is DiMaggio's longtime pal, "they come out of the woodwork to ask for his autograph. He signs and signs and signs."

It is as if DiMaggio has been preserved for those who remember that summer before the war. There are thin streaks of gray in his black hair, but give him two weeks in the batting cage and he could take his cuts against Frank Lary. As a dresser, he never succumbed to the sport shirt, seldom to the single-breasted suit; to him, baseball was a business, and he looked then as he looks now, like a businessman: expensively tailored in dark-blue double-breasted suits, custom-made French-cuff shirts, hand-painted ties, highly polished black shoes. He dines in the best restaurants. He escorts beautiful women.

On May 14, 1941, DiMaggio was struggling at .306. The Yankees were struggling with him. They had lost four games in a row and seven of their last nine; they were in fourth place, five-and-a-half games behind the league-leading Cleveland Indians.

The next day, in a game at Yankee Stadium with the Chicago White Sox, DiMaggio hit a first-inning single off stocky left-hander Edgar Smith, but the Yankees lost again, 13–1. The start of the historic streak was a routine sentence in the game reports. The team slump was the story: YANK ATTACK WEAKEST IN YEARS, said the New York *Journal-American*. DiMaggio, of course, was the culprit. The two previous seasons he had won the American League batting championship, with .352 in 1940 and .381 in 1939. He also had been given the league's Most Valuable Player award in 1939, his fourth straight year on a pennant-winning Yankee team. He had succeeded Babe Ruth and Lou Gehrig as the big hitter of the Yankees, but in mid-May of 1941 he wasn't really hitting.

The streak sputtered along. In the seventh game, however, Detroit manager Del Baker showed what little regard he had for DiMaggio's bat despite Joe's two early-inning hits. With the score 4–4, the Yanks had the winning run on third in the ninth with nobody out. Ordinarily this situation called for an intentional walk to a slugger of DiMaggio's stature, since even a long fly ball would win the game. Instead, Baker ordered right-hander Al Benton to pitch to him. DiMaggio grounded out. The Yanks won in the 10th, but there were those at the Stadium who said, "Joe Dee don't scare 'em like he used to."

Actually, DiMaggio was slowly adjusting his wide-legged stance and regrooving his sweeping swing. On May 24 the Yanks were losing, 6–5, to the Boston Red Sox. In the seventh they had runners on second and third, DiMaggio up. "You can get him out, don't walk him," Red Sox manager Joe Cronin told left-hander Earl Johnson. On the first pitch DiMaggio singled for the winning runs. This hit stretched his streak to 10 games, but hardly anybody was aware of it yet, not even DiMaggio. "This damn swollen neck is driving me crazy," he told his roommate, Vernon (Lefty) Gomez, a few days later. "But don't say anything about it."

DiMaggio kept getting his hits, but in the Memorial Day doubleheader in Boston he made four errors. Normally a superb defensive outfielder, he dropped a fly ball in the first game; in the second he booted a grounder and twice threw wildly. "If you're not going to say anything about that neck, then I will," Gomez told him. The secret was out, but DiMaggio shrugged it off. "I get it every year," he said. "It'll go away." It did, and on June 7, as the Yankees opened a weekend series with the St. Louis Browns, manager Joe McCarthy sat in the dugout at Sportsman's Park and predicted, "The boys are just waiting for Joe to show 'em how to do it."

That day, DiMaggio began to show the Yankees how to do it. He got three hits. The next day, in a doubleheader, he slugged three homers and a double to spark an eight-game winning streak. "I knew I was hitting the ball well," DiMaggio says now, "but I wasn't conscious of the streak until after that series in St. Louis, when the writers started digging out the records I could break. But at that stage I didn't think much about it."

As the streak moved steadily through mid-June, DiMaggio broke the Yankee record of 29 games, shared by Earle Combs and Roger Peckinpaugh. *That* record hit came on a sharp grounder that took a bad hop and struck White Sox shortstop Luke Appling on the shoulder—one of the few times luck helped. By now, DiMaggio was more than a bigname ballplayer. He was a national celebrity. The next night he went to the first Louis-Conn fight at the Polo Grounds. "He nearly started a riot," says George Solotaire. "There were so many people asking for his autograph that he had almost as many cops around him as the fighters."

Other forgotten streaks were dug out by the statisticians. In 1897, it was discovered, Wee Willie Keeler—aided by the

old rule that foul balls were not strikes—hit in 44 games for
the Baltimore Orioles, then in the National League. In 1922
George Sisler went 41 games for the American League record and Rogers Hornsby went 33 for the then-modern
National League record. "To look at Joe," recalls Lefty
Gomez, "you'd never think he had any pressure on him. I
never saw a guy so calm. I wound up with the upset stom-
achs."

As DiMaggio approached Sisler's record, it was no longer
a one-man story. His teammates rooted openly in the dugout. On the other clubs the pitchers bore down more than
ever against him—they all wanted to be the man to stop him.
The fielders, too, were more on their toes. For better or
worse, human nature had become part of the plot. In the
36th game, for example, an eighth-inning single saved the
streak against Bob Muncrief, a rookie right-hander for the
Browns. Later, Browns manager Luke Sewell asked Muncrief, "Why didn't you walk him the last time up to stop
him?" Muncrief glared. "I wasn't going to walk him," he
said. "That wouldn't have been fair—to him or to me. Hell,
he's the greatest player I ever saw."

Two days later, after the Yankees finally had climbed to
first place, they were leading the Browns, 3–1, in the eighth
inning, but DiMaggio was hitless. He could easily have
missed a last chance. "That was the trouble at the Stadium,"
DiMaggio says. "On the road I knew I always had nine innings, so I was almost sure to get up at least four times. But
at home, if we were winning, I only had eight innings." He
was the fourth man up in the eighth, against Eldon Auker,
a submarine-ball right-hander. Johnny Sturm popped up,
but when Red Rolfe walked, Tommy Henrich turned back
from the on-deck circle and talked to Joe McCarthy. "If I
hit into a double play," he said, "Joe won't get up. Is it
O.K. if I bunt?" McCarthy agreed. After Henrich's sacrifice, DiMaggio doubled to left on Auker's first pitch.

In the 40th game the Yankees faced Johnny Babich of the Philadelphia Athletics in Shibe Park. Babich, a right-hander who had pitched in the Yankee farm system, had a reputation as a Yankee-killer. The previous season, he had bested the New Yorkers five times to ruin their pennant chances. "He was out to stop me," DiMaggio says now, "even if it meant walking me every time up." In the fourth, after Babich threw three wide fastballs, DiMaggio glanced at third-base coach Art Fletcher. "McCarthy had given him the hit sign," Joe recalls. "The next pitch was outside, but I caught it good and lined it between Babich's legs into center field. After I made my turn at first, I looked over at him. His face was white as a sheet. McCarthy was great to me during the streak," Joe added. "He let me hit the 3–0 pitch quite a few times, but that's the one that I remember best."

The next day, in a doubleheader in Washington, DiMaggio doubled off Dutch Leonard in the sixth inning of the opener to tie Sisler's record at 41. Between games, however, a fan jumped on the field near the Yankee dugout and snatched DiMaggio's favorite bat. In the second game, against Arnold Anderson, DiMaggio twice lined out and then flied out. In the seventh, he picked up Henrich's bat—an old DiMaggio model that Tommy had borrowed—and singled to left. All over the country radio announcers interrupted programs to say, "Here is a sports bulletin: Joe Di-Maggio today set. . . ."

In the Yankee dining car on the way to New York that night DiMaggio ordered beer for all his teammates and told a reporter, "I wish that guy who stole that bat would return it. I need it more than he does. Most of my models are 36 inches long and weigh 36 ounces, but I had sandpapered the handle of this one to take off a half to three-quarters of an ounce. It was just right."

The bat was returned. "The fellow who took it lived in Newark," DiMaggio says, "and I guess he was bragging around how he had the bat. I had some good friends in Newark. They heard about him and got the bat back for me."

In the opener of a doubleheader wtih the Red Sox, DiMaggio hit a tricky grounder to third baseman Jim Tabor in the fourth inning. Tabor, hurrying his throw, fired wildly past first base. As Joe coasted into second, everyone in Yankee Stadium waited for the official scorer's decision: Was it a hit or Tabor's error? In the press box, Dan Daniel, the veteran baseball writer of the New York *World-Telegram* who was scorer that day, raised his right arm, signaling a hit. The crowd of 52,832 roared, and DiMaggio sighed. "That was one of the few times I got a break from the scorer on a questionable play," he recalls. "Instead of giving me the benefit of the doubt—not that I was asking for it— they usually made sure it was a clean hit. The next spring I was talking about that to Dan, and he told me, 'There was just as much pressure on me and the scorers around the league not to cheapen the streak.' "

In the second game that day, DiMaggio's first-inning single tied Keeler's record, and on Wednesday, July 2, he had his chance to break it. Before game time it was so warm —94.8 degrees—that 41-year-old Bob (Lefty) Grove, then nearing his 300th win, begged off and the Red Sox started Heber (Dick) Newsome, a rookie right-hander who won 19 games that season. First time up, DiMaggio hit a liner to right field, but Stan Spence, after momentarily misjudging it, ran back to make a leaping catch. In the third he grounded out to Tabor. But in the fifth, on a 2–1 count, he hit his 18th homer of the season into the lower left-field stands. With that long stride of his, DiMaggio rounded the bases, tipped his hat as he neared the dugout and clattered down the concrete steps into a swarm of back-slapping teammates. "You not only broke Keeler's record," said Gomez, "you even used his formula—you hit 'em where they ain't."

After the game, DiMaggio calmly sat in front of his locker and puffed a cigarette. "I don't know how far I can go," he said quietly, "but I'm not going to worry about it now. I'm glad it's over. It got to be quite a strain the last 10 days. Now I can go back to swinging at good balls. I was swinging at some bad pitches so I wouldn't be walked." Then, picking up a stack of fan mail, he added, "The pressure has been as tough off the field as on it." Later, he needed a police escort to get to Gomez's waiting car for the ride back to his apartment. "It was like that everywhere," DiMaggio says now. "It was a great tribute to me, and I appreciated it, but it had its drawbacks, too. I got so much fan mail—there was some kind of a good-luck charm in every letter—that I had to turn it over to the front office."

A few days later, in the Log Cabin Farm, a nightclub north of New York City, a 29-year-old disc jockey named Alan Courtney (now a Miami radio commentator) scribbled some song lyrics on a tablecloth. "See if you like this," he said to bandleader Les Brown:

Who started baseball's famous streak
That's got us all aglow?
He's just a man and not a freak,
Jolting Joe DiMaggio.
Joe . . . Joe . . . DiMaggio . . . we want you on our side.
From Coast to Coast, that's all you hear
Of Joe the One-Man Show.
He's glorified the horsehide sphere,
Jolting Joe DiMaggio.
Joe . . . Joe . . . DiMaggio . . . we want you on our side.
He'll live in baseball's Hall of Fame,
He got there blow-by-blow.
Our kids will tell their kids his name,
Jolting Joe DiMaggio.

"Not bad," Brown said. "I'll get Ben Homer to do the arrangement. Hey! That's a helluva name for a guy arranging a DiMaggio song." They laughed, and Courtney said, "I'll work on it some more, but if we can get it on the market quick, it might sell. Let's hope he keeps hitting."

He did—for two weeks more—and Joe DiMaggio became, in a sense, a side-show freak. On July 10 the Yankees opened a weekend series in St. Louis, and the Browns took three-column ads in the newspapers that read: "The Sensational Joe DiMaggio Will Attempt to Hit Safely in his 49th Consecutive Game!" On July 16 in old League Park in Cleveland, DiMaggio had three hits in the 56th game. Late the next afternoon, he and Gomez got into a cab outside the Hotel Cleveland for the short ride to the ball park. The driver glanced in his mirror. "Joe," he said, "I got a feeling that if you don't get a hit the first time up, they're gonna stop you tonight." DiMaggio said nothing, but Gomez barked, "What the hell is this? What are you tryin' to do—jinx him?"

Al Smith, a veteran left-hander, was the Indians's pitcher. There were many in the record night-game crowd of 67,468 who hoped that DiMaggio would get a hit so that, the following night, Bob Feller could stop him. In the first inning third baseman Ken Keltner moved back to the edge of the infield dirt for DiMaggio. "He dared me to bunt on him," Joe says. "I didn't bunt during the entire streak." On a 1–0 count, DiMaggio smashed a drive past the third-base bag. Keltner lunged to his right, made a backhand stab and, from foul ground, threw DiMaggio out. On the bench, Gomez growled, "That cab driver . . . that lousy cab driver."

In the fourth, DiMaggio walked, and in the seventh, Keltner made another good play on a hot shot directly at him. In the eighth, the Yankees knocked out Smith and, with DiMaggio coming up, Indian manager Roger Peckinpaugh brought in right-handed Jim Bagby Jr. On a 2–1 pitch, Di-

Maggio hit a sharp grounder at shortstop Lou Boudreau. It took a bad hop, but Boudreau picked it off near his shoulder and fliped to second baseman Ray Mack to start a double-play. "DiMaggio," Herb Goren wrote in the New York *Sun* the next day, "rounded first base, picked up his glove and trotted to center field. There was no kicking of dirt, no shaking of the head." In papers all over the country the next day there were head shots of Smith, Bagby and Keltner, side by side, like the three assassins of a king.

The streak had ended but, for DiMaggio and millions of others, the memory lingered on. In August, as the Yankees increased their lead—they won 30 of their last 35 games, won the pennant by 17 games and then whipped the Brooklyn Dodgers in the World Series—Tommy Henrich, Bill Dickey, George Selkirk and Johnny Murphy were discussing DiMaggio's contribution. "We ought to do something special for Joe," Dickey said. "He won the pennant for us."

On August 29, after a tiresome train ride from St. Louis, the Yankees checked into their rooms in the Hotel Shoreham in Washington. It was a night off, but in room 609D, Selkirk was on the phone calling the other players and the newspapermen. Meanwhile, Gomez was taking a long shower.

"Let's go, Lefty," DiMaggio urged. "All the steaks will be gone."

Gomez, however, refused to be rushed. On the way to the elevator he told DiMaggio, "I just remembered something. I've got to go by Selkirk's room."

"I'll get us a table and order," DiMaggio said. "I'll meet you downstairs." "No, no, stay with me," Gomez said. "It'll take only a minute."

"O.K.," DiMaggio grunted, "but hustle it up."

From behind the door of 609D, Selkirk peeked down the corridor. "Here he comes," he whispered. As DiMaggio entered the room he was met by nearly 40 men with raised champagne glasses. There were cheers and songs, and Go-mez presented DiMaggio with a gift-wrapped package. It was a sterling silver humidor. Perched atop the cover was a statuette of DiMaggio in his classic swing. On one side was the No. 56 for the streak; on the other, 91 for the number of hits during the streak. The inscription read: "Presented to Joe DiMaggio by his fellow players on the New York Yankees to express their admiration for his consecutive-game hitting record, 1941." Below that there were the engraved autographs of all his teammates. "We got it at Tiffany's," Murphy said.

9

Lou Gehrig

Most managers have their best hitter bat third, so he will always get to the plate in the first inning. But if he gets on, someone has to drive him in. Lou Gehrig was that someone —the perfect clean-up hitter.

He would have been the best hitter on 99 percent of the baseball teams ever assembled, but he played on the Yankees in Ruth's era. Gehrig was one of the game's great home-run hitters; he hit more than 30 for ten seasons. He wasn't just a slugger, though. He had a lifetime average of .340, just two points below Ruth. Most important, he drove in runs. For 13 years in a row, he drove in more than 100; in 1931 he had 184 RBIs, still the American League record.

A clean-up hitter must also be dependable—someone who can be relied on to do his job with consistency every day. Gehrig did his job with great consistency for 2130 consecutive games.

Having Gehrig hit behind him helped Ruth. If he didn't have a hitter of Gehrig's stature batting clean-up, Ruth would have been walked much more often. With Gehrig coming up next, a pitcher had to think twice before walking the Babe.

Gehrig might also have been helped by having Ruth on his team; being the No. 2 man takes pressure off a player. It also meant, though, that Gehrig didn't get the recognition he merited. He not only had to compete with Ruth as a player, but also as a personality. And it does take some sense of the theater, which Gehrig lacked, to be recognized by the newspapers as an interesting story.

Gehrig wasn't the only great player who was overshadowed by a teammate. In recent history I can think of Don Drysdale, who was a truly great pitcher for the Dodgers, but not as great as his teammate Sandy Koufax. And Willie McCovey was probably never appreciated as much as he would have been if he hadn't played for the Giants at the same time as Willie Mays.

But Lou Gehrig, more than anyone else in the game, epitomized the player who does the job but isn't noticed until he's gone.

THREE VIEWS OF LOU GEHRIG

Winning Acceptance

•

Robert Smith

The only really authentic hero for the Yankees in the prewar age was Lou Gehrig, the solid young man from Columbia who dogged Ruth's steps in almost every home-run race for several seasons, and who earned himself the nickname "Iron Horse" for his durability.

Lou, like Babe Ruth and many another young star, had to grow up in public—although, because he was quiet by nature, his adolescent personality was never exposed to the full glare of the light. But men who met him in the 1920s, when

he was just a big strong boy with a mighty bat and a rudi-
mentary knowledge of how to play first base, were sometimes repelled by him. Lou was a boy who had been made
much of by devoted parents (all their other children had
died). Perhaps in consequence of this he was driven, as
many such boys are, by an excruciating sense of inadequacy,
into painful self-consciousness. Scared speechless by the
great men who gathered to interview him, he seemed able
to do little more than grunt and growl. His teammates were
irritated by his utter naïveté—his bringing packages of good-
ies, such as pickled eels from mama's kitchen, to regale his
mates, and his coming to after being knocked cold in a fist
fight to ask, in Boy Scout fashion: "Who won?"—and they
used to mimic and make fun of him until manager Huggins
shut them up.

Lou was driven by grim ambition and by dogged thrift.
He was determined to succeed at baseball in spite of the
devil, and he was consumed with a desire to keep himself
secure with all the money he could save. It was Gehrig's
smoking ambition that kept him playing ball day in and day
out, season after season, despite colds, headaches, broken
thumbs and charley horses; that turned him from an awk-
ward kid who, one coach thought, was too pigheaded to
learn, into a finished infielder. It kept him hiking and skating
throughout the winter so his body would never go flabby.
Lou did not miss a ball game for 14 years, and he was never
out of condition summer or winter.

It was Lou's private vanity, or superstition, that exposure
to the elements hardened his body and made it impervious
to ills. He could be seen at a football game, in near-zero
weather, sitting in the stands without overcoat or vest to
warm him. It was Lou's thrift that prompted him to walk
all the way from his hotel to the training park and thus save
the fare, to conserve expense money, to avoid having to give
a tip. These habits did not sit well with his free-spending

mates or with newspaper writers who met him when he was a recruit.

Success brought a gradual loosening up to Lou. Not that he ever became easy on himself. He was a man who could never stop trying, no matter how bleak the outlook or how long the road. If he seemed to be weakening he knew only that he must deal more harshly with himself and thus get back into top physical trim. His teammates soon learned to appreciate Lou's willingness to do whatever needed to be done to bring his club home first, and he was eventually accepted as an intimate even by those who had at first made the most bitter fun of him.

But it was not Lou's home-run records (he twice led the league and once tied for the leadership) or his incredible string of consecutive games (2130) that made Lou truly great. He became a hero off the diamond by the quiet and courageous way he faced the fact that he was dying of an incurable disease, by his utter sincerity when, after his enforced retirement from the game, he accepted a tumultuous tribute from fans, political leaders, peanut sellers, ushers, umpires, ballplayers, and sportswriters by modestly disclaiming any virtue except that he was "the luckiest man in the world." He meant that to have a devoted wife, as he had, good friends, a fine record, financial success, and to have been able to provide handsomely for his beloved parents—all this bounty was more to him than the fact that at the age of 36 he was the victim of a crippling disease, with only an even chance to live. Gehrig died in 1941, just before his 38th birthday. He is the only baseball player to have had a New York street named after him. The blue and white street signs just outside Yankee Stadium in New York now carry the inscription: Lou Gehrig Plaza.

The Babe might have been coming off a hard night, but his eyes were wide open when he hit the ball.

The ball's moving at close to 100 mph. Hank Aaron's bat is moving about as fast. Result: his 707th home run.

United Press International Photo

Ernie Banks could wait until the last instant to whip his bat around, then power the ball out of the park with his strong wrists.

Wide World Photos

It looks as though Johnny Bench has connected with a right hook, but he has the ball in his hand and so it's legal.

United Press International Photo

Roberto Clemente not only made dramatic catches, but he made dramatic catches that *looked* dramatic.

Wide World Photo

Some say Ty Cobb sharpened his spikes before every game. This third baseman apparently believed those tales.

Culver Pictures

Joe DiMaggio was graceful even when striking out, but here he gracefully follows through on a home run.

United Press International Photo

Overshadowed during his career, Lou Gehrig had to be forced into retirement by a fatal disease to win his place in the sun.

United Press International Photo

Thousands saw Josh Gibson play in the 1944 Negro All-Star Game in Comiskey Park. Millions never saw him play.

International News Photos

Gil Hodges was a formidable man to argue with. I don't envy the umpire here.

In 1924, Rogers Hornsby hit .424. In 1962, as batting coach for the original Mets, he would have settled for one .300 hitter.

A great fielder, like Al Kaline, sometimes has to take great tumbles.

It may look like fun, but after you've signed a few hundred thousand autographs, as Mickey Mantle has, it gets wearing.

Willie Mays rarely disputed umpires, but in last year's Series he argued with passion. Who knows, maybe he was right.

Associated Press

Stan Musial's batting stance may have seemed a little funny to some people, but not to pitchers.

Frank Robinson, experienced as a kangaroo court judge, could make a
good manager—if he'd stop wearing silly wigs.

Associated Press

One way to psych a pitcher is to threaten to steal home—and then steal it, as Jackie Robinson is doing here.

Wide World Photos

Honus Wagner was strong enough to belt the ball, but in his day a carefully placed single was more the style.

Culver Pictures

Ted Williams studied hitting like Einstein studied math, and his figures added up to a .344 lifetime average.

Wide World Photos

In Ruth's Shadow

●

Arthur Daley

Lou Gehrig was a tragic figure in so many ways.

To me a part of the tragedy of his career was that he never escaped from the shadow of Babe Ruth. It was his fate to remain under that shade. If there had been no Bambino, the Iron Horse might never have been challenged as one of the brightest of all stars. He had a lifetime average of .340. But Ruth's was .342. See what I mean?

In 1931 the home-run champion should have been Gehrig with 47 to Ruth's 46. So what happened? With Lynn Lary on base Larrupin' Lou larruped one into the stands. Lary inexplicably let the notion creep into his head that the fielder had caught the ball. Since there were two out at the time, he rounded third base and headed for the dugout. Gehrig modestly jogged with downcast eyes around the paths and never looked up until he'd crossed the plate. That made him out for passing a base-runner and his home run disappeared from the books since it had been nullified. So all he could do was tie the Babe for the home-run championship. That's the way it always seemed to go.

But here was the crusher, the most graphic illustration imaginable of the way Destiny seemed to conspire against him. On June 3, 1932, the Iron Horse performed that rarest of feats, hitting four home runs in one game. Here was a red-letter achievement of such sheer magnificence that it was worthy of a front-page spread in every newspaper in the country. An unbelieving nation would read of his amazing exploit and gasp. Acclaim was his alone at long last.

But Gehrig's four home runs landed on the sports pages, buried alongside the want ads. On June 3, 1932, John Mc-

Graw resigned as the manager of the Giants, the most stunning sports story of the century. McGraw stole away all the front-page headlines, all the front-page space. No one even noticed that the Iron Horse had hit four home runs in one game.

That was Lou Gehrig for you.

Prototype Yankee

•

Jack Mann

In 1925, the year Ruth was marked absent, the Yankees were trying to make do with ordinary, first-magnitude stars like Bob Meusel, Earle Combs and Wally Pipp. One day the veteran Pipp violated the corporate precept that it is dangerous to take a day off because it may show the management how unnecessary you are. He was replaced at first base by the rookie Gehrig, who took his job. That sort of thing will happen from time to time, but the veteran always assumes it will be all right because the kid will play himself off the team after a while. And Gehrig did. On May 9, 1939, in Detroit, when Pipp was 46 years old, Gehrig benched himself. He had played 2130 consecutive games. (The "Iron Man" label was tainted once, when Gehrig was indisposed and couldn't have played but they let him bat leadoff in the first inning, to keep the record intact, then put in the shortstop for whom Gehrig was, in effect, pinch-hitting.)

Gehrig spent the first decade of his career in Ruth's shadow. Playing on the same team with the Babe was enough to obviate any possibility of being top banana, but hitting immediately behind him in the batting order was like following Judy Garland in a vaudeville show. All the magnificence of the stolid No. 4, displayed while the applause for the charismatic No. 3 was still echoing in the stadium rafters, did about as much to distinguish Gehrig as Wendell Willkie's "me too" campaign against Roosevelt in 1940.

A case can be made that Gehrig, and not Ruth, was the prototypical Yankee, clubbing the opposition into submission with an inexorable consistency and performing the task with dispassionate, if not completely humorless, efficiency. He, more than Ruth, set the distinguishing tone that would obtain through 15 years of Yankee teams to follow him. Attempts by Yankee publicists and broadcasters to sell the idea of traditional rivalries, or even feuds, with the Red Sox, Tigers or White Sox were doomed to failure because the men executed in their gray flannel rompers in the manner in which John L. Lewis once said F.D.R. had cussed out labor and management: "With equal fervor and fine impartiality." The fervor was usually as feverish as that of a hangman springing the trap. This very aloofness, manifested almost as indifference, was as maddening to Yankee victims as the frustration of defeat itself.

Being beaten by the Yankees could be as insulting as being spanked by a parent who wasn't angry. ("All right, all right—if I should hit him, I'll hit him.") Gehrig in his indestructible, imperturbable way was the model Yankee for 14 years, making all the necessary plays at first base and very few spectacular ones, hitting 493 home runs and very few tape jobs that anybody remembers. His 184 runs batted in in 1931 still stands as the American League record, topped only by the 190 RBIs by Hack Wilson the year before, playing for the Cubs. . . . Lou Gehrig was a great baseball player. But never in baseball history have so many been so unexcited about so much.

In 1927, Gehrig's first season of what should have been recognized as superstardom, he batted .373 and drove in 175 runs, which had never been done before. But you know what Ruth did that year. . . . In 1936 Ruth was gone and

Gehrig was the undisputed Big Guy of the Yankees, for a little while. He led the league with 49 homes runs and 152 RBIs that year, and was the Most Valuable Player. But there was this rookie, an Italian kid from San Francisco, and he was a natural if you ever saw one. By the end of the season the name DiMaggio was first on the lips of the Yankee followers, and Lou Gehrig's magnificence was being taken for granted again.

Finally, on an afternoon in 1939, Gehrig was given the recognition he had always deserved, but he had to die for it. There was something wrong with him during the 1938 season. He played all the games, as usual, but his hitting fell off to a mediocre .294 and he seemed sluggish. It couldn't be his age, because he was the Iron Horse and, well, he'd always be there. But there came the day when the picture on the back page of the New York *Daily News* was of Gehrig, sitting on the steps of the third-base dugout in Detroit, watching Babe Dahlgren take infield practice. Gehrig had told manager Joe McCarthy that he realized he wasn't helping the team, and asked to be benched after 2130 games. At the Mayo Clinic they told him it was lateral sclerosis, a pernicious degeneration of the spinal cord. Whether or not they told him he was going to die, Gehrig must have known it when he stood at home plate in Yankee Stadium that July day, responding to the cheers of a full house of Yankee followers, many of them seeing him as a human being for the first time as they saw him in the gray pinstripes for the last time. . . . They made a movie of Gehrig's life and it was about as bad as most baseball movies. But they called it *Pride of the Yankees*, and that wasn't too bad. No man ever gave the Yankees more to be proud of.

10

Josh Gibson

I never heard of Josh Gibson until I reached the major leagues, yet he was one of the great sluggers in baseball history. Gibson played at the same time as Jimmy Foxx, Mel Ott and Hank Greenberg, and he possibly was better than any of them. But he was black.

Willie Mays told me that Gibson could hit a ball as far as anyone he's ever seen, and he's seen many great players—not only in the majors but in the Negro leagues where he started.

Think of what we would have missed if Willie—or Hank Aaron or Roberto Clemente—had been born 25 years earlier. That's what we missed because Gibson played when racism barred blacks from organized baseball.

People who claim that baseball has diluted its talent by expanding the leagues forget just how much greater the pool of talent is today compared to 25 years ago when the majors had no blacks or Latin-Americans—and black kids had no black major-leaguers to make heroes of.

It means so much to kids to have athletes as heroes. Sports stars are people kids can relate to and who can provide them with an ideal to achieve. But Henry Aaron was 13 before Jackie Robinson entered the majors. And the professional black teams received little publicity—no radio broadcasts and meager newspaper coverage. It's a wonder that, when the racial barriers were finally let down, so many great black ballplayers were ready to step in.

Josh

•

Robert W. Peterson

There is a catcher that any big-league club would like to buy for $200,000. His name is Gibson . . . he can do everything. He hits the ball a mile. And he catches so easy he might as well be in a rocking chair. Throws like a rifle. Bill Dickey isn't as good a catcher. Too bad this Gibson is a colored fellow.

—Walter Johnson

There is a story that one day during the 1930s the Pittsburgh Crawfords were playing at Forbes Field in Pittsburgh when their young catcher, Josh Gibson, hit the ball so high and far that no one saw it come down. After scanning the sky carefully for a few minutes, the umpire deliberated and ruled it a home run. The next day the Crawfords were playing in Philadelphia when suddenly a ball dropped out of the heavens and was caught by the startled center fielder on the opposing club. The umpire made the only possible ruling. Pointing to Gibson he shouted, "Yer out—yesterday in Pittsburgh!"

Gibson fans of those years might concede that there was an element of exaggeration in the story, but not much. Josh Gibson was not merely a home-run hitter; he was *the* home-run hitter. He was the black Babe Ruth, and like the Babe a legend in his own time whose prodigious power was celebrated in fact and fancy. But while it is relatively easy to separate fact from fancy in Ruth's legend, Gibson's suffers from the paucity of certified records about the quantity and quality of his home-run production. Old-timers credit Gibson with 89 home runs in one season and 75 in another; many of them, of course, were hit against semipro competition.

Whatever the truth of these claims, a strong case can be made for the proposition that Josh Gibson, a right-hand batter, had more power than the great Babe. The clincher in the argument is the generally accepted fact that Gibson hit the longest home run ever struck in Yankee Stadium, Ruth's home for 12 seasons.

Baseball's bible, *The Sporting News* [June 3, 1967], credits Gibson with a drive in a Negro league game that hit just two feet from the top of the stadium wall circling the bleachers in center field, about 580 feet from home plate. It was estimated that had the drive been two feet higher it would have sailed out of the park and traveled some 700 feet!

Some old Negro league players say that Gibson's longest shot in Yankee Stadium struck the rear wall of the bullpen in left field, about 500 feet from the plate. But Jack Marshall, of the Chicago American Giants, recalls an epic blast by Gibson that went *out* of the stadium—the only fair ball ever hit out of the Yankees' park.

In 1934, Josh Gibson hit a ball off of Slim Jones in Yankee Stadium in a four-team doubleheader that we had there—the Philadelphia Stars played the Crawfords in the second game; we had played the Black Yankees in the first game. They say a ball has never been hit out of Yankee Stadium. Well, that is a lie! Josh hit the ball over that triple deck next to the bullpen in left field. Over and out! I never will forget that, because we were getting ready to leave because we were going down to Hightstown, New Jersey, to play a night game and we were standing in the aisle when that boy hit this ball!

. . . Unlike Babe Ruth, whose swing was awesome and whose body wound up like a pretzel when he missed the ball, Gibson's power was generated with little apparent effort. Judy Johnson, who was Gibson's first manager, said:

It was just a treat to watch him hit the ball. There was no effort at all. You see these guys now get up there in the box and they dig and scratch around before they're ready. Gibson would just walk up there, and he would always turn his left sleeve up, and then just before he swung he'd lift that left foot up.

And when Gibson raised his front foot, the infielders began edging backward onto the grass. If he met the pitch squarely and it came to them on one hop, they knew the ball would be in their glove before Gibson could drop his bat.

Josh Gibson was born December 21, 1911, in Buena Vista, Georgia, a village not far from Atlanta. His father scratched a bare living from a patch of ground outside the village. Josh, the first child of Mark and Nancy Gibson, was named Joshua after his grandfather.

At intervals of three years, two other children were born to the Gibsons: Jerry, who would follow Josh into professional baseball as a pitcher with the Cincinnati Tigers, and Annie. By 1923 the Gibson youngsters were growing up, and it became clear to Mark that if they were to have better opportunities than he had had he must join the swelling migration of black men to the North. And so, late that year, he went to Pittsburgh, where he had relatives, to find work. He quickly got a job as a laborer for Carnegie-Illinois Steel, which was later absorbed by U.S. Steel. In early 1924, Mark sent for his family. Josh was 12 years old when the Gibsons settled down in Pleasant Valley, a Negro enclave in Pittsburgh's North Side.

While equal opportunity was only a pleasant dream for a Negro boy in Pittsburgh, still, the change from the oppressive atmosphere of a southern small town was welcomed. "The greatest gift Dad gave me," Gibson said later, "was to get me out of the South."

Baseball was new to the migrant from Georgia, but he was soon the first one chosen for sandlot pickup games when he began demonstrating a talent for hitting the ball. He was always looking for a ballgame, to play or to watch, and he thought nothing of strapping on rollerskates and skating six miles downriver to Bellevue to see a game.

The young Josh did not care especially for football or basketball, the other neighborhood sports, but swimming caught his interest and as a teen-ager he brought home a number of medals from the city playground pools. At 16 he was on his first uniformed baseball club—the Gimbels A.C., an all-Negro amateur team playing in Pittsburgh. He was already a catcher, as he would be throughout his career, except for an occasional game in the outfield.

His education was over. Josh had gone through fifth grade in the Negro school in Buena Vista and continued in elementary school in Pittsburgh. He dropped out after completing the ninth grade in Allegheny Pre-Vocational School, where he learned the rudiments of the electrician's trade. He immediately went to work as an apprentice in a plant that manufactured air brakes. But by this time it was clear that Gibson's vocation would be baseball. He was nearing his full size of six feet, one inch and 215 pounds. He had a moon-round, trusting face, a friendly disposition, and the body of a dark Greek god. His broad shoulders sloped down to tremendous arms, thick with muscle, and his barrel chest tapered in the athlete's classic mold to a deceptively slim looking waist. Like his arms, Gibson's legs were heavily muscled.

For a Pittsburgh Negro boy who loved baseball, his goal would have to be the Homestead Grays. He could envy the Pirates's heroes of his youth—the Waners, Lloyd and Paul, and Pie Traynor and Burleigh Grimes and Rabbit Maranville—but he could not hope to step into their shoes. The next best thing was the Homestead Grays, who had started 20 years before in the steel town a few miles upriver and were beginning to emerge as a national Negro baseball power. They had Smoky Joe Williams and Johnny Beckwith and Sam Streeter and Vic Harris and Martin Dihigo— names that meant nothing to the typical Pirate fan but that loomed large in Negro baseball.

In 1929 and 1930, when the Grays were strengthening their position as one of the best Negro ball clubs in the country, Josh Gibson was catching for the Crawford Colored Giants of Pittsburgh. This was a semipro club that Josh had had a hand in organizing around a city recreation building in Pittsburgh's Hill District. The Crawfords (not to be confused with Gus Greenlee's powerhouse, which was formed in 1931) played other semipro clubs in and around Pittsburgh for a few dollars a game. No admission was charged for their games and the collection rarely brought in more than $50, although crowds of 5000 attracted by the growing awareness of Gibson's power at the plate, were not uncommon.

The Grays, naturally, soon heard of the big, raw slugger. Judy Johnson, who managed Homestead in 1930, said:

> I had never seen him play but we had heard so much about him. Every time you'd look in the paper you'd

see where he hit a ball 400 feet, 500 feet. So the fans started wondering why the Homestead Grays didn't pick him up. But we had two catchers. Buck Ewing was the regular catcher, and Vic Harris, an outfielder, used to catch if we were playing a doubleheader.

In late July the Kansas City Monarchs, Negro National League champions of 1929, came to Pittsburgh for a series with the Grays, bringing along their new portable lighting system. On July 25, the Grays and Monarchs were battling under these uncertain lights in Forbes Field. Johnson remembers:

> Joe Williams was pitching that night and we didn't know anything about lights. We'd never played under 'em before, and we couldn't use the regular catcher's signals, because if he put his hand down you couldn't see it. So we used the glove straight up for a fastball and the glove down—that was supposed to be the curve.
> Some way Joe Williams and the catcher got crossed up. The catcher was expecting the curve and Joe threw the fastball and caught him right there, and split the finger. Well, my other catcher was Vic Harris and he was playing the outfield and wouldn't catch. So Josh was sitting in the grandstand, and I asked the Grays's owner, Cum Posey, to get him to finish the game. So Cum asked Josh would he catch, and Josh said, "Yeah, oh yeah!" We had to hold the game up until he went into the clubhouse and got a uniform. And that's what started him out with the Homestead Grays.

Gibson got no hits that night, but he made no errors, either, and that was strange, for he was still a raw-boned, 18-year-old and clumsy with the mitt. For the rest of that season, Johnson said, "Josh would catch batting practice and then catch the game, he was so anxious to learn. He wasn't much of a catcher then, but he came along fast."

Despite his shortcomings as a catcher, Gibson became an instant regular on the Grays, although he was often used in the outfield during his first year in top competition. His bat simply had to be in the lineup somewhere.

There remains a wide division of opinion among ball-players who played with and against Gibson during his prime as to his skill as a catcher. Many maintain that he became a good receiver, but never a great one. They hold that he never learned to catch foul pop-ups, that his arm was adequate, but no more than that, and that as a receiver he was not in the same class with Bruce Petway, who threw out Ty Cobb twice trying to steal second in a series in Cuba in the winter of 1910, or Biz Mackey, whose career began in 1920 and spanned 30 years on top clubs, or Frank Duncan, Kansas City Monarchs catcher of the 1920s.

Walter Johnson's description of Gibson as a rocking-chair catcher with a rifle arm suggests otherwise. Joining Walter Johnson in his opinion that Josh was a superior catcher is Roy Campanella, who was beginning his career in professional baseball with the Baltimore Elite Giants in 1937, about the time Gibson reached his peak. Campanella said that Gibson was a graceful, effortless receiver with a strong, accurate arm. He was, said Campy, "not only the greatest catcher but the greatest ballplayer I ever saw."

The middle ground between these extreme opinions is held by Jimmie Crutchfield, an outfielder who was a team-mate of Gibson on the Pittsburgh Crawfords from 1932 through 1936:

I can remember when he couldn't catch this building if you threw it at him. He was only behind the plate because of his hitting. And I watched him develop into a very good defensive catcher. He was never given enough credit for his ability as a catcher. They couldn't deny that he was a great hitter, but they could deny that he was a great catcher. But I know!

In 1931, Josh Gibson was an established star on the Homestead Grays. He was credited with 75 home runs that year as the Grays barnstormed around Pennsylvania, West Virginia, Ohio, and into the southern reaches of New York State, feeding the growing legend about the young black catcher who could hit the ball a country mile. The next year he was lured to the Pittsburgh Crawfords by the free-spending Gus Greenlee to form with Satchel Paige perhaps the greatest battery in baseball history. Gibson stayed with Greenlee's Crawfords for five summers, his fame growing with each Brobdingnagian clout. In 1934 his record was 69 home runs and in the other years his homer production, although not recorded, was from all accounts similarly Ruthian. Or perhaps Gibsonian.

As Greenlee's dream of a baseball dynasty soured, Gibson jumped back to the Grays near the end of the 1936 season. In 1937 he was listed on the Crawford's spring roster, but by mid-March he was described as a holdout. . . . Gibson did not come to terms with Greenlee and was then traded back to the Homestead Grays. Spring training had hardly begun when he heard the siren call of the dollar to be made with Satchel Paige in the Dominican Republic. He heeded the call. The *Pittsburgh Courier* reported, most improbably, that Gibson had gone to Trujillo-land with the consent of the Grays. In any event, he stayed only until July, returning in time to help the Grays win their first Negro National League championship.

For the next two years, Gibson's big bat was the pile-driving punch on the strongest club in Negro baseball. Boasting Buck Leonard, Sam Bankhead, Vic Harris, and other sluggers in addition to Josh, the Grays dominated the league and toyed with their foes on the barnstorming trail. It was such a powerful and well-balanced team that it could survive the loss of Gibson and continue its mastery over the NNL in the 1940 and 1941 seasons after Gibson had jumped to the Mexican League. He earned $6000 a season with Vera Cruz, according to the *Courier*, $2000 more than he was paid by the Grays. If Cum Posey and Sonnyman Jackson had looked on with favor when he had gone to the Dominican Republic in 1937, they were not pleased by his contract-jumping in later years. They won a court judgment against Gibson for $10,000 and laid claim to his Pittsburgh home. But when he signed with the Grays for 1942, all was forgiven and they dropped the suit.

Josh Gibson was at the height of his fame and near the peak of his incredible power, envied but popular with other Negro professional ballplayers, and the toast of Pittsburgh's black community. There was nowhere to go but down, and the slide would soon begin.

He had come into big-time Negro baseball 12 years before as a rookie of uncommon rawness, a young man so shy and retiring that when he visited in another player's home he spent the evening looking at his shoes. Now he was self-assured, the main attraction at any party, and he had developed a fondness for the bottle. Gibson's drinking never reached the point where he failed to show up for ball games —or to hit with power—but in his final five seasons he was occasionally suspended for a few days for "failing to observe training rules."

Another, more ominous, portent of the dark days ahead appeared when he began suffering from recurring headaches. On January 1, 1943, he blacked out, lapsing into a coma that lasted all day and hospitalized him for about ten days. The diagnosis was a brain tumor. Doctors at Pittsburgh's St. Francis Hospital wanted to operate, but he would not permit it, according to his sister, Mrs. Annie

Mahaffey. "He figured that if they operated, he'd be like a vegetable."

Gibson's knees, too, were giving him trouble, apparently the result of cartilage damage, and he was slowing to a snail's pace compared with his former speed. In his heyday, Gibson, despite his size, had been one of the fastest runners on the Grays. Yet, even while his troubles were pyramiding, Gibson was still the symbol of power. In 1944 he led the Negro National League in homers with six while batting .338 in 39 league games. The next year he was again home-run champion with eight and boasted a league-leading .393 average in 44 games. As a matter of course, he was chosen as the East's catcher in the East-West all-star games in 1944 and 1946. He missed the 1945 all-star game because it was played during one of his periodic suspensions for violating training rules.

Josh Gibson had played baseball the year-round every year from 1933 through 1945, spending the winter seasons in Puerto Rico, Cuba, Mexico, and Venezuela. His greatest thrill, he said, had been winning the batting title and the Most Valuable Player award in the Puerto Rican League in 1941. (He was without doubt the most valuable player in the Negro National League for several seasons, but no MVP award was ever given in the NNL.)

Now, in the winter of 1946, his headaches and blackouts were increasing in frequency and severity, and for the first time since 1933 he stayed home in Pittsburgh. Outwardly, he remained a cheerful, easy-going giant, gregarious and friendly, and only his increasing attachment to liquor betrayed his concern about his illness. "He never got drunk so that he was staggering or anything like that," Mrs. Mahaffey recalled, "but still it worried you, because he wasn't really a drinking man."

On the evening of January 20, 1947, Josh came home and told his mother that he felt sick. He said that he believed he was going to have a stroke. Mrs. Gibson said, "Shush, Josh, you're not going to have no stroke," but she sent him to bed. The family gathered around his bedside and waited for a doctor while Josh laughed and talked. Then he sent his brother Jerry to the homes of friends to collect his scattered trophies and his radio and bring them home. "So Jerry came back about ten-thirty," Mrs. Mahaffey said, "and we were all laughing and talking, and then he had a stroke. He just got through laughing and then he raised up in the bed and went to talk, but you couldn't understand what he was saying. Then he lay back down and died right off."

Gibson died the year after Jackie Robinson had broken organized baseball's color line at Montreal and only months before Robinson would become the first Negro in the major leagues since Fleet and Weldy Walker in 1884.

11

Gil Hodges

When Gil Hodges first came to the Mets in 1968, he was disliked by virtually everybody. He was an aloof person who didn't relate well to people he didn't know. Many of the players—myself included—would have preferred someone they could chat with more easily. But Gil didn't really care if the players liked or disliked him. All he wanted was for the players to respect him and his position. He made it clear that, as manager, he ran the ship.

By the end of his second year, we were World Champions, and we had learned that Gil Hodges was exactly what the team needed. In very difficult situations, he was the strong, dominant figure who could be depended on to make the decisions. He had made us feel that if everybody did his job, then, with the talent we had, we would succeed. After seeing what he had accomplished, we respected the man tremendously.

Gil never really changed in the years he managed the Mets, except for becoming just a little more mellow and compassionate after his first heart attack. When you reached the point where you enjoyed working for him, you could begin to see his more human side. But you never forgot that he was the boss.

Once I was pitching against Cincinnati at Shea Stadium and we were ahead, 3–2, with two out in the top of the ninth. Lee May was the batter and I walked him on four pitches low and away. I didn't walk him intentionally, but I wasn't going to give him a pitch that he could hit for a home run.

By the time May reached first, Gil was at the mound. He had a rule that we were never to put the tying run on base. All he said was: "You pitched to him like you wanted to walk him."

Very early I had learned that you didn't lie to Gil. Most of the time he knew the answer anyway and was just feeling you out. So I said, "Just about." He looked at me, then went back to the dugout.

The next batter was Jimmy Stewart. I had struck him out the time before and I thought I could do it again. I did, on three pitches, and we won the game.

Still, I was worried about Gil's reaction, so I stuck my head in his office and said, "You don't agree with me about walking May, do you?"A big smile appeared on his face, and I felt as if a whole ton of bricks had dropped off my back. "If I knew you were going to strike out Stewart, I never would have come to the mound," he said. We both chuckled, then I went to my locker, much relieved.

That was the thing about Gil. He never said much, but you always felt his presence. Partly it was his massive strength. He was so strong he could inspire physical fear in players. I was never very aware of Gil as a ballplayer when I was young, but I knew what kind of hitter he must have been as soon as I met him; he had the biggest, strongest hands of any man I'd ever seen.

In a sense, he was the Lou Gehrig of the Brooklyn Dodgers. He didn't get very much recognition. The Dodgers had a whole group of great hitters—Duke Snider,

Roy Campanella, Jackie Robinson—and Gil was so quiet off the field. But he was a dominant force. For seven years in a row, he hit more than 100 RBIs and for 11 years in a row he hit more than 20 home runs. He holds the National League lifetime record for most grand-slam homers—14. Hodges was the dependable backbone of the Dodgers.

Once in a while, Gil would take batting practice with the Mets, and you could still see that old Ebbets Field swing. He was a dead pull-hitter, always looking for an inside pitch to pull into the left-field stands. After I got to know him a little better, I used to rib him when he stepped into the batting cage. "I'd strike you out every time," I once told him. "I'd throw it to the outside corner on your knees, and you'd never even make contact."

"I'd just move up on the plate, Tom," he answered.

"Then I'd bust it right at your hand," I said.

"You'd better not miss," he warned, "or I'd pull it into the stands."

After Gil died, we missed his strong presence. It was difficult not to be constantly thinking about him those first couple of months. He had so many strong qualities you could almost feel that some of them were still there in the clubhouse. He passed on a measure of his strength and dedication to his players. We all learned from Gil what it really means to be a professional.

One Stayed in Brooklyn
•
Roger Kahn

Late spring is the time to see Gil Hodges work. Not summer. Then heat sits on the cylinder of Shea Stadium and a baseball season, like New York summer, grinds down strong men. Not September. The weather cools, but then the final pressures of a pennant race clamp Hodges into a vise. He manages the New York Mets, contenders like the Dodgers, but a generation younger than he, people playing the same game in a different time, and by September his face shows leather strain lines and his soft voice becomes ever more tightly controlled. But in late spring Hodges watches his ball club settle in. He almost relaxes. There are no baseball irrevocabilities in the month of May.

During August of 1968, Hodges suffered the forewarnings of a heart attack. The Mets were moving from ninth place to eighth amid dizzying waves of adulation. Hodges, the still point, smoked heavily and tried to bury tension within his large frame. On about September 19, 1968, he felt what he calls "pain like a drill boring into my chest." It was not excruciating, but neither did it go away. For five days he ignored the boring, the way his old roommate Carl Furillo might have done, although the pain disrupted sleep and shattered concentration. "Did I know what it was?" Gil Hodges says. "I suppose so. Yes. Did I *want* to know what it was? No." He continued managing for a week. Then, during the second inning of a night game at Atlanta on September 24, he excused himself from the dugout, walked into the dressing room and lay down on a training table. His skin was ashen and he felt chilly. "I got to rest," he told Gus Mauch, chief trainer of the Mets, who had followed him inside.

A local physician put a stethoscope to Hodges's chest, and said he thought Gil could go home and check into a hospital the next morning. Mauch, who is not an M.D., was more cautious. He had suffered a heart attack himself. He urged Hodges to ride a taxi with him to Crawford W. Long Hospital, which is named for the man who first mastered the use of ether. By midnight Hodges lay under intensive care. He had suffered a myocardial infarct, a heart attack of so-called "mild" proportions. He had walked about for a week, hit fungoes, pitched batting practice, with a developing coronary. The strongest of the Dodgers was fortunate still to be alive at 44.

As far as researchers can tell, six specific factors contribute to the heart attack that strikes a man in his mid-40s: poor diet, insufficient exercise, overweight, heredity, smoking and—catchall for most ills of modern man—stress. Only the last two considerations apply directly to Hodges. Still two out of six were enough. He built an outer barrier of calm, but he churned beneath the way the sea churns below a pale, rippled surface. "And the smoking got out of hand," he says. "I knew I was smoking too much. Don't write I've stopped. I sneak one every so often. But I'm fine. I do sit-ups, push-ups, run. I do everything I ever did except pitch batting practice. I'm perfect, if you can overlook a few mental hang-ups."

"Such as?"

"You have one of those things, you don't forget it."

Gil Hodges the ballplayer cast a sense of strength. He stood six feet two, and with no extra fat he weighed more than 200 pounds. After playing cards once, he returned to his compartment on a train and found Dick Williams reading in the lower berth. "How did you do?" Williams asked.

Hodges smiled faintly. Then he slipped both arms under Williams, 190 pounds himself, and lifted him into the upper bunk.

He had the largest hands in baseball. "Gil wears a glove at first because it's fashionable," Pee Wee Reese said. "With those hands he doesn't really need one." People were always kidding about his physical powers.

Hodges has to be the strongest human in baseball.

What about Ted Kluszewski?

If he's stronger than Hodges, he ain't human.

Did you hear what went on after Hodges hit the beach at Okinawa?

The Japs surrendered.

Not only that. Half our Marines did, too.

You know what happens when big Gil squeezes that bat?

No. What?

Instant sawdust.

Beyond the jokes stood a large, quiet, intense man, somewhat surprised at his own success and damned to cringe before tough, right-handed pitching. Remembering Hodges against Sal Maglie or Allie Reynolds, I see a man hating to come to bat against such intimidating stuff and hating more the fact of his own fear.

One's response to a curveball and its allusion of impending concussion is almost reflex. One wants to duck. Some, like Billy Cox, conquer the reflex with comparative ease. Most do not. Athletes as heroic as Jim Thorpe never learned to control the reflex well enough to hit a good curve. Without precisely knowing—good hitting remains as mysterious as any other art—I suspect a mild phobia is at play. Mild, because batting is genuinely a high-risk occupation. It is normal for a hitter to be aware of the danger.

Few of us are anxious to paint bridges; real risk exists and our sense of self-preservation asserts itself in distaste for high winds that keen through suspension cables. Conversely, the fearless bridge painter may himself be discomfited by tunnels or by ocean breakers. No one is a coward because he shuns suspension towers, or because he draws back from a baseball hurtling toward his head. Rather it is a measure of courage that Hodges fought his cringe reflex year after year. To taste fear as he did and to choke it down and make a fine career is a continuing act of bravery.

Hodges hit 370 home runs, four in a single game. Swinging hard, he batted .273 across 18 seasons. But his conflict, the reflex to duck contending with the desire to hit, almost snipped his career before he was 30.

On September 23, 1952, the day on which the Dodgers

clinched a pennant, Hodges singled off Karl Drews, a Yankee reject who had joined the Phillies and threw hard sinkers. Hodges did not hit safely again that week. Humiliation came with the World Series. Hodges went to bat 26 times, and during these tense games, when men about him rose to the drama of the days, he suffered in a public impotence. He walked five times, but he made no hits in any of the seven Series games.

The spring brought no relief. Hodges outran a ground ball for a single on opening day, but by the middle of May he was batting .187 and Charlie Dressen sent him to the bench. The fans of Brooklyn had warmed to the first baseman as he suffered his slump. A movement to save him rose from cement sidewalks and the roots of trampled Flatbush grass. More than 30 people a day wrote to Hodges. Packages arrived with rosary beads, rabbits' feet, mezuzahs, scapulars. One man wrote that pure carrot juice would restore the batting eye. "Vitamin A," he explained.

Charlie Dressen knew what was wrong. He ground his teeth and swung his arms. "The trouble," he said, "is they won't let ya teach 'em till they is real down." Without telling Hodges, Dressen asked Barney Stein, the team photographer, to shoot hundreds of feet of movies. A few days after the benching, Dressen thought Hodges was ready to be taught and called him into his office, beside the clubhouse.

In the most telling strip of Stein's film, Hodges was hitting and Andy Seminick was catching for Cincinnati. As the ball approached, Hodges drew back his bat, and stepped toward the third-base dugout. His stride carried him away from home plate. He followed the pitch into Seminick's glove, certain that it was outside. It was a strike. Had Hodges swung, his weight would have gone toward the safety of a dugout, while his arms and bat moved toward the ball. He was off balance. His timing suffered. He got neither weight nor accuracy into the swing. "See it, see it," Dressen cried.

"Mmmm," Hodges said, for "yes."

"Now ya been stepping that way for a long time and maybe ya ain't gonna stop," Dressen said, "but I can fix it so a step like that don't hurt ya, if you're willing to listen."

"I'm listening right now, Charlie."

"Keep your front foot where it is, but move the back foot farther from the plate. See what I mean. Now when ya pull back, the way ya do, you'll just be stepping into line. It won't hurt ya so much, stepping outa the way like ya do, cuz ya won't be really stepping out of the way, you'll really be stepping into it. I wancha to overcompensate, or some word like that."

That season, 1953, Hodges batted .302. In the World Series of 1953 he led all the Dodger hitters with .364. His weakness persisted, but his career was saved.

"I remember that slump very well," Hodges said softly, as we left his house on Bedford Avenue near Avenue M. It is a large, unpretentious, comfortable home—the Hodges have four children—in a quiet neighborhood that has shown little outward change since the 1940s. We were going to drive from the house to Shea Stadium, where that night the Mets would play the Chicago Cubs. "Having had to fight slumps, does that help you manage?" I said, as we climbed into my car.

"Not by itself," Hodges said, "although I understand you can't help a man until he's willing to be helped. I probably would have understood that anyhow. Charlie's way isn't the same as mine. Take the man in the other dugout tonight, Leo Durocher; not in any way criticizing, he makes noise. I'm not built that way. I communicate through my coaches. I have rules that I want obeyed, but I keep the coach between myself and the player, which establishes a distance that I like and prevents arguments. You don't want to be arguing with them yourself when you're manager."

"How is it working with people of a different generation?"

Hodges mused. "Go left up here," he said. "We want to hit the Shore Parkway. Then into Van Wyck. That'll take us in."

Silence. Hodges uses silences. He seems to enjoy them.

"Is it tough working with kids?" I said.

"Oh," Hodges said. "That's right. You had a question in there, didn't you? No. I haven't found it all that tough."

"Your background is different from theirs. You came out of the mines."

"No. I was never down in the mines. My father never would let me go down in the mines."

"Mining country."

"That's true."

"Well, you came out of hard times, and when you broke in, the game was all white. Now you're managing men who've gotten good money to sign, and they're black and and white."

Hodges looked over oncoming traffic as we pulled onto the Shore Parkway. "I can honestly say that color was never a problem to me," he said. "It wasn't to Pee Wee or the others either. And it isn't now." He puffed his lips in a faint sigh and began to talk easily about his background.

Princeton, his hometown, lies below the White River in the southwestern corner of Indiana. You can make a triangle from Anderson to Princeton to Louisville—Erskine, Hodges and Reese—and plot the Dodgers from the Middle Border. Princeton was coal country, and (as Gil remembers) his father rode down to deep veins in order to support his family and died slowly, one part of his body at a time. An accident cost an eye. Another cost some toes. At 54 he injured a knee and as Big Charlie Hodges lay in a hospital recovering from surgery, an embolism stopped his heart in 1952.

"Did *you* want to go down into the mines?" I said, as we drove beside the foul blue waters of Jamaica Bay.

"I didn't want to go down," Hodges said. "I didn't want to ever work down there."

Charlie Hodges had two sons, Gil, called "Bud," and Bob. Both were big and well coordinated and Charlie taught them what he knew about playing ball. If he could not escape the mines himself, at least he'd show the boys a better way. After high school they went to St. Joseph's College near Indianapolis. Bob, 14 months older than Gil, entered the army in 1942. Gil, who ran track, and played football, basketball and baseball, caught the attention of Stanley Feezle, the scout and sporting goods man who signed Carl Erskine. Feezle sent Hodges to a tryout camp at Olean, New York. From there Hodges went to Brooklyn, for personal examination by Branch Rickey. He was, as someone has said, "the kind of prospect who secures a scout's job for life."

Over three morning workouts, Rickey moved Hodges through eight positions, every one but pitcher. "You ever think of catching, young man?"

"No, sir."

"You have a little hitch in your throw at shortstop. Catching would be a marvelous opportunity."

Hodges signed for a $500 bonus and joined the 1943 Dodgers, a team of Durocher, Luis Olmo, Mickey Owen, Billy Herman and a waning Dolph Camilli. Hodges played one game—at third. He walked once, stole a base and struck out twice. Then he was drafted into the marines, where he spent the next 29 months. Whatever heroics he may have worked, he keeps to himself. He says only that he started smoking "to have something to do sitting in those holes in Okinawa."

Bob Hodges's baseball career ended with a bad arm in the low minors. Then he went to work for the U.S. Rubber Company. When Gil returned to baseball, Rickey gave him another $500, and sent him to Newport News to master catching. A year later Hodges leaped to Brooklyn and became catcher No. 3.

The next season, 1948, the outlines of the team began to

show. Billy Cox took over third. Jackie Robinson moved to second base. Snider and Shuba appeared in the outfield. Roy Campanella caught and Hodges, handed Robinson's discarded mitt, was assigned to first.

He had to struggle. That season he batted .249. But he hit 23 home runs for the pennant winners of 1949 and led the league in fielding. In 1951 he hit 40 homers, the second highest total in baseball. He seemed to have arrived. Then the slump seized him.

"With me," he said, as we parked close to the players' entrace at Shea Stadium, "it was a battle. I *always* had trouble with the outside pitch. Some don't. I did." He shrugged.

We walked through the Mets's dressing room, carpeted and empty, into Hodges's office, a large underground room without windows. "Did you plan on managing?" I said.

"How can you plan on getting a job that may not be offered? I suppose I hoped, but when George Selkirk asked me to take over Washington, I didn't jump. I called some people. Talked to my wife, Joan."

"Do you find it hard?"

"Sending out an older player, telling him he's released, is hard."

"How about strategy?"

"Most is simple logic. I don't think it calls for any great thinking."

"Hello, Dad," called Gil Hodges II, a cheerful, chunky boy of 19. "I thought me and my friend Jack here could work out."

Hodges looked at his oldest son. "Since you got a haircut, okay." Someone appeared and began to talk to Hodges about the jewelry he could get wholesale and Hodges nodded and said he had to go out for a minute and look for Rube Walker, his pitching coach.

The two boys dressed quickly. "Hey," the younger Hodges said to Jack, "what kind of spikes you wearing?"

"What do you mean what kind?"

"They got white tops."

"That's right. The uppers are white."

"Well, you can't use them here. My father's a kind of conservative man."

"He don't seem bad."

"He isn't. He's just kind of conservative."

Hodges returned. "Your hair should be even shorter," he said. Young Gil grinned and shook his head. The father dressed silently. "I'm not a Durocher type," he repeated at the batting cage. "I can't get that worked up all the time."

"Or even talk that much," I said.

"You got it," Hodges said.

I turned and suddenly he was gone. I found him back in his office, speaking with Harold Weissman, the Mets's publicity director.

"Tommie Agee," Weissman said, "is having chest pains."

"How old is Agee?"

"Twenty-seven."

Hodges looked pale and concerned. "Don't tell the papers just yet."

"A city edition will be closing," Weissman said. "We can't withhold something like that."

"Don't tell them," Hodges said.

"You're losing points with me, Hodges."

"If it was a matter of needing your points, I wouldn't be behind this desk. You're losing points with *me*."

"Give a man an office," Weissman said, "and he goes wild."

"We should wait," Hodges said. "Wait for the cardiogram. Then if it's nothing, you can announce it as chest pains that *weren't* a coronary."

"Got you," Weissman said.

"The word scares people," Hodges said.

"We'll wait," Weissman said.

"Rube out there?" Hodges asked.

"Ru-u-ube!" someone called.

Rube Walker, the catcher who backed up Roy Campanella, has grown bald and portly.

"How's Koosman?" Hodges said.

"No complaints," Walker said.

"Good," Hodges said. The phone rang on his desk. Someone from the front office was calling. "Yes," he said. "Yes. I've taken care of that. Long distance? Sure. Put it on the other line."

Gil Hodges's salient quality, strength, works a strained contrast against the tension of his silences. A slim fierce infielder named Don Hoak appeared with the Dodgers during Walter Alston's first year and established himself as a neurotic. Hoak liked to be called "Tiger," and he raged several times a day, as others might take meals, or yawn. Hoak had fought professionally in Pennsylvania and when he became angry—at a train schedule, at an umpire or at the color of the sky—he cocked his fists. Visiting the clubhouse once, I saw him chattering at Hodges, then suddenly throw two punches to the upper arm. Hodges is fair-skinned. The blows left small red marks. Expression flowed from Hodges's face. He stared at Hoak, his pale eyes the more menacing because they showed no emotion. Hodges himself did not so much as make a fist, but before the gaze Tiger Hoak retreated.

A sense of strength stays with a man. When Hodges managed the Washington Senators, he learned once that four players were violating a midnight curfew. Hodges believes in curfews and he convened his ball club and announced: "I know who you were. You're each fined one hundred dollars. But a lot of us are married and I don't want to embarrass anyone. There's a cigar box on my desk. At the end of the day, I'm going to look into that box and I want to see four hundred dollars in it. Then the matter will be closed."

Hodges gazed. At the end of the day, he looked into the cigar box. He found $700.

Against this sense of power and command beat the serious silences of Gil Hodges. Always (it seemed to me) the silences were tense. Yes, he could lift Dick Williams, flatten Don Hoak, physically awe an entire team. But he knew how weak physical strength really was. He had learned that watching his father die one part at a time. And he learned it again, when smaller, weaker men mixed fastballs at his head with curves. It was fine for Reese to talk about flattening a pitcher, as if flattening one man would work. But the game was played by rules and one rule commanded him to stand in and take it and he believed in rules. He practiced a devout, quiet Catholicism and he sought humility, but he drove himself to move ahead and drove himself to fight down fear, and what can give a strong athletic man a frightful heart attack at 44 is the war he wages within himself, even if he is soft-voiced, like Hodges, and blankets the conflict under casual remarks, a hard blank look, bantering ways and the faint, almost casual smile.

Tommie Agee had not suffered a coronary. By nine o'clock he was back in Shea Stadium. "Chest pains," Harold Weissman announced in the press box, "which were probably caused by indigestion. We had a precautionary cardiogram and it proved negative." A crowd of 50,586 appeared, but it was not an easy night. The Cubs scored three in the first inning when Jim Hickman, an original Met, who was traded in 1967, hit a home run. After one of Koosman's pitches in the second inning, Jerry Grote, the catcher, called time. Hodges walked toward the field and Grote said, "He had nothing on it. Something must be hurting." At the mound Koosman admitted that his arm ached and came out of the game. Later a downpour stopped play for 55 minutes. The Cubs stayed ahead and won, 6–4.

Hodges had promised to talk on a Chicago television program after the game. Still in uniform, sweating from the sultry heat, concerned about Koosman, reminded of heart pains by Agee, he made his way up runways to the corner of the press box that would serve as the studio.

"Yes," he told the announcer, an ebullient man named Jack Brickhouse, "I'm disappointed in the loss, but the Cubs played well. Agee is fine. He'll play tomorrow. Koosman? We'll have to wait a day. We're hoping it's nothing." Then, "Thank you, Jack. Thanks for having me. I've enjoyed talking."

The television lights blinked off. We started down the runway, myself and the manager of the Mets, a 45-year-old post-coronary. In the half light his face seemed dry and gray.

"Tough night?"

"They're *all* tough. I mean it. I'm being serious. In this job the days don't get easier. I thought maybe we could sit up a while, but with the rain and all the problems, when I go home, I better go to sleep. The one thing after a heart attack is you don't want to overtire yourself."

I said, "Sure. You need a lift back?"

"I'll go with Gilly. You can go home. I guess you're tired, too."

I said yes, but I wasn't. We parted, and in the large empty ball park I tried to imagine how this job and night and life felt to a man with mine deaths in his past and a heart condition in his present and I missed a sense of joy. He has been close to the peaks of baseball for a quarter of century and, though he has gained things he wanted, Hodges has paid. He had seemed more tranquil as a player struggling to hit Maglie than as a pennant-winning manager. In the empty ball park, where my footfalls on cement made the only sound, I wondered whether Gil Hodges truly was better off with the satisfactions and fierce strains of his success or whether sometimes he envied his older brother Bob, who always talked a better game, but disappeared into the chasm of corporate life during the 1940s when all his talk and scheming ended with a dead arm on a Class D ball club playing in West Central Georgia. And here it was, only May.

12

Rogers Hornsby

Rogers Hornsby was one of baseball's great hitters, but not one of baseball's great batting coaches. At least not judged by the performance of his last pupils—the Mets of 1962.

Ed Kranepool is the only player still with the team who played on that original Mets team (for three games at the end of the '62 season) and he remembers Hornsby well. Ed was a bonus baby drafted out of a New York City high school, and the Mets, a team of fading players, were eager for their young prospect to make it as quickly as possible. When he was playing for Auburn in upstate New York that summer, Ed heard that the Mets were sending Hornsby up to help him with his hitting. Ed, only 17 at the time, was awed that one of baseball's all-time greats was coming just to help him.

Hornsby stayed at Auburn just long enough to tell Ed two things. First, he informed Ed, "I don't think much of modern players." Then Hornsby advised him on his hitting. "Go up there and swing at strikes," he said. Then he left.

Maybe it's just as well that Hornsby didn't tell Ed anything more. The Rajah had some peculiar ideas about how a batter should keep himself in shape. As far as I'm concerned, Hornsby's theory of never reading or going to a movie in order to save your eyes hurts an athlete more than it helps him. Part of being a professional athlete is being able to use your mind well and think quickly. Reading and seeing movies helps you train and stimulate your mind while also helping you relax. As for Hornsby's refusal ever to drink beer, well, it's fine to take care of your body but nobody likes a fanatic.

Return of the Rajah
•
Robert M. Lipsyte

Rogers Hornsby, a hard-bitten, heavy-set man of 66, is an active witness this season [1962] to baseball's 38th annual attempt to better his major-league batting record (.424, set in 1924). The Rajah is watching from the inside this year, as batting coach for the new Mets.

During his playing career, from 1916 to 1937, Hornsby never smoked ("Cuts down your wind," he would growl); never drank ("Highballs are bad enough, but beer goes right to the legs and slows you up"); never went to the movies ("Might affect my batting eye"); and never stayed out late with girls.

"I gotta get my sleep," he would explain petulantly. "The people pay money to see me at my best, not tired and hung-over. I go out with girls. I'm human, but I figure if I don't get the pitch I want between seven P.M. and midnight, forget it."

Despite this credo, and a lifetime batting average of .358 (surpassed only by Ty Cobb's .367 in the American

League), Hornsby was one of the game's most controversial and unpopular characters.

In 11 years with the St. Louis Cardinals, he set a dozen records; managed the team to its first world championship; was named in a divorce action (his own first wife subsequently divorced him on the grounds of general indignities); punched his predecessor as manager, Branch Rickey; told the owner to mind his own business and let him run the team, and advised the commissioner of baseball to go to hell when the latter asked him to give up gambling on the horses.

In 1927, he was traded to the New York Giants. At dinner one night, accompanied by a player named Ed Farrell, he was asked if the Giants could win the pennant. "Not with Farrell playing shortstop," he retorted.

In 1928, he was sold to the Boston Braves. He won his seventh batting championship that year. When asked if the Braves had a chance to win the pennant, he snapped: "These Humpty Dumpties?"

And in 1952, when he was fired from his position as manager of the St. Louis Browns (they were the 11th team for whom he worked), the club owner who fired him received a 24-inch silver trophy from the players inscribed: "To Bill Veeck for the greatest play since the Emancipation Proclamation, June 10, 1952."

Hornsby's parting remark was characteristically blunt and succinct: "When you work for a screwball, you gotta expect screwball tactics."

In spring training this year, Hornsby gave ample proof that age had mellowed him only slightly. He made disparaging remarks about Roger Maris, baseball's current hitting idol, and displayed the old dedication: First man on the field, last one off; no liquor, no smoking; and if there had been movies in the past 25 years, he couldn't recall the titles.

In the evenings, he was always available in the hotel lobby to amplify the batting instructions he had imparted on the field during the day. (His hobby, as listed in the *Baseball Register*, is lobby-sitting.)

"Baseball is my life, the only thing I know and can talk about, my only interest," he said recently, sitting in a corner of a hotel lobby, his broad hands folded across the front of an open, double-breasted jacket. "I'm easy to get along with —if you're on the up-and-up, of course—but I'm not a good mixer. I get bored at parties and I bore other people. I don't like to get dressed up and go out.

"I enjoy the right kind of people, my kind of people, but I don't like to do the sociable things. I think it's undignified, a man of my age going around in short pants, for example, and I don't think I'm old enough to play golf. I'm used to other people chasing balls I've hit; damned if I'm going to run after a little ball myself."

He still looks the man who hit baseballs other people chased. Six feet tall, 200 pounds, he walks erectly and briskly. His large, square face is tough and humorless, his lips thin, his eyes very blue and very cold.

He says he still regards his greatest moment as the time the Cardinals won their first championship.

"I always was a hard-boiled guy who could keep his mind on the game no matter what. In the spring of 1926, the year we won it, we were playing a game in San Antonio and I visited my mother. She took me out on the porch, and you can call it mother's intuition or whatever you please, but she told me that the Cards were going to win and that she would die on the day we clinched the pennant. And she said I should play the World Series before I came home to bury her.

"Well, on September 26, 1926, we beat the Giants in New York to clinch, and when I got back to the Alamac Hotel, there was a wire waiting for me. She was dead. We played and won the Series, and on the way back to St. Louis I changed trains and went home and buried her."

He leaned forward slightly in his chair (the only movement he makes while lobby-sitting) and said: "I'm kind of cold-blooded. When I put on the uniform, that's it. I'm out there to play to win and that's it."

He leaned back again. "The horses was my relaxation after a game, and you can believe I had some pretty big paydays, more than the stars these days make in a year, and I lost big, too, sometimes. But it was nobody's business but mine because when I got out there on the field there was nothing but baseball on my mind."

Hornsby was born on April 27, 1896, on his father's Hereford ranch outside Winters, Texas. At 15, he was a batboy for the local meat-packing-plant team in North Fort Worth (where the family had moved after his father died) and won some acclaim when he filled in for absent regulars. Within a short time he was playing regularly with Hugo, and then Denison, in a lower minor league.

In 1915, the Cardinal second team, barnstorming through the Southwest, played an exhibition game with Denison. Hornsby's skill in the field was commended and remembered. He was purchased for $500 several months later and in September was brought up to the big leagues.

"I couldn't hit much," he recalls. "I was six feet tall and weighed 130 pounds, and the bat was so heavy I had to choke up on the handle. Miller Huggins, he was the manager, he looked at me and said, 'Hornsby, I'm going to have to farm you out on account of your size.'"

This is Hornsby's favorite story and he almost smiles at the reminiscence. The 19-year-old infielder thought Huggins meant that he would literally have to go to a farm. So he did. He spent the winter of 1916–17 on his uncle's farm in Lockhart, Texas, sleeping 12 hours a day and consuming gargantuan quantities of ice cream, steaks, milk, cheese and potatoes.

When he reported back to the Cardinals in the spring, he weighed 165 pounds and could grip the bat at the end. He hit .313 that year, a winner in any league, and began batting out his niche in the record books, in baseball folklore and, 25 years later, in the sport's Hall of Fame.

He acknowledges that he has made many enemies along the way, but claims that he wouldn't want them for friends anyway. He does not quite understand why he has been variously called narrow, provincial, bigoted, suspicious, arrogant, old-fashioned and hostile by men who have worked with him.

"Maybe because I'm not two-faced," he says, "because I'm sure no diplomat."

The off-seasons and the periods when he was out of pro baseball were hard on him, he says. He has never read a book and rarely looks at newspapers. Since the end of the horse-parlor days, he has lost some of his interest in gambling.

In the winter he sometimes visits his son, a beer salesman in Tennessee (another son, by his first wife was killed in a military plane crash). Mostly, he just sits in the Chicago luxury apartment he shares with his third wife, whom he married five years ago, and waits for spring.

He was especially pleased, he says, to come back to the major leagues with the New York Mets.

"Casey Stengel [the manager] and George Weiss [club president] are real old-line baseball men, you can trust them. They're not like these new clowns, these promoters who make a circus out of the sport. Weiss and Stengel, they keep it on the level of the National Pastime, they set a fine, clean example for our youth, which is the most important thing people in baseball can do."

He drew a shallow breath at the passion he had expended, then lapsed into succinct, sharp, pure Hornsby when a lobby passerby asked if he were happy.

"That's a stupid question," he snapped. "You know damn well I wouldn't be here if I didn't like the set-up."

13

Al Kaline

Al Kaline made a serious error early in his career: He won a batting championship, hitting .340 with the Detroit Tigers, when he was only 20. Even though Kaline never again won a batting championship, he has established himself as one of the great hitters in baseball history. Entering his 22nd year as a major-leaguer, he had 2861 hits, only 12 behind Babe Ruth's career total; 1519 runs batted in, ten more than Mickey Mantle; and 386 home runs, more than Joe DiMaggio or Hank Greenberg.

He has also been one of the great defensive outfielders in the game. Jim Fregosi, who has played in both leagues, rates Kaline on a par with Clemente as a right fielder.

But Kaline's career has been shadowed because even more had been expected of him. It isn't fair, because you can't evaluate a player on just one season, even if it is a championship year at the age of 20.

I didn't make the same mistake. When I was 20 I was pitching for the University of Southern California. I was 22 the first time I faced Kaline. During spring training of my rookie year with the Mets, I pitched in a game against the

Tigers in Lakeland, Florida. Kaline hit a double off the left-field wall. And he wasn't the only Tiger who got a hit. In an inning and a third, I gave up something like ten runs. It was the first time I had been manhandled in a major-league uniform and I was in tears. I felt that the whole world had collapsed around me.

Spring training is the only time I've ever pitched to Kaline. He's a very aggressive batter who will go after the ball with that long bat of his, and he has always hit well off me. I'd be interested to see how I'd do against him in regular season play. But, of course, that won't happen.

I think it's a shame that so many of the top players never face each other in regular competition. I believe that interleague play would help baseball greatly. All major-league teams should be able to play each other occasionally. Then fans in American League cities would get a chance to see the National League stars and vice versa. And there'd be many great natural rivalries—the Mets and the Yankees, the White Sox and the Cubs, the A's and the Giants, the Angels and the Dodgers. Also, interleague play would cut down on the traveling we players have to do.

And I would have a few more chances to get even with Kaline for embarrassing me in my rookie training camp.

The Torments of Excellence

•

Jack Olsen

In a world fraught with inconstancies, unpredictabilities and galloping variables, it is a pleasure to report that spring [1964] has sprung in the traditional manner in Detroit. The flowers are popping up in Belle Isle park, the automobile plants are booming night and day, and everybody is wondering what's the matter with Al Kaline. Everybody has been wondering what's the matter with Al Kaline ever since he made the tactical error of winning the American League batting championship at the age of 20, the youngest player in history to make that mistake. To understand why this is a mistake, one must first understand a baseball truism most recently re-expressed by that skilled practitioner of brush-back and typewriter, James Patrick Brosnan, as follows: "Fans want the player to be not what he inherently is but what they think he ought to be." Fans think that anybody who wins the batting title at 20 should win it again four or five or 12 times. Kaline hasn't. Therefore something must be wrong with him.

If there has been any change at all in Detroit's attitude toward the lean and shy outfielder, it is merely quantitative. Of late, the Kaline enigma has been discussed more and more loudly and more and more persistently by college professors and semiskilled seat-spring assemblers, waitresses and *grandes dames*, by everyone in Detroit who can tell a baseball from a free balloon. As a result of all this discussion, the expectable human reaction has begun to set in. What people cannot figure out they tend to dislike. And Al Kaline, the best all-round ballplayer the Tigers have had since Charley Gehringer, is finding himself disliked. Not long ago he stepped to the plate in a home game to the accompaniment of a Shostakovich symphony of boos and catcalls. One would have thought that Joe DiMaggio had put the old pin-stripe back on and returned to hit against the Tigers with the bases loaded; not even Liberace has been booed like that.

While these hostilities were being ventilated, a kindly and gifted sportswriter, long addicted to the wonders of the Tigers and their star right fielder, was stomping about the windswept press box announcing to all who would listen: "As far as I'm concerned, Al Kaline can go take a jump. I've had 10 years of Al Kaline and that's enough!" A few feet away, another expert was collecting his own thoughts about Kaline and coming to a conclusion that he was later to proclaim over radio: "Personally, we feel Kaline should be traded now before his value to the team diminishes even more." The ultimate in non sequiturs was expressed by someone who should know better, and who therefore shall remain nameless. "Maybe the Tigers *should* trade Kaline," this man observed. "After all, they've never won a pennant with him!" [*Ed. They were, finally, to win one in 1968, but haven't repeated since then.*] This particular approach to the laws of cause and effect would have made a shambles of the good names of Baron von Richthofen, Haile Selassie and Chuck Klein, but rationality has never been the long suit of the disgruntled baseball fan.

In fact, there are no villains in the Al Kaline story. Not the fans who booed; they only know what they see, and they have been seeing a slumping Kaline. Not the insiders, the habitués of the press box; Kaline has indeed been a difficult subject for them, combining reticence and taciturnity with a seeming indifference and, lately, even rudeness. And certainly nobody can blame Al Kaline himself, the party of the first part, a child who was thrust full-blown into a world in which nothing he ever did was good enough and excellence brought its own torments.

Kaline is one of the last of an almost prehistoric type of ballplayer, the kid who makes it not because of physique but in spite of it. Walk into a baseball clubhouse nowadays and you see The Body Beautiful all around you: Smoothly muscled, superbly built young men like Sandy Koufax, Frank Robinson, Mickey Mantle. But not many years ago you would see bandy-legged little guys who make it on gristle and shank, on skills honed in thousands of games on sandlots that no longer exist, on guts and drive and gall.

Al Kaline is not bandy-legged, but neither is he a strong athlete, and he has had to overcome physical limitations that would have driven a lesser man to pack it in long ago. He has always had osteomyelitis, a persistent bone disease, and when he was eight years old doctors took two inches of bone out of his left foot, leaving jagged scars and permanent deformity. This slowed Kaline down only slightly, and only temporarily. His father, Nicholas, his uncles, Bib and Fred, and his grandfather, Philip, had all been semipro catchers from the Eastern Shore of Maryland, a place that had spawned major-leaguers as Miami Beach spawns gaucherie. One may assume that the first long discussions heard around the family hearth by the infant Albert William Kaline were not about the repeal of the Volstead Act or high protective tariffs. The Kaline family was poor, proud and hungry—no Kaline had ever graduated from high school—and before long the whole clan had decided that little Al was going to be something different.

Down the street from the family's brown-front row house in south Baltimore was a vacant lot (such things are now extinct in cities) where the men of the gas and electric company assembled at lunchtime to sneak in 30 or 40 minutes of softball. After the games Kaline's mother would see the boy, not yet old enough for school, running pell-mell around the bases, all alone, ruining his pants with daring slides to beat throws that were never made. At the ripe old age of six he was adjudged skilled enough to be permitted to shag flies and warm up pitchers for the lunchtime frolickers, and within a few years he was welcomed into the game as an equal. At 11 he flung a softball 173 feet six inches to set a new elementary school record. The judges did not believe their eyes; so he repeated the feat. Naturally, he became a hard-ball pitcher; the best ballplayer in any neighborhood always seems to be asked to pitch, no matter what his natural position is, *e.g.*, Stan Musial, Babe Ruth. In a league of 10-to-12-year olds, Kaline's record was 10-0. In high school the coach reckoned the boy was too small to make it as a pitcher and too fragile to make it as a second baseman; so he planted Kaline in the outfield. In four years he hit .333, .418, .469 and .488 and made the All-Maryland team each year, a feat last accomplished by Charlie Keller.

By now the Kaline family had staked the boy's whole future on baseball, the way Lower East Side families used to stake a son's future on the violin. On Sundays he would play in two and sometimes three games, with his father and his uncles shuttling him from game to game while he changed uniforms in the car. For one team he was hitting .824 at midseason, but tailed off to .609 at the end. By the time Kaline was signed to a $30,000 bonus-salary arrangement with the Tigers at 18, he had played as much baseball as the average major-leaguer plays in five or six seasons, a fact that goes a long way toward explaining why he was able to win the batting championship at 20 and has not won it since. He was at his peak at 20, and the pitchers, looking at the raw young kid of 150 pounds, simply could not bring themselves to admit that he was as good as he was. As Kaline says, "They've been cuter with me ever since."

A childhood like Kaline's may produce a star ballplayer, but it is not guaranteed to produce a barrel of laughs. Says Kaline: "I suffered a lot as a kid playing in all those games. You know how Baltimore is real hot in the summer? When everybody was going on their vacations, going swimming with all the other kids, here I was Sundays playing doubleheaders and all because I knew I wanted to be a ballplayer and my dad always told me, 'You're gonna have to work hard and you're gonna have to suffer if you're gonna be a ballplayer. You're gonna have to play and play all the time.'

"There was a couple times when I told my dad I wasn't gonna play Sunday, I was gonna go down to the beach with my girl or with a bunch of the guys to go swimming. And he says, 'Now look, like I told you in the beginning when you agreed to play for these people, they're gonna be counting on you, so if you're not gonna play tell 'em to tear your contract up.' So I would go play, but it was these things he did to me that showed me the right way and pushed me the right way."

Kaline was a dutiful son; when the Tigers thrust something in the neighborhood of $15,000 in cold cash on him (with $15,000 to come later in salary), he turned every penny of it over to his father, who was working in a broom factory, and his mother, who was scrubbing floors. The mortgage was paid off on the house, Mrs. Kaline's failing eyesight was saved by an operation, and young Al drove up to Connie Mack Stadium to take his maiden cut as a major-leaguer. He flied out to center on the first pitch, and was so nervous that he has no memory of going to the plate, swinging or returning to the dugout. Within a few years Ted Williams was saying: "There's a hitter. In my book he's the greatest right-handed hitter in the league. There's no telling how far the kid could go." Said a well-known manager: "This fellow is amazing. You ask yourself four questions. Can he throw? And the answer is yes. Can he field the ball? And you answer yes. Is he active on the bases? Yes, you'd have to say yes. And then, can he drive in the runs? The real test. And again you say yes. So he is an amazing fellow."

He was, in his early years in the majors, more amazing than even Casey Stengel realized, and at the same time he did everything with fluid ease. Dale Mitchell rapped a ball into right field and Kaline barely missed a sprawling shoe-string catch. The ball rolled a few feet away and Mitchell scooted for second. Kaline threw him out from a sitting position. In a game against the White Sox, when he was 19 years old, Kaline threw out Fred Marsh trying to score from second on a single, Minnie Minoso trying to stretch a single into a double and Chico Carrasquel trying to go from first to third on another single. The only people who believed it were those in the ball park, and they were not sure. At Yan-

kee Stadium, with the Tigers ahead by one run and the
Yankees threatening with two outs and two on in the last
of the ninth, Mickey Mantle hit a ball so hard and so far that
Mel Allen's broadcasting assistant whooped, "The Yankees
win five to four!" as he counted the base runners coming
across. In the Tiger clubhouse the equipment man angrily
flipped the radio off and waited for the Tigers to mope in.
They came in yelling and laughing. Kaline had raced to the
auxiliary scoreboard, leaped and twisted high in the air,
supported himself against the scoreboard with his bare hand
and caught the ball backhanded to end the game.

But the question, in his first few years, was not whether
he was a good enough fielder, everybody knew he was that.
"I was there because I was a fielder," Kaline says. "That's
what kept me in the league. The question was: Did I have
enough bat?"

His first season as a regular, 1955, answered that question.
At .340, he outhit Mickey Mantle by 34 points and Willie
Mays by 21. Among other feats of batsmanship that year,
he made four hits in five at-bats one day against the Kansas
City A's; three of the hits were home runs and two of the
home runs came in a single inning, a feat accomplished by
only five other American League players. He was compared
to Ty Cobb, and after that everything was bound to be
Bridgeport.

Looking back, Kaline cannot help feeling resentment.
"The worst thing that happened to me in the big leagues
was the start I had. This put the pressure on me. Everybody
said this guy's another Ty Cobb, another Joe DiMaggio.
How much pressure can you take? What they didn't know
is I'm not that good a hitter. They kept saying I do everything with ease. But it isn't that way. I have to work as hard
if not harder than anybody in the league. I'm in spring training a week early every year. I've worked with a heavy bat
in the winter, swinging it against a big bag. I've squeezed

rubber balls all winter long to strengthen my hands. I've lifted weights, done push-ups, but my hitting is all a matter of timing. I don't have the kind of strength that Mantle or Mays have, where they can be fooled on a pitch and still get a good piece of the ball. I've got to have my timing down perfect or I'm finished. Now you take a hitter like me, with all the concentration and effort I have to put into it—I'm not crying about it, it's just a fact—and imagine how it feels to be compared to Cobb. He was the greatest ballplayer that ever lived. To say that I'm like him is the most foolish thing that anybody can make a comparison on. Do you realize there's old people that come to Tiger Stadium and they saw Cobb play ball, and they look at me and they say how can I be as good as Cobb? They threw all this pressure on my shoulders and I don't think it's justified and I don't think it's fair to compare anybody with Cobb. I'll tell you something else: I'm not in the same class with players like Mays or Musial or Henry Aaron, either. Their records over the last five seasons are much better than mine."

In the first few years after he won the batting championship, Kaline went into frequent depressions over his inability to give the fans what he knew they expected. He would come into the clubhouse after a game and slump in front of his locker, speaking to no one. "But I didn't really sulk, the way the newspapermen said I did," he claims. "I was just quiet, and when a newspaperman came up to me and said, 'Nice game,' or something like that, I'd just say, 'Thank you.' I would never prolong the conversation, and the guys who didn't know me would say, 'Look at this stuck-up kid.' But it was just my way. I don't talk much. I don't like to make people mad at me, and if you talk too much you're gonna put your foot in your mouth sooner or later."

On top of these pressures, the front office began to apply the screws to Kaline. "They told me to be more colorful, that I could bring more people into the ball park if I was more colorful. But how could I do that? I could jump up and down on the field and make an ass out of myself arguing with umpires, but I'm not made up that way. I could make easy catches look hard, but I'm not made that way either."

The result of all these subtle difficulties is The Al Kaline Problem, the certain harbinger of spring in Detroit. But is there a genuine problem or is it ersatz? Charley Dressen votes for ersatz. "He's not hitting now," says the cherubic little manager and gourmet, "but what does that mean? Nothing. When a man is an established hitter like Kaline, you know what he's gonna do. The pitchers are getting him out now, but later on in the season somebody's gonna suffer."

It is true that Kaline at 29 seems overplayed, tired both physically and emotionally. He does not have a rapport with Dressen; although each publicly equates the other with Alexander of Macedon, there is antipathy underneath, and it will be a long time healing. Kaline was one of three or four players who complained vehemently about the firing of manager Bob Scheffing last year. "He made me a good ballplayer," Kaline says, "and I was really devoted to him." Scheffing did not make Kaline a good ballplayer; that job was accomplished years before by Nick Kaline and Al's uncles, but Kaline's veneration of Scheffing is nonetheless real.

But the main difference in Al Kaline is that the new 1964 model does not seem to be having any fun. To be sure, he claims that he is—"when it gets to be no fun you'll know it, because I won't be playing anymore." Not every man is gifted with the ability to know himself, and Kaline does not appear to be one of them. You might suppose that a man with a .309 lifetime batting average (same as Mantle's) and a place in the record books alongside Babe Ruth and a

$62,000-a-year salary and plenty of outside income would be having the time of his life, an orgy of joy. But talking to Kaline is like making funeral arrangements. In one breath he provides all the proper, time-honored remarks: "Detroit fans have really been good to me. . . . I think that Charley Dressen knows more about baseball than any manager I've ever had. . . . I owe everything to baseball. Without it, I'd probably be a bum today." But his more meaningful comments are made between the lines, almost *sotto voce*: "The owners want you to eat baseball, drink baseball, think baseball. It's too much to expect. . . . The season should be cut in half. Doubleheaders should be banned. It takes me three days to get over a doubleheader. . . . Spring training is over-rated. I'll admit I'm bored with it. . . ." He sounds, at times, like an old lady with sore feet, and, in fact, he is a young man with sore feet. Very sore feet. No one except Kaline himself will ever know the agonies that have accompanied his long career as an athletic cripple, mostly because he has kept his mouth shut about it. When the doctors operated on him, they left him with a set of sharply swept-back toes on his left foot. Only two of those toes touch the ground when he walks, which has forced him to develop a special running style: on the heel and toes of his right foot and on the side of his left foot. The fact that he gets to line drives with the style and skill of a Mantle or Mays is one of the athletic miracles of the ages. All Kaline will admit publicly is that his foot sometimes hurts him—"It's like a toothache in the foot." But there is a clearly discernible difference in his running as the game goes on. The Kaline who lopes out to his right-field position in the first inning runs almost normally; the Kaline who comes in after the last out is in pain and favoring the left foot. He is forever having his foot rubbed by trainer Jack Homel to restore the circulation and relieve the pain. On top of that, he has suffered more than the average number of injuries, among them depressed frac-

tures of both cheekbones, two beanings and a broken collarbone. Baseball has not been a frolic through sylvan glades
for Al Kaline, and if a lot of Detroiters do not know it, at
least one person does: general manager Jim Campbell of
the Tigers. "Al Kaline has had more reason to jake it than
almost any ballplayer I know," says Campbell, "but I have
never seen him give less than everything he had. That's the
way he learned to play baseball, and that's the only way he
knows how."

And what about all the suggestions that The Al Kaline
Problem be solved by trading him off while he is still a
valuable commodity? "Well, I'll tell you," says Campbell.
"I would consider it. Yes, sir, I would. If the Giants would
offer me Mays and Marichal and Cepeda for Kaline, I would
have to give it some consideration." In the meantime, Campbell and Charley Dressen and the good people of Detroit
will have to live with their problem. With a couple more
problems like Al Kaline, the Tigers would be the Yankees.

14

Mickey Mantle

When you think about Mickey Mantle, you think about tape-measure home runs and the glory and pain of a fabulous career on the diamond. But the following article shows a part of Mantle's life that wasn't often written about —the terrible demands that were made on him off the field.

The hero-worship of fans can be very satisfying, but constant invasions of your privacy can be tough to handle. I don't mean signing autographs for the kids waiting outside the locker room, but being approached on the street and in restaurants and even having strangers knock on your hotel-room door. Since you can't wear disguises, you have to learn to live with it. Unless you're a really exceptional person, though, you never really accept all the demands that are made on your time. Before you go out for dinner on the road, you have to anticipate being interrupted while you eat. It doesn't help your digestion.

Players react in different ways to this. Some have short tempers, others a great deal of patience. My moods vary. Sometimes I can be very patient, but other times I can be irritable. The worst times for me have been at the end of seasons when the Mets were in a pennant race. Then, I couldn't go anywhere without having to sign my name or talk into a microphone. There's only so much of this a person can take. When I reach the end of my patience and want some privacy on the road, I often go to a park and sit on a bench reading a newspaper; surprisingly enough, that's where I can be the most inconspicuous.

And it's not just the fans who invade your privacy, either. Before pitching the sixth game of the '73 World Series in Oakland, I was sleeping soundly at seven in the morning when my phone rang. A broadcaster in Boston was calling to ask me to tape a five-minute radio interview. "You woke me up and I'm pitching today," I told him, and not-so-politely declined to do the interview. He didn't seem to understand my reaction at all—after all, he was awake and working back in Boston. Naturally, I couldn't get back to sleep after that interruption.

So I can understand just how tough Mantle must have had it when he was the most idolized player in the game on a team that was always in the pennant race.

I pitched to Mantle in the last year of his career, at the 1968 All-Star Game in Houston. He was never a particular hero of mine growing up because I rooted against the Yankees and for the underdogs, which was every team the Yankees played back then. But I always respected him as one of the greatest players ever to come along. And as a kid I liked him for that great big grin of his I'd see in newspaper and magazine photographs.

The All-Star Game was, of course, a big moment for me. My parents and wife were in the stands at the Astrodome and I was high as a kite being out on the mound. Mantle came up to pinch-hit and was given a standing ovation. That didn't make my job any easier. I didn't try to out-think him or even pitch to spots; I just fired the ball in there. I threw four fastballs. Three of them were right down the middle of the plate, but I struck him out. At his peak, Mantle probably would have hit one of them through the dome. But this was '68 and age had caught up with him. He took that beautiful swing of his, but he wasn't even close. By the time he swung for the second time, I could tell how far behind the ball he was. I was just in my third year of pro ball and it made me feel sad to see a guy at the end of a great career.

On the Trail of a Hero

•

Ed Graham

At nine P.M. Saturady night, July 13, 1963, the first knots of Mickey Mantle fans began to form in the lobby of the Kansas City airport. Word was buzzing that the New York Yankees's plane would not arrive from Los Angeles until just before midnight. Most of the well-wishers were kids from nine to twelve years old, but some clutched the hands of younger brothers and sisters less than three. As the crowd grew, I noticed that most of the kids had pens and pieces of ruled paper clutched in their hands. I began setting up my flash equipment. A girl asked me if I was going to take pictures of Mickey Mantle. "Yes," I said.

Had I ever met him personally, she asked? I guessed her age at ten. "Yes," I said. "But only once."

Could she have *my* autograph? I thought she was kidding, but she was not. A small boy wanted me to sign on the same folded piece of paper where he already had "Jerry Lumpe," "Ed Charles," and "Norm Siebern," all Kansas City players. I told him I'd spoil the page. "But you've met Mickey Mantle," he said. "What's he really like?"

"A very nice fellow," I answered. But secretly I was not sure. I had only met him for a few minutes to get his permission to follow him for one full 24-hour period. But it was a disturbing few minutes.

For one thing, I was ready to like him because I am a Mickey Mantle fan. In fact, I am such a fan that when I wrote to the Yankee office—outlining my idea for a story —I didn't care if I sold it or not. Not that I told that to the Yankees. My secret ambition to meet the Yankees personally had started at just about the same age as that of the fans now clustered in the airport. For 24 years I waited for it to go away, but it never did. So I looked up the name of the public-relations director for the Yankees and sent him a letter suggesting I do a story on "A Day in the Life of Mickey Mantle." I was stunned when, two months later, I got a phone call saying the idea had been discussed with Mickey, and now Mickey himself wanted to discuss it further with me. If I never got any farther than a talk with Mickey Mantle—so what? What more did life have to offer anyway?

The meeting was set for a day in late June. It was the day that Mantle flew to New York to have the cast removed from his broken foot. I sat waiting in his dressing cubicle at Yankee Stadium and stared at the famous pinstriped shirt hanging above me with an actual No. 7 on the back. It really existed! And there hung his mitt with M-A-N-T-L-E scribbled in indelible ink on the back. I wondered why some younger player like Phil Linz didn't steal it and take it home and keep it in his drawer. Then Mantle himself limped in on aluminum crutches, with reporters, photographers and radio interviewers all around him. I overheard one reporter ask Mickey if he'd heard the big news. For the first time in history Commissioner Ford Frick was going to name an "honorary" member to the All-Star team. Although Mantle couldn't play, he'd still be an official member of the 1963

American League team. I was glad for Mantle, and I expected him to let out a whoop of excitement. But instead he drooped. "Does that mean I have to go?" he asked.

I was silently outraged. To think that only moments before I had idolized this travesty of an American hero! What I did not realize was why Mantle drooped. Now I do. Watching what he goes through during one 24-hour period on the road made me realize that playing ball is the easiest part of it.

But back to my "fallen idol" stage. When I asked Mantle if I could follow him for 24 hours, eat with him, travel with him, take pictures of him and perhaps see if I could get a story based on a typical day in his life, he drooped at that, too. He didn't say no point-blank—perhaps because the Yankee office might have asked him not to. But I had the definite feeling he wished I'd go away.

"Maybe Kainsas Cihty," he said in the voice I always assumed Li'l Abner spoke with. "We'll be thair for a double-hayder in the middle of July." Kansas City in the middle of July! This must be one of his bucolic jokes—and with a touch of meanness, I thought. Well, if he's going to make it rough on me, I'll show him I can take it. "O.K.," I said, "but no chickening out after I get there." "I won't," he said.

Now a rumor swept the airport lobby that the Yankee plane was about to land at Gate 2. A bus was already out on the field waiting to spirit the players away. Even at midnight in Kansas City, obviously a mob was anticipated.

The crowd rushed to Gate 2. After one person showed it could be done, we all poured through the gate and onto the airfield itself. Soon a light appeared in the west. It drew closer. A searchlight flicked on. With a roar the "Yankee Special" touched down and taxied to within 50 feet of us. A ramp was rolled up, the door burst open and down streamed the ballplayers, Cletis Boyer first. Swiftly they moved through a gauntlet of fans which extended from the base of the plane ramp to the door of the bus. The first Yankees signed autographs as they moved rapidly along.

Then Mantle appeared at the door of the plane. His crutches were gone now. As he came down, there was only a faint trace of the limp. A cheer went up. The gauntlet dissolved to re-form in a circle at the base of the ramp. It swallowed Mantle up. He too began to sign, but the size of the crowd made it impossible for him to move as rapidly as the others. I noticed that his first autograph was for the boy with the piece of ruled paper that boasted "Jerry Lumpe," "Ed Charles," "Norm Siebern"—and almost me.

Finally Mantle made it to the bus. The mass formed up again outside his window and began thrusting things in at him. He signed them quickly and seriously. I noticed that he was very much at ease with the kids. He admonished one who thrust the same piece of paper back for a second autograph. Once he noted that a hand reaching for a ball he had just autographed was not the same hand that had thrust it at him in the first place. Suddenly there were loud shouts of "Look out!" "Stand back now!" "This bus is leaving!" The engine was gunned. The crowd shrieked and scattered and the world champion baseball team rolled off into the night.

I took a cab to the Muehlebach Hotel in downtown Kansas City and beat the bus there. It took Mantle 10 minutes to work his way through the packed lobby, and then 15 minutes to pick up his keys. The jostling at the big, brown desk reminded me of pictures I had seen of the crowds fighting near tellers' windows when banks went broke during the depression.

By 1:30 A.M. it was all over. The players were on the sixth floor, Mantle and Ford in adjoining suites with an open door between. I was on the seventh floor with manager Ralph Houk, the coaches, other members of the press and the radio and TV crew. The phone operator would not ring Mantle's room. But through Whitey Ford, who acts as his social secretary, I made a date for the next morning at 10.

I am one of the world's easiest sleepers. But this night I lay awake the way I used to as a boy on Christmas Eve, wishing for the daylight. Also my pillow was very small (not much bigger than Ford's resin bag). And, furthermore, fate had placed me in an adjoining suite to Mel Allen. Our connecting door remained locked, but his voice carried. At home when the "Voice of the Yankees" grows too loud I can turn down the volume knob. But this night there was no knob to turn.

At exactly 10 A.M. (I had been hovering in the hall outside) I knocked on the door of room 638. Mantle opened it. He was wearing a pair of Bermuda-length jockey shorts that said M-A-N-T-L-E in an undignified stencil on the rear. When he saw my camera, he pulled on a pair of blue slacks and a blue polo shirt. There was a table with his breakfast in the center of the room. He asked if he could order me something. I was tempted to say, "Yes, I want to start my day with the same energy-packed breakfast that Mickey Mantle eats." But then I wouldn't have been able to take pictures.

What is the breakfast that Mickey Mantle eats? If you'd asked me to guess I think I would have said, "A sirloin steak, 11 flapjacks, four fried eggs and a pound of link sausages." But I was shocked to see that in reality he was eating a piece of melon, a tiny box of cereal (from one of those 10-pack assortments) and coffee.

Our talking must have awakened Whitey Ford. I looked up to see the pitcher with the highest won-lost percentage of all time stumble sleepily through the connecting door in a pair of blue silk pajamas. He took a bite of Mantle's melon, and studied it like a wine taster. "Pretty good Cranshaw," he said and went to the phone to place an order himself.

"Do you always eat in your room?" I asked Mantle.

"He doesn't get to eat much if he goes downstairs," Ford answered.

The phone rang, and Mantle answered it. He said, "Hello," then listened for what seemed a long time. "Well, I'll sign at the door," he said. "But they can't come in. It's room 638." As Mantle hung up, Whitey Ford asked, "Who was that?" His tone indicated the great pitcher sensed trouble. Like any Yankee fan, I knew that Ford relied on an uncanny ability to outthink his opponents. Now I was seeing a touch of it here in the room

"It was a fella," Mantle answered. "Said he's a friend of my brother Frank's. And he's got a couple of kids with him."

"You don't have a brother Frank," Ford said. Was this an old Abbott and Costello act they were putting on for my benefit? "I know I don't," Mickey said. "I figured the fella'd be embarrassed in front of the two kids and all."

There was a knock at the door. Mantle opened it and greeted a man with two boys who wore Yankee caps. Each got an autograph and a handshake. Then the man led them away. Breakfast was resumed.

Within five minutes it struck. First screams down the hall. Then the tread of fast-running feet. The words "room 638" could be heard amid the babble. Then suddenly there was pounding on the door. It grew more furious. Occasional bodies hurled themselves at the door. We actually seemed to be living a scene from Hitchcock's *The Birds*— the one in which millions of the tiny creatures pecked and hurled themselves at a door until they splintered the wood, burst through and pecked out the eyes of their victims inside.

I opened Ford's door and told the kids they would have to leave. They ignored me. I told them Mantle's room was 738 (Mel Allen's). But they did not believe me. Some had fallen to the floor and were peeking under the door. "I can see his shoes!" one boy called up triumphantly. "Yeah, and they're moving!" another shouted.

Perhaps because they decided it couldn't be any worse, Mantle and Ford decided to join their teammates in the coffee shop. After all, they had to go downstairs sometime. After a harrowing elevator ride—definitely over capacity —we reached the lobby. The scene there reminded me of another movie. It was one in which American families fought with each other to leave Manila in 1941.

Inside the coffee shop there was comparative relief. Anyone not eating was not allowed inside. But a boy whose chair was back to back with Mantle's stopped his own breakfast to stand up and breathe over the star's shoulder. A lady with a Polaroid camera asked Mantle to pose with his cup not in front of his face. And would Ford please get up because he was blocking the view?

Outside, word was now going around that Mantle would soon be coming out the coffee-shop door, and the biggest crowd yet began to form. Ralph Terry told Mantle and Ford that the bus was loading. The two of them plunged off into the sea of people—Ford in front, attempting to part it, with less spectacular results than Moses.

Inside the bus Mantle signed more autographs for the hands that reached inside the window. I clocked him at 12 autographs per minute. He signed for about 20 minutes. That would be 240 autographs outside the Muehlebach. I figured that he must sign over 1000 a day. My wife says she'd sign a lot of autographs for $100,000 a year, and so would I. But then I remember the time I had to write "I will not talk in class" only 25 times on the blackboard. My hand still aches. Could I have done it every day both on entering and leaving class and before and after recess? And while sitting around listening to *The Shadow*?

Riding to the park, Mantle and I talked about his personal feelings toward the public adulation he receives. "These are nice kids here in Kansas City," he said. "I just wish there weren't so many of them." I wondered if he was just saying that so I would play him up as a kid lover. But he named another city where the kids do not affect him as warmly.

"After all these years have you been able to adjust to the crowds, at least to a point where you can have some privacy?" I asked him.

"No," he said, and there was a wistful quality about the way he said it. There are moments when he smiles a very natural smile—not at all like the pictures you usually see of him. In those moments I found myself wishing things would go better for him—fewer worries, fewer injuries, more time to relax and enjoy the money he makes.

"Do you ever wish you could be a nonfamous guy like me and just walk around and do some special thing without people bothering you?"

He looked at me. "Have you got any kids?" he asked. I told him, yes, two boys. "You ever hear of the Six Flags Over Texas place?" he asked. "No," I said.

"It's like Disneyland, only near Dallas," he explained. "My boys, they love it, you know? Merlyn, my wife, has to take them there alone. Just once I'd like to be able to go and watch them on those rides."

The doubleheader with Kansas City had been sold out weeks in advance. When Mantle came out of the dressing room and into the dugout he was besieged by men who wanted special autographs and pictures. Even while thinking, "Why don't they leave him alone?" I found myself asking him to pose with a special greeting sign for one of my boys. He was nice about it. So to show my gratitude I took further advantage of him. Would he come out of the dugout for a picture of the two of us together on the field?

(My neighbor, who bores me with his sales achievements at Lily-Tulip Cup company, would faint.) Another man agreed to take the picture with my camera, and I tried to think of something to do. "Feel my muscles," I said, rolling up my sleeves. Mantle feeling *my* muscles seemed like a funny idea to me, since he's certainly the strongest man since Samson. I assumed he'd snicker at my comparatively puny arm. But Mickey Mantle is not a guy for the type of joke where a person says one thing and means another. He took me at my word and felt my arm. "You know, that's pretty strong," he said. Now I was embarrassed. I decided to push the humor to such an extent it would be more apparent.

"I'd challenge you to an Indian hand-wrestling contest," I said, "but I'd probably pin you so fast it would injure you and you'd be out the whole season."

"You know who you ought to challenge?" he said. "Dick Stuart. He's the world champion. At least he says he is."

We talked of other strong ballplayers, and I reminded him that people have said he's the only active player with a chance to hit a ball over the upper facade at Yankee Stadium. He had hit just below the top of the right-field facade a week before he broke his foot.

"You know something?" he said. "I always called those things 'fah-kaids.' "

I don't mean to imply that Mickey Mantle is stupid. He's not. But he seems to want to cling to the country-boy side of himself. I had thought of the big stars of the game as men who grow aloof and seek the special dignity befitting their positions. Joe DiMaggio seemed to become a sophisticated New Yorker—a smooth, big-city hero. But not Mickey Mantle. He told me it still bothers him when he hits a home run in New York and eight people show up with the ball to get it autographed.

Jerry Coleman, the ex-Yankee second baseman turned broadcaster, has described Mantle as "the biggest name in show business—bigger than Elizabeth Taylor." Yet I noticed that when a voice pipes out from the stands, "Hey, Mickey! Turn around!" he does. He assumes it is a friend calling. At least he assumed it in Kansas City.

By the time the Yankees took batting practice, the stands were pretty well filled. Elston Howard knocked a ball over the left-field fence. There was a smattering of applause. Johnny Blanchard put one over the right-field fence and scattered the sheep that graze on the hill beyond. More applause. Joe Pepitone hit two out of the park. He stepped out of the cage, delighted. Like all fans, I am a fair-weather friend. So I dropped Mantle and began complimenting Pepitone on his power.

"Mickey kids me about this park," he said. "We opened here and when I got a homer I told him I was going to be the first person in history to hit 162 home runs in one season. Now he won't let me forget it."

Bobby Richardson stepped out of the cage and Mantle went in. Suddenly there was a different sound in the stands. On the first pitch Mantle pushed a bunt. Tony Kubek, standing near by with his bat, rushed in front of the cage and bunted the ball back at Mantle. Mantle picked up the ball and threw it at Kubek. As the next pitch came in, Yogi Berra threw his bat at it from outside the cage so it passed across Mantle's line of vision as he swung. The ball went over the hill where the sheep graze and disappeared completely. I dropped Joe Pepitone immediately. Mantle hit six of the next seven pitches out of the park, all of them farther than any of the other drives hit that day. During this display the crowd reacted with the particular sound I associate with people watching fireworks displays on the Fourth of July.

As the ball would head out they'd go "oooooooooh." Then as it passed over the Cyclone Fence they'd change to "ohhhhhhhh!" Then as it left the park altogether they'd switch to "ahhhhhhhh!" mingled with applause. By that time the next one would already be on its way.

As Mantle came out of the cage, Pepitone tried a joke. "Will you ever realize your potential?" he asked. It was obvious that he is a Mickey Mantle fan too.

Unlike some teams, the Yankees are a very close group. It is Mantle who is the cohesive force. Although Ford is his personal pal, Whitey does not monopolize him on the bench. Mantle has as many upper-arm punches for Phil Linz as he does for Yogi Berra. If someone like Joe Pepitone strikes out, Mantle moves over and sits with him when he trots back. Soon you see the two of them laughing.

Just before the first game young Tom Tresh, who had been in a minor slump, was the target of some Mantle rough-housing. He went on to hit two home runs. I don't know if there was a connection or not, but at the time Tresh looked as proud to have been sitting next to Mickey Mantle as I was.

Between the two games Mantle took a whirlpool bath. It seemed like a spot to relax. Instead, the time was assigned to answering written requests for autographed pictures. At the start of the second game there was more autograph signing along the runway that leads from the dressing room back to the bench. The game was in progress, but not for anyone near the section.

After the game a crowd formed outside the players' exit. A knot of boys gathered around the ventilator that fed air into the dressing room. Someone had discovered that if you looked through the top of the ventilator you could see a portion of the dressing room inside. "Can you see Mickey Mantle?" one kid yelled. "No," another answered, "but I can see Yogi Berra. And he's naked!" As each Yankee boarded the bus, I interviewed him for "background on the story I was doing." I asked the players if it was like this always, wherever Mantle went. "Sometimes worse," they said.

Cletis Boyer told me he had tried to go deer hunting with Mantle after the last World Series. "It was ridiculous," he said. "Crowds trooping around through the woods after us, asking for autographs. I think even a couple of deer recognized him." I asked Yogi Berra, "Ever go into a restaurant with Mantle?"

"Sure," he said.

"What usually happens?" I asked.

"We eat," Yogi said.

"He means with the people who come over to the table," Phil Rizzuto told him.

"Oh!" said Berra. Then he told me about sitting facing Mantle at a table in Minnesota. A drunk approached Mantle from the rear. "Just as Mickey was cutting into his steak this guy slaps him one the back and says, 'Mickey Mantle!' and the steak slid off the plate right on the floor."

"Did the drunk apologize?" I asked.

"I don't think so," Berra answered. "I just remember he pulled up a chair, sat down and started asking Mickey who was better—himself or Ted Williams."

I asked Ford about the mob pounding on his hotel room door. "Is there a friend of Mickey's brother Frank who tips people off in the other towns too?" I asked him. "No," he said. "Usually somebody just gives a bellboy a buck for the room number."

"Couldn't the two of you get off away from the team hotel and relax somewhere?"

"If there's a night game, sometimes we'll go to a movie in the afternoon. But on summer vacations, school kids see him coming in, and then they all sit behind him and ask questions. The first 10 minutes of *Dr. No* were great. But then some kid hollered out, 'Hey! Mickey Mantle's sitting in this row right here!' Then a whole bunch started crowding around and making remarks, you know. When we left the theater, this same kid hollered, 'Mickey Mantle's leaving! Big deal!' "

When the bus arrived back at the hotel, it pulled up to a side entrance. It was almost 11 P.M. Riding up on the elevator with Mantle, Ford and Houk, I asked Mantle what his plans were for the night.

"I'm going to call my motel in Joplin [a place called Mickey Mantle's Holiday Inn]. My wife said she might come up from Dallas. If she did, I can get there in less than an hour. Otherwise, I'm going to go to bed."

The door opened for the sixth floor. Mantle and I shook hands, and he left. As the elevator door closed I heard a whoop and the now-familiar stampede of feet. "It's Mickey Mantle!" kids shouted. "Hey, Mickey!"

It felt nice to be getting off at Ralph Houk's floor instead.

15

Willie Mays

Probably nobody ever had greater baseball instincts than Willie Mays. He was a marvelous natural athlete whose reflexes, strength and coordination were perfectly suited for the game. But most people never realized that Mays was a thinking ballplayer as well as a natural one. He wasn't an intellectual by any means, but in his own way he studied the game and kept learning all through his career.

In the clubhouse, you could mention a pitcher who hadn't played in 15 years and Willie would tell you, "Oh, he had a good curve. Once I hit it for a double into right-center." He'd remember not only what a pitcher threw but individual pitches he'd been thrown at particular times. Willie seemed to have almost total recall of his baseball experiences.

One thing that surprised me when he joined the Mets was how well thought-out his defensive play was. You'd think, here was a guy who ran so fast and got such a good jump on the ball that playing center field was easy for him. It might have been, but he thought about it too. He'd come up to me with a list before a game I was pitching and ask me how I was going to pitch to each batter. Was I going to keep the ball away from this guy, and would I change my tactics if a runner was on second? I'd tell him in detail and he'd decide just what he'd do with each player in each circumstance. "I'll play this man about four steps to the left; that guy I shade to the right and move in if someone's on first." He'd put the list in his back pocket. And if I looked around during the game, there he was, just where he said he'd be.

When I first pitched to him, Willie was already in his 17th major-league season, but I never dared to treat him as a has-been. The book on Mays was never to give him any soft stuff. In the All-Star Game of 1970, when we were teammates, Willie and I were yakking—he's so great to talk to, he laughs so hard that tears run down his cheeks—and he said to me in that high, squeaky voice: "Man, when you going to throw me a changeup? You throw me that fastball away, then that slider away—I can't hit that stuff. I never hit a home run off you. I'm an o-o-old man. Throw me a changeup right up here." I laughed and agreed, "Okay, next time I pitch to you, I'll throw you a nice high changeup."

Next time we played the Giants I threw him nothing but sliders on the outside corner. Old man, my foot!

One thing that never worked against Willie was to throw at him. You couldn't hit him if you wanted to. He could duck so quickly. I was chatting with our pitching coach Rube Walker about it once. Rube used to be with the Brooklyn Dodgers, and he said that in the old days of the beanball battles between the Giants and Dodgers, nobody could hit Willie. He'd take a quick dive, get up and say, "Don't you be throwing at me," and then he'd rip the ball off the wall.

That was Willie. I'm sorry I couldn't have played with him in his great years. But it's something very special to me that, for two seasons, I was a teammate of Willie Mays.

Autumn

•

Murray Kempton

He was 20 when he began these voyagings, and he is supposed to have said then that this first trip around the league
was like riding through a beautiful park and getting paid for
it. Out of all those playgrounds, only Wrigley Field in
Chicago is still used for baseball; everywhere else he is
older than any piece of turf upon which he stands.

All has changed save him. No one else is still playing in
the major leagues who was there when he arrived. Five
managers are younger than he. In his first spring he saw the
Braves in Boston; in his golden summer, he met them in Milwaukee; now, with the turning of his leaves, he finds them in
Atlanta.

Before the New York Mets had ever played one game as
a team, Willie Mays had already hit more home runs than
all but six players then in the Hall of Fame. By now, he has
stolen more bases than Rabbit Maranville, hit for more bases
than either Ty Cobb or Babe Ruth, caught more fly balls
than Tris Speaker, scored more runs than Honus Wagner
and driven in more than Ted Williams.

You have to come early to the Mets's warm-ups to be
certain of seeing Mays; more days than not, his most exten-
sive exposure to the public gaze comes at batting practice
with the other pinch-hitters, those "extra men" left over
after the starting lineup has been named. He takes his cuts
two hours before game time with the Jim Beauchamps, the
Dave Marshalls, the Ed Kranepools; he has hit more than
four times as many home runs as all three of these playmates
put together. It is very soon noticed that Willie Mays is the
only one among them who runs to the box when his turn

comes. "I'm gonna *kill* you cockseekers today," he laughs. He fouls off two pitches then drives one to the grass just past the infield. "That's a hit," he cries. "You *got* to give me that." They rule him out. "Cockseekers," he grumbles and wanders away to pick up balls for coach Eddie Yost to hit to the fielders.

Here there bounds intact his image as eternal child. For here he takes his ease; he need fear no tests this night. But then there arrives an afternoon when he has been inscribed to start; and there falls upon him in the batting cage a desperation like the prisoner's in his cell. The face cherished by his countrymen along with Ernie Banks's as the last unaffectedly accommodating black one suddenly evokes some photograph from Attica, the nostrils flared, the eyes hot, the temper sour and nothing between him and despair except self-esteem.

Negroes who went young into the world put on and never quite took off a mask that carried them through the ordeal of inspection by great numbers of white people; Louis Armstrong was over 60 before he gave way to those occasional dark flashes that suggested how ancient was his bitterness and how often renewed by the condescensions of the middle class. Willie Mays had generally kept the mask of careless joy whenever the audience was larger than two dozen persons; still a private reputation, of having grown sullen with the years, had followed him back to New York and his new teammates had been surprised to find him exerting himself to please them.

He had been especially cheerful after the first evening he had suited up with the team and the occasion had arisen for a pinch-hitter and manager Yogi Berra had sent in John Milner instead of the Willie Mays for whose sight the crowd was crying. Happiness, then, must be an arrival at some place when everything is no longer expected of you; and contentment some assurance that this could be a workday when nothing at all is asked of you except to sit and watch.

But this day he was down to play and the young Mets who had joked with a man-child a few hours before looked now upon a brooding god. His life has been one long responsibility, more often met than not, but always feared. For nearly 18 years he had carried the Giants. His memory is scarred by the recollection of fainting spells in locker rooms; of the team collapsing around him in 1959 while he alone held the gate with a broken finger and hit five home runs in the last two dreadful weeks of the season; of the arrival at the third game of last year's championship series so exhausted that, with no one out, a run already in and Tito Fuentes on second, he could only bunt and leave the decision up to Willie McCovey.

He does not want the load. He shouts for the bat boy to hurry and help him with his warm-up throws—"fuggin kids"—the playmate any other time, but now the imperial despot at bay.

Berra had him leading off. Mike Torrez, the Montreal pitcher, was not yet five years old the afternoon in 1951 when Willie Mays threw out Billy Cox from center field in the Polo Grounds, a ball traveling 360 feet to catch a fast man who had to run only 90. Torrez paid his respects to this shrine by throwing two balls, the first wickedly close to the cap, the second evilly close to the chest. Willie Mays then watched a strike and another ball—he seemed as squat, as archaic, as immobile as some pre-Columbian figure of an athlete—then melted to protect himelf with a foul tip and walked at last.

Ted Martinez came up to drive a long ball to right center and two outfielders turned and fled toward the wall with a gait that at once informed the ancient glittering eyes of Willie Mays that men run like this when they have given up on the catch and hope only for a retrieval from the wall. Mays gunned around second and then, coming into third, quite suddenly slowed, became a runner on a frieze, and turned his head to watch the fielders. He was inducing the mental error; he had offered the illusion that he might be caught at home, which would give Ted Martinez time to get to third.

And only then did Willie Mays come down the line like thunder, ending in a heap at home, with the catcher sprawled in helpless intermingling with him and the relay throw bouncing through an unprotected plate and into the Montreal dugout. He was on his feet at once; his diversion had already allowed Martinez to run to third and he jumped up now to remind the umpire, in case he needed to, that when the ball goes into the dugout each runner is entitled to one more base. Ted Martinez was waved home and those two runs were the unique possession of Willie Mays, who had hit nothing except one tipped foul.

You remembered how often it had been said that Willie Mays knows more ways to beat you than anyone who ever played the game. But that was no more than comment; and here was presence; and all historical memory was wiped out for this moment when Willie Mays had paused at third as if to array himself as proclamation of an army with banners. It was beyond any mere note of excitement; it was the tone of absolute authority. When we hear it in the blues, it comes less often from the Delta than from Kansas City. It grows in the bones of scuffling, isolated country childhoods. It is much more broadly country Southern than it is uniquely black. The only baseball player before Jackie Robinson and Willie Mays who played with that almost brutal abandon we call the black style was Enos Slaughter of the Cardinals, a native of Roxboro, North Carolina. You read the tone in Faulkner when Boon Clatterbuck stands beside the wagon "turbaned like a Paythan and taller than anyone there. . . . 'Them that's going,' he said, 'get in the goddam wagon. Them that ain't get out of the goddam way.'" You can hear it in the old Venuti-Lang record of *Farewell Blues*, where there is a deal of slush and then a kind of stuttered note on the trombone and Jack Teagarden pushing everyone else aside. Boon Clatterbuck throwing his whiskey bottle away, Jack Teagarden almost clearing his throat, Willie Mays arraying himself for the charge—three pauses to assemble the irascible, occasionally even vicious dignity of the Southern country boy's announcement that he is taking command of the city ones.

Those were all the runs the Mets would have that afternoon; and they would be just enough to win. Willie Mays did nothing else except catch two fly balls and thus twice routinely set a new record for total putouts by an outfielder in the whole 20th century. In the locker room Yogi Berra did one of the minor managerial duties he was taught by Casey Stengel, in this case catering to the susceptibilities of the journalists for mythmaking. "I think Willie timed that throw," he attested. "I've seen him do that before. He slows down and tries to hit the plate at the same time as the throw to make it hard on the catcher." "Yogi lies a lot," said Willie Mays affectionately. "You can't time no throw like that."

And he departed for Philadelphia and on Saturday drove in the first run with a double and scored the winning run after a walk, and the next day he beat the Phillies with a home run; the next Wednesday he scored the only run in a Met defeat; and Thursday he singled to break a tie with the Cubs after having played 14 innings. He had returned to New York from San Francisco as half a pensioner; yet he had played six games and had produced or scored the winning run in five of them. In Chicago he hurt his finger, scrambling for some fragment of first base; he was healing and infrequently seen for the next two weeks. By June 8, he was healthy and marked down to start against the Reds. By then he had come to bat 37 times as a Met and gotten on base 19 of them: Even so, as the shadow of responsibility came once more toward him, he again withdrew into that brooding silence from which no diplomatic jape of his teammates could coax him forth. Isolated in the rubbing room, he left them to wait on the field until just before the game began.

It began and would end most alarmingly. The commissioner of baseball had come to Shea Stadium in May to wonder aloud what sort of dynasty was being built here; but Bowie Kuhn is the stockholder type, which is to say that he fell off a horse when he was four years old, or suffered some such blow to his reason, and has since been conditioned to see in any transient rise of an issue the promise of unbreaking ascent. The Mets had since settled back to the scrabbling of the accustomed existence of teams able to trust their arms and their gloves more than their bats; and now they would win a close game and then they would lose another. And this day, in the first inning, the Reds fell for four runs on Tom Seaver, the league's most effective pitcher last year. The Mets built a run in the first. Seaver righted himself thereafter but the game remained at 4–1 until the fifth when Mays singled off the pitcher's shoulder and there followed two runs. Tony Perez hit a home run, and the Mets came to the bottom of the ninth behind, 5–3. Ed Kranepool pinch-hit a gentle single; and then Willie Mays was up. He swung so hard at the first pitch that his hat flew off; the respect of two successive balls was offered him and then, more viciously than before, he swung and shot a single like a 40-mm shell to left field. As often happens with him, you felt that the pitch had fooled him and that, in his passion, he had simply overpowered it. The note of authority had been struck; he was on first and Kranepool on second and there were no outs. The note vibrated in the air and there it died. Bud Harrelson bunted and Perez came down from first and seized the ball and threw out Kranepool at third. That killed it; the next two hitters expired on infield grounders and Willie Mays was left at third.

He had had two hits for three official bats yet afterward

his solitary gloom was impenetrable. It had been an afternoon to stir uneasy prospects. There were so many small things: lead runner thrown out at third base, the foundation stone of the pitching staff inexplicably shaky, such big hitters as the roster holds failing—all signs that the Mets would never know the comfort of being enough ahead or the resignation of being enough behind. No, it would go on all summer, one more of those desperate adventures with an incomplete team that Willie Mays had known so often before with the Giants until the familiar horror of those final weeks whose reiterated torment had brought him, as long ago as 1965, to confess how permanently drained he was: "No. There is nothing in baseball that can get me excited anymore." And yet there is not another Met who has known the ordeal of a close pennant race more than once in his career; and Willie Mays has been there eight times before. So, more and more, they would have to turn to him with too much of the load, and this would be another one of those cruel summers that, for just a little while, in the sun with the extra men, he had been able to entertain the illusion of escaping. Scowling, he strode through the children who had waited for him at the gate and alone he drove away; his face fixed in its contempt for destiny; everything that he had proved through all those years was worthless to appease him; nothing was ahead of him but the implacable duty of needing to prove everything all over again. Fuggin kids.

16

Stan Musial

One thing that sticks out in my mind about Stan Musial is seeing him on a bad day near the end of his career. He grounded out to second four times in a row, but each time he hustled down the first-base line—on 40-year-old legs—as if his life depended on it. He already had over 3000 hits and he seemed as eager for another as a rookie. That showed me something about what makes a great ballplayer.

I ran into Musial at a golf tournament during the off-season and commented on his amazing number of hits—3630, second only to Ty Cobb. He said, "Yeah, but people forget that I also made more than seven thousand outs." That kind of modesty is typical of Stan—and comforting to a pitcher.

Musial not only was dangerous at the plate, but he looked dangerous in that peculiar coiled stance of his. As a pitcher, though, I would have tried to pay little attention to his stance. Stance is only a starting point. What matters to me is the first movement the batter makes. How does he move his foot, and in what direction? What does he do with his front shoulder, and what does he do with his hands? How he moves, not how he stands, is what I'm worried about when I'm trying to figure out a way to pitch to a batter.

Stance, though, is very important to a batter. And Musial knew just how peculiar his was. I remember hearing him say, "Don't copy your hero's stance. Get something you like and are comfortable with and stick with it. Someone else's way won't work for you."

I always took his advice. I never did a "Stan Musial" stance—except in the bullpen when we were playing "guess who?" Musial's was the only one I could ever imitate.

Stan the Man

•

Jerry Izenberg

It is September 29, 1963, and the ball park is old and tired. The ball park was there before the big jets began to carry the players off into uncharted time zones . . . it was there when the team called the Browns lived in St. Louis . . . it was there when the transients in the visitors' clubhouse pulled on blue-gray uniform shirts with names like Brooklyn and Boston in bold letters across the chest. Today, in 1963, the hard-baked infield is the worst in baseball. It is half kangaroo and half concrete. The ball park is old and tired and used up and its wake is already planned for sometime next season.

The hitter is tired, too. He is pushing 43 now. Like the park, he was there before the jets. He was there when the Braves lived in Boston and the Athletics in Philadelphia; when the Browns lived in St. Louis along with the Cardinals; when the Dodgers lived in Brooklyn and the Giants lived in New York. His name is Stanley Frank Musial and the first time he saw the park was 3629 hits ago, and now more than anything else he wants to make it an even 3630.

The Cardinals are closing the 1963 season at home against Cincinnati. It is superfluous to say that Stanley Frank Musial is a Cardinal. All his adult life he has never worked for anyone else. He began working for them back in 1938 in a hardrock coal-mining town called Williamson. West Virginia. He took a dive on the point of his left shoulder for them back in Daytona Beach, Florida, and he left a modest pitching career there, in the uneven outfield grass. He hit baseballs so hard and so often for them in Springfield, Ohio, and Rochester, New York, that they brought him up to play the outfield for the big team before he was old enough to vote. He set 17 major-league records, 29 National League records and six All-Star Game records and now the end is just minutes away and all he wants is one more hit.

It is a dark, gray day. This is a game for the young, and the hitter knows it. The young man whose fastball will come wheeling in out of the gloom is named Jim Maloney. He is the same age as the hitter's son. The man on second base can score if Stanley Frank Musial gets his hit. The man on second is Curt Flood and he was born the same year the hitter reported to Williamson in the Mountain State League. The Mountain State League is gone and the ball park will be gone next season and the world in which the hitter lived most of his adult life is gone, too. All he wants is one more hit.

There was always a strange geometrical defiance in the way Stan Musial stepped into his office to hit. It was almost as though he were two very different people hitched together at the waist, a kind of afterthought. The lower torso bent slightly but the upper half of his body was positively tilted by the latent power in his forearms, the massive concentration and the odd way he had of cocking his head like a man trying to shoot a rifle around a corner. But it was fluid and when television began to poke its big red eye into the ball parks for the first time, thousands and thousands of anonymous youngsters watched in places like Boise, Idaho, and Culpepper, Virginia, and took it out to the sandlots with them. And who is to say how many nine-year-olds shouted at other nine-year-olds:

"It's my ball and if I can't be Stan Musial, you can't play."

So with a count of two balls and one strike, Stanley Frank Musial looks around that corner one last time and Jim Maloney, who has won more games in this particular year than at any time before or since in his major-league career and who at age 23 could, indeed, be the hitter's son, sends a curveball breaking up there out of the shadows. The hitter is left-handed. His right foot strides forward and the man looking around a corner uncoils in that magical, poetic motion for the very last time as a major-leaguer.

The ball is heading for the hole between first and second and on through to the outfield. The hitter is running now and the tired, old ball park catches the sound of a crowd which is neither tired nor old. It is the sound of innocence and absolute trust and gratitude that Stanley Frank Musial, who has been so much a part of this town, is going out like the solid gold Frank Merriwell he is. Curt Flood scores. Musial leaves the game for a pinch-runner. It is over.

No, not really over. The lines and lines of agate type are still in the record book. There is still the restaurant out on Oakland Avenue and the bank and the other giant footprints around St. Louis and the sure knowledge that here in this town—and wherever else baseball is played—Stanley Frank Musial is going to remain as the measuring stick for generations of summer heroes yet unborn.

There is a paradox to all of this. Just because a man can hit a baseball, our society is inclined to imbue him with the honesty of a Boy Scout, the loyalty of Rin Tin Tin, the motivation of Jack Armstrong and the modesty of Li'l Abner. This is a terrible burden. Hang around the locker rooms long enough and you have to realize that nobody can live up to this. But then the conversation comes up Stan Musial and who is to really say no?

They are going to vote him into the Hall of Fame. Well, he belongs there and the record says so . . . things like 3630 major-league hits . . . 475 home runs . . . 1956 runs-batted-in . . . a lifetime batting average of .331. But the rest of it, well, the rest of it is positively incredible. How can you play 23 major-league seasons and never once get kicked out of a ball game by an umpire? Somehow, Musial did it.

Or consider the town in which he played those 23 years. This is a smart baseball town. It cannot be conned. Baseball in this town has never been subtle. It was Pepper Martin sliding in spikes high, and the Dean boys telling you to get the hell away from their plate unless you wanted to go through life with a baseball sticking out of your ear, and Leo Durocher filling the air with the kind of sweet-nothings which have emptied many a barroom.

And yet here comes Stan Musial, who in 23 major league seasons had only one near baseball fight. A Dodger pitcher named Les Webber—at Durocher's urging—tried to chop Musial down with a fastball and then Musial's teammate, big Walker Cooper, lifted him up bodily for his own protection. Here in this baseball-wise town, Stan Musial gets booed one night and a group of citizens take a newspaper ad the next day to apologize. This was, indeed, Stanley Frank Musial, whose fluid grace was all the color he ever needed to make himself a folk hero.

Talent? Well, nobody ever said it better than Leo Durocher. Just before Willie Mays played his first game against the Cardinals, Leo ran down the batting order for him. He told him how to play the first two hitters and then he skipped to the cleanup hitter.

"Hey," Willie said, "you left out No. 3."

"The third hitter," Leo replied, "is Stan Musial. There is

no advice I can give you about him. He will show you why the first time he gets to bat."

Stan Musial was born in Donora, Pennsylvania, on November 21, 1920. Donora is 28 miles south of Pittsburgh and the first thing you are going to ask is why Stan Musial did not wind up playing for the Pittsburgh Pirates. This is a foolish question. Why did the Steelers draft Sid Luckman and trade him before he ever played a game for them? Why have the Pirates only won one pennant since the Ice Age? Pittsburgh is an entirely different story and it is not about winners. It is about survival.

The Pirates, as a matter of fact, did try to sign Stan Musial to a contract. They timed it exactly like, well, the Pirates. They didn't bother to ask him until after Branch Rickey's commandos had already signed, sealed and delivered him for St. Louis.

A long time ago, the late Stanley Woodward angered a great many western Pennsylvanians by writing "there is no flora in Donora." Well, there ain't. And when Stan Musial was growing up, it was blast furnaces and galvanizing mills and a zinc plant. It didn't matter what color you painted your frame house. In the end the smoke stacks and charcoal gray won out. You lived on pierogi and baked beans. It wasn't exactly Duncan Hines but you made it.

A man named Joe Barbao made Stan Musial a pitcher. Musial was the batboy on the Donora Zinc Works A.A. baseball team which Barbao managed. When they ran out of pitchers one day, left-handed Stanley pitched six innings and struck out 13 hitters. The hitters were men . . . not boys. Stan Musial was convinced he was going to be a major-league pitcher.

In a way these were very good times for young men who wanted to play baseball. Not satisfied with one farm system —which happened to be the first in baseball—Branch Rickey was filling two and three clubs with prospects in the same minor league. If he could lift a baseball, Rickey told his army of birddogs, sign him. At these prices we can afford to find out.

They signed Stan Musial and he went off at age 19 to Williamson, West Virginia, for a magnificent 65 bucks a month. He spent two mediocre seasons there. Not that his won-lost record was bad. His trouble was control, and when you trace the peculiar web of "ifs" which go into the making of a folk-hero, you had best start by picking up on a conversation between the late Dickie Kerr and another manager in the Cardinal chain.

This was down south, where they were sorting out the wheat from the chaff and the prospects from the lukewarm bodies. They had considered sending Stan Musial, boy pitcher, to another minor-league club and the man who managed it did not exactly stand up and sing the Donora Zinc Works Fight Song.

"I'll take him for Daytona Beach," Dickie Kerr volunteered.

"You can have that wild sonofagun," the man said with much relief. "He's no pitcher."

So Musial went to Daytona Beach, where it was soon to be the end of Stanley Musial, boy pitcher, and the beginning of Stan Musial, pitcher-destroyer. The first pitcher he destroyed was Stan Musial. He was playing center field one August night when he dove for a low line drive, his spikes caught in the grass and he landed on his pitching shoulder. Exit Stan Musial, pitcher.

By the end of the season it was obvious that if Musial were going to remain in baseball, it would have to be as an outfielder. Dickie Kerr believed he could make it and so did most of the scouts who sent reports trickling back into the main office in St. Louis. Scouts are like that. Once he eliminated himself as a pitcher, they began to notice one of the truly genuine hitters in the game. If he hadn't taken that spill, he probably would have been developed by them into a dandy Triple A relief pitcher.

Things moved quickly after that. The next season he hit .379 at Springfield, Ohio, in the Western Association and led the league in home runs with 26. Which brings us to 1941 and the night Musial and a minor hitter of major reputation named Erv "Four-Sack" Dusak joined the Cardinals's Triple A farm at Rochester in the International League. They joined the club at Syracuse. Benny Bergman, for many years a Cardinal scout and now a scout with the Seattle Pilots, managed Syracuse. He will never forget that evening.

"My pitcher," Bergman recalls, "was named Jack Tising, and before the game I thought we ought to go over their two new players. I knew about Dusak because he had the good reputation. But I knew about Musial, too. I had seen him at Springfield. We ran down Dusak and then we got to Musial."

Tising told his manager: "Dusak's the one to worry about. Don't be concerned about the other guy, skipper. He's just a broken-down pitcher." This ties a record for casual death wishes originally set by the cavalry scout who told Custer: "Beats the hell out of me where they are. They must have all gone up to Expo for the winter season."

A very fine fielder named Buddy Hassett was playing first base for Syracuse that night. The first time Musial came to bat, all he did was to separate Mr. Hassett's glove from Mr. Hassett's hand with a line drive. The second time, Bergman went to the mound.

"Don't worry, skipper," Jack Tising told him. "I'll just throw him low and outside." Wham! A man named Red Julick who had the misfortune to be playing third base was nearly decapitated by Musial's two-base hit. The third time, Tising told Bergman: "I'm going to throw one right down the gut." Wham! The ball shot past where the pitcher's head had been a fraction of a second earlier. The fourth time, Musial hit the fence for three bases.

"I was somewhat impressed," Bergman says, "but the night wasn't a total loss. Four-Sack Dusak went o-for-4."

Musial didn't stay in Rochester very long. He played 54 games and hit .326. The Cardinals, plagued with injuries that season and striving desperately to catch front-running Brooklyn, brought him up to the varsity. On September 17, 1941, Stan Musial walked into the clubhouse at old Sportsman's Park for the first time. Center fielder Terry Moore immediately recognized him. "Hey," Terry said, "you're that humpty-dumpty pitcher I hit the home run off down south last year." It is always nice to be wanted.

That same day, Stan Musial played the outfield against the Boston Braves. Jim Tobin threw Musial two knuckleballs during the game. Musial missed the first and fell down swinging. The second one, he popped to the infield. He had never seen a knuckleball before. The next time at bat, Stan Musial hit a knuckleball against the wall in right field to drive in two runs. He got two hits that day. And he never looked back.

In 1942, the Cardinals platooned him most of the season with a man named Coker Triplett. They won the pennant and Musial hit .315. They won three in a row and Musial hit .357 and .347 before the military service took him away for 1945.

There is a sameness to the Stan Musial story after that. After all, he hit .340 or better in seven seasons. He won seven batting titles and two RBI crowns. He won the MVP award three times and was chosen by the *Sporting News* as the player-of-the-decade. He once made nine hits in 11 at-bats against the Dodgers in a two-game series. He won the 1955 All-Star Game with a 12th-inning home run. He . . . well, you could go on and on and on.

There was, for example, the time he hit five home runs

against the Giants during a doubleheader and was greeted by his 12-year-old son with the comment: "Boy, that's some crummy pitching staff they've got."

And there was the day at breakfast when a Cardinal third baseman named Tommy Glaviano told him: "Stan, I prayed for you before I went to bed last night and this morning at church I lit a candle."

"Well, gee, thanks," Musial said with obvious embarrassment. "I really appreciate you thinking of me, Tommy."

"What thinking of you?" Glaviano shot back. "It's that World Series money I'm protecting."

But legends and folk heroes both are made of "ifs" and there was, indeed, a moment in this incredible career when it all could have turned the other way . . . a moment when it would have turned for most other people.

In 1946, Jorge Pascual may have come a lot closer to changing the course of Musial's future than even Stan is willing to admit to himself. Pascual was a Mexican millionaire, and he liked baseball so much that he wanted to buy it. He damned near did.

This was the year of the outlaw Mexican League. Pascual reasoned that he could not bring major-league baseball to Mexico without major-league players. Since all the major-league players in the world were in residence in the United States, Senor Pascual would not go to the mountain, he would take it with him. In this case the mountain was made out of fresh, green money.

He swung into the spring training camps with all the subtlety of a forward observer for Hell's Angels. He wore flashy clothes and a very flashy pistol the size of a howitzer. He ran through hotel lobbies beating players over the head with $100 bills.

He nailed Mickey Owens out of the Dodger camp. He nailed four players right out of the Giants's locker room, including a minor-league pitcher named Sal Maglie. He grabbed others. Then he went to work on the Cardinals. He worked pretty good. He got second baseman Lou Klein, then pitcher Max Lanier, who had won six straight games during the young season. Finally he went after Stanley Frank Musial.

He sent his brother, Alfonso, and Mickey Owen to see Musial. No deal. He had Lanier call from Mexico. No deal. Finally, Alfonso and Owen visited Musial at the Fairgrounds Hotel in St. Louis. For openers, the junior Pascual threw down five cashier's checks of $10,000 each and said, "This money is simply for the bonus. Now we talk contract."

There are several versions of what followed, but some facts are beyond dispute. Stan Musial was then earning $13,500 a year from the Cardinals, a ball club which paid so little that the players around the league referred to it as "wetbacks North." The Pascuals were offering Musial $125,000 in addition to the bonus money if he would sign for five years.

But Musial didn't accept it. Some people say Eddie Dyer, then the Cardinal manager, talked him out of it. Some say that Musial made the decision on his own, repelled by the thought of breaking a contract, no matter how miserly the contract may have been. Subsequent events proved how correct Musial was in refusing.

Owen was destroyed as a ballplayer and returned disillusioned and unemployed. Lanier jumped back to the Cardinals before the commissioner's deadline expired. The rest accomplished nothing except for Maglie, who at the time had not really developed as a pitcher. In late August of that year, Sam Breadon, the Cardinal owner, tore up Musial's contract and raised him $5000. A small price, indeed, for loyalty.

There were, of course, other dynamic moments in a career so long and incredible. There was 1959, and 1959 was not a vintage year. Musial was out of shape and never caught up. When the final numbers came up .255, logical people reasoned that at age 39, Stan Musial had had it. The following year, there was talk of trading him to Pittsburgh. In mid-season, Stan Musial began to hit and, despite a poor start, he finished at .275. Two years later he hit .330.

He didn't go out until 1963. A man remembers 1963 very well. The Cardinals were not going to win the pennant that year, but it was not for lack of trying. After a slow start they chased the Dodgers and chased them hard. In mid-September they had a shot to catch them right in that same old ball park. They didn't make it, but there is a story about that week and it tells a great deal about Stan Musial and what he means to St. Louis, Missouri.

We came from all over the country for that one. Although the three-game series consisted entirely of night games, which would make it impossible for Eastern columnists to make most of their editions, we still went because it was exciting and St. Louis was the place to be.

That first night, as we began making our way from the field to the press box, I noticed a man with a folding chair walk out onto the roof in right field. He opened the chair and sat down.

"What's he doing out there?" I asked an usher.

"He's waiting to catch Stan Musial's home run."

"What?"

"Stan Musial has hit 474 home runs and when he hits the 475th he will retrieve the ball so Stan gets it . . . unless he hits it out of the park."

"How do you know he'll hit one?"

"He's Stan Musial . . . he'll hit one."

And he did in the seventh inning.

So it has been over these five seasons now for Musial, who occupies an executive suite for the Cardinals. The old ball park was abandoned to the city and now there is a spanking new magnificent structure down by the super-slick Gateway Arch. Beyond the outfield entrance to the park there is a nine-foot statue of Stan the Man, with his body bent and a bat in his hand and his head tilted like a man trying to shoot a rifle around a corner. It cost $40,000. It was raised by public subscription.

"I don't know about statues," a visitor to the new ball park remarked when he first saw it.

"Why not?" a native St. Louisan asked.

"Well, you know, pigeons and all. . . ."

"No St. Louis pigeon," the man said with great feeling, "would even dare consider it."

17

Frank Robinson

Trades are a popular topic of conversation when we're sitting around the clubhouse. Sometimes we have contests to see who can name the most one-sided trades ever made. The one that sent Frank Robinson from Cincinnati to Baltimore for Milt Pappas and two throw-ins always gets first mention (except from Ray Sadecki who thinks the Sadecki-for-Orlando Cepeda trade was the most one-sided).

The season after that trade, 1966, Robinson won the Triple Crown and led Baltimore to a World Series victory, while Pappas had a 12–11 record with a 4.29 ERA for Cincinnati. The trade also helped Robinson set a record by becoming the only player ever to be named MVP in both leagues. That's only one of the impressive facts in Robinson's career. He has also knocked in 1710 runs and he's fourth on the all-time home-run list with 552.

The first time I faced Robinson outside of spring training was in the '69 World Series. Our book on him said that he was a pull hitter who liked inside pitches. He often got hit by pitches because he stood almost on top of the plate, but you did yourself a disservice by knocking him down. If you upset him, he'd get up and hit the ball twice as hard. I tried to keep the ball away from him, throwing him mostly breaking pitches on the outside corner. I had good success with Robinson in the first Series game and until the ninth inning of the fourth game.

We had a 1–0 lead with one out. With the count 2–2, I threw him a fastball on the outside corner, which he fouled off. Then he fouled off another outside fastball. I figured he'd now be set up for an inside fastball. I knew I really shouldn't throw him inside, but I did. He hit a vicious rope to left field for a single; it went out there like a rocket.

That's one example of a predicament a pitcher often gets himself into. You want to pitch to a batter's weakness, but at the same time you don't want him to know what's coming and be laying for it. So you're tempted to throw to a batter's strength just to keep him honest. Often, it doesn't work. Stu Miller tells a story about this kind of situation. Stu had struck out Frank Howard something like seven times in a row by pitching soft floaters to him. Howard was getting frustrated but he predicted, "One time he's going to give me a fastball and I'll hit it eight miles." Soon after that Miller did serve him up a fastball and Howard did hit it into the next county. Asked why he threw the fastball, Miller explained, "I'd struck him out so many times with soft stuff, I figured he'd be getting ready for the slow pitch—so I thought I'd surprise him with a fastball."

That's one thing about great hitters. They're hard to surprise. When Robinson returned to the National League for a season with the Dodgers, I pitched him outside, consistently.

Robinson is highly respected by ballplayers today, not only for his skills, but also for his leadership and his knowledge of the game. I wouldn't be surprised if he became a manager. And I think it's about time we did have a black manager in baseball. Players certainly aren't the ones who demand that a manager be white; they only care that he be competent. And from what I know about him, Frank Robinson might be a very competent manager.

A Good Leader Slides Hard and Carries a Big Stick

●

Bard Lindeman

Just having him in the lineup was bound to do something for team morale—he was an established major-league star and a prototype of the "big hitter" managers like to build batting orders around. But the Baltimore Orioles's new outfielder began to lift his ball club this spring in ways that sometimes startled both the opposition and his own teammates. He was on first base in Washington one night when another Oriole hit a soft fly to shallow center; after the catch, he startled everyone by tagging up and sliding safely into second base ahead of the routine throw from the outfield. On the next pitch he stole third. Against Detroit, he scored all the way from first base when a teammate lined a single through the middle on a hit-and-run play. Then there was the big play in Yankee Stadium. Baltimore had a two-run lead with two out in the last of the ninth, but the Yankees had two men on base, and New York's Roy White hit a long drive toward right field that would win the game if it reached the seats.

Frank Robinson drifted back against the waist-high barrier, made a half-turn and leaped, reaching as high as he could. With the ball stuck in his glove, and the game saved, he tumbled backward into the stands and disappeared into the crowd.

More than any other factor, Robinson has made the differ-

ence in Baltimore, where the young Oriole teams of recent
years have established a reputation as talented also-rans.
They were good enough to be contenders, but they were
inconsistent and seemed to lack the kind of swaggering, intimidating confidence that is characteristic of a championship ball club. This year the Orioles have dominated the
pennant race to lead the American League by a dozen games
in late July—and Robinson's impact only begins with the
fact that he has been hitting over .300 and is among the
league leaders in home runs and four other offensive categories. The headlong style of play that sent him sprawling
into the seats at Yankee Stadium seems to be reestablishing
another, older Baltimore tradition of tough, combative baseball that dates back to the "old Orioles" of the 1890s.

"The way Frank plays," says Paul Blair, the young center
fielder, "he makes you hustle. He'll make a great play and
the rest of us will follow." Robinson has played much of the
season with a pulled thigh muscle and then a badly strained
right knee, but manager Hank Bauer has kept him in the
lineup. "I'd like to rest Frank," he says, "but just his being
in there peps up the other guys."

Curt Blefary, the tough-talking left fielder, speaks for all
the 1966 Orioles when he says, "This is the year we don't
foul up."

Robinson's presence in Baltimore could hardly be felt
more keenly than his absence in Cincinnati. In a 10-year
career with the Reds, he batted .303, averaged 32 home runs
and 101 runs batted in per season, and in 1961 led the team
to its first pennant in two decades. Despite these credentials,
Cincinnati president William O. DeWitt traded him last December for starting pitcher Milt Pappas and two lesser Orioles, on the theory that the team needed pitching more than
power for the 1966 race. But the Reds, picked to win in the
Associated Press preseason poll, were in eighth place at
midseason. "If we had Robinson here," Cincinnati relief

pitcher Bill McCool told reporters, "we'd be in the race, or even in the lead."

Hank Bauer remembers that he was at home in Prairie Village, Kansas, when the trade was announced. Bauer happily began to practice writing a lineup card with Robinson in the order. First he made him the cleanup hitter; then he wrote him into fifth spot, and finally decided to have him hit third, bringing him to bat in the first inning in every game. A friend called from New York to poke fun at his good fortune.

"Have you gone out and gotten drunk yet?" the friend asked.

"No," Bauer said. "I wanted to put the kids on the school bus first."

But there was one small worry. Like other American Leaguers, Bauer had heard reports that Robinson was not only a ruthless competitor on the field but a troublemaker off it. People who passed on this rumor always spoke of the time five years before when Robinson had been arrested for carrying a gun.

Robinson's reputation was not helped by DeWitt when he explained to newsmen last spring why he traded away his best offensive player.

"Frank is an *old* thirty," said DeWitt. He went on to say that Robinson was certain to slow down dramatically one of these days, because as a young player he had led a fast life.

Jim Brosnan, the baseball author (*Pennant Race*, *The Long Season*), was Robinson's teammate from 1959 to 1962, and he says this is untrue and only "DeWitt's excuse." He laughingly describes Robinson as a bowler, a movie-goer, a big television fan and a tireless baseball talker. These were his pastimes off the field, according to Brosnan.

But the Orioles were wondering what Robinson would be like when he showed up in training camp this spring. The man they watched closely seemed to be extraordinarily confident, in a relaxed way, hardly fitting the "trouble-maker" image. He showed this the day he appeared for extra hitting practice, principally to work with several of the younger players. The only time anyone saw him lose his temper was when he wanted to make a point about aggressive baseball. Paul Blair, who became his protégé in time, was slow coming in on a short fly ball one afternoon. Everyone who saw Robinson correct Blair remembers the scene well.

"He chewed him out right there," says one Baltimore newspaperman. "Right there on the field he gave it to Blair. He was so mad you could see his head bobbing up and down."

"I believe," Robinson says, "that every ball that stays in the park ought to be caught."

Once the season began, he did most of his leading by example. In his first Sunday doubleheader in Baltimore he hit a single, double, triple and two home runs. The second home run was the first ball ever hit out of Memorial Stadium. It stopped rolling 540 feet from home plate in the black-topped parking lot that is called Babe Ruth Plaza.

Later, as Robinson talked about the home run with reporters in the clubhouse, he used his big hands to help illustrate what he was saying. With each movement, the ridges of muscle that begin at his shoulder, and are still sharply defined halfway down his back, rippled and swelled.

Bob Johnson, the utility infielder, watched Robinson giving the interview.

"Frank is an exhibitionist," he said, shaking his head. "He's such an exhibitionist they should lock him up. See those muscles? He did thousands of pushups as a kid to get them."

"He still squeezes a rubber ball for his wrists," said Blair.

"But look at those ridiculous wheels," Johnson said, pointing at Robinson's legs, which are long and slender, almost girlishly thin for a big man.

"If Frank's legs didn't have those big feet on them," said pitcher Dave McNally, "they'd stick in the ground when he walked."

He has always had skinny legs and always he has been teased because of them. On Myrtle Street, in Oakland, California, where he lived as a boy, and in the Tompkins School playground where he first played the game, he was called "Pencils."

Robinson was the youngest of 10 children. His mother, Mrs. Ruth Shaw, who was separated from her husband, raised the big family alone and, while he remembers "things were pretty good," Frank was 12 before he owned his first glove. Five years later, in 1952, he was graduated from high school and signed with Cincinnati for $3000—which he gave his mother.

There were three minor-league seasons then, two of them at Columbia, S.C., where he was called "Nigger" when he didn't hit. In 1956 he moved up to the Reds. "I was in a shell in those days," he says, "and I didn't have a friend on the club. That was the dark side of baseball for me."

In successive years he was the National League Rookie of the Year, Sophomore of the Year and "Gold Glove" winner as the leading defensive left fielder. Somewhat dazzled by this immediate success, he indulged a new fondness for cash money. He spent as much as $140 for sports-clothes outfits, bought a new car at least every year—he traded in one model after only 1000 miles—and he walked around with from $500 to $2500 wadded up in his stylish slacks.

He was carrying a good-sized cash roll the February night in 1961 when he and two other young Negroes fell into an argument with three white men in a Cincinnati drive-in restaurant. The police were called and asked the whites to leave the place. What happened next is confusing. Robinson says the restaurant cook so provoked him that he challenged the man to "come on, try me out."

The cook started toward him, carrying a butcher knife. Robinson took a .25 caliber Italian hand-pistol out of his pocket and held it in his left palm so that the cook could see it.

"He's got a gun!" the man screamed. Robinson was arrested and charged with carrying a concealed weapon. He spent the night in a detention cell because Bill DeWitt went back to bed after a newspaperman had told him the story over the phone. The Reds's president said the middle of the night was no time to have to deal with a bail bondsman and a desk sergeant.

Robinson was indicted and pleaded guilty, explaining to the court that he kept the gun as protection against the threat of robbery. He was fined $250. And everywhere he went that '61 season, he had the "gun incident" hurled at him. From dugouts and grandstands he heard, "Hey, ump. Frisk him . . . it's Pistol Packin' Frankie."

But he played as though he had to atone for his act. He hit .323 with 37 home runs and drove in 124 runs. He was named the league's Most Valuable Player and it was no coincidence that the Reds were the surprise pennant winners.

"I've never seen such a dramatic change in one player," Jim Brosnan says. "Frank became the club's leader that year."

In late October of that year, Robinson married 20-year-old Barbara Ann Cole of Los Angeles, and now his life began to change. He went two years without buying a new car, he lived on a budget, and 11 months after he was married he became the father of an adopted infant son, Frank Kevin.

"Having a child then," he said, "did us a lot of good. It filled out our lives, gave us a little more responsibility and made us a complete family. That's what life is all about, isn't it?"

The shadowy story of the old gun incident followed Robinson to Baltimore—"I guess I'll never be free of it"—and so did his reputation as a vicious baserunner, a man some National Leaguers said would deliberately try to maim an infielder with his spikes. One day recently he sat slouched in a canvas chair in front of his locker in Baltimore and talked about his approach to the game.

"I don't know where all that 'mean' stuff about me got started," he said. "I believe you should do everything to win, short of hurting someone deliberately. If you're going into second on a ground ball, you've got to break up the double play. If you just go in there with one of those easy slides because you and the shortstop are having dinner afterwards, you're letting your teammates down.

"They don't play football halfway and nobody criticizes them. When you hit a man in football, you put a shoulder into him. That's the way I play. Sometimes somebody gets hurt. A few times it's been me."

Proof of this is on his body. Along his smooth, brown forearms is a series of ugly scars. They are mostly four or five inches long, the length of a tear in the flesh from a steel baseball cleat.

"Baseball, all baseball," he said. "That's where they came from."

He was holding out both his forearms and he began to finger the scars, one by one. "This is 1956, this one is '57, here's '63 and another '63.

"This one," he said, holding his forefinger on a scar halfway up the left forearm, "I got trying to steal home."

"You were out?"

"They said I was," he said.

As he told it, the scars had simple, undramatic histories. Almost all of them, he said in this matter-of-fact voice, resulted from plays around second base. He would slide in hard, intent on dumping the fielder, and the defensive man would come down on top of him, spiking him on the arm.

The longest scar fills the crease of his left arm. It is a raw-looking, ribbed line, remnant of a punctured biceps which took 30 stitches to close. He got it at second base three seasons ago. The Mets's Ron Hunt was the fielder.

"Funny thing," Robinson said. "He laid the arm right open only it didn't bleed much."

"Was it deliberate?"

He shook his head. "There was no way he could do it intentionally."

"Why not?"

"He doesn't know where I'm going to slide," Robinson explained, "but I know how he's going to cover the bag because I've studied him."

There is a professionalism about his style which has nothing to do with showmanship, even though he is one of the game's most exciting players. After his big catch in Yankee Stadium, he did not hold the ball over his head in the usual gesture as he headed for the dugout. Later a reporter told him, "Mantle thinks you should have shown the ball, so there was no doubt you had it."

"You go tell Mantle to catch them his way," Robinson said. "I'll catch them mine." He said it without resentment; what he meant was that showmanship was unnatural for him.

"There's only one way for me to play," he says. "I bear down all the time, and I've got this drive that makes me always want to be the best."

The pride which marks Robinson is evident the moment he arrives at the park. He doesn't smoke, nor does he drink during the season. He dresses slowly, with an almost ritualistic care. As he walks toward the plate his pants are evenly bloused below the knees and he is unwrinkled. The shirt is tucked in tightly, so deep inside the trousers that his No. 20 is almost at belt level. Now he steps quickly into the batter's box, and here Robinson makes his challenge. No one in baseball stands closer to the plate. His left foot is up against the forward chalk line. It can go no farther. His head is cocked around, defiantly over the plate. The bat is held straight up, and his left elbow juts out, aimed straight at the pitcher's belt buckle.

"He's out to get me," Robinson says, "and I'm out to hit him. When I got to the majors, I figured I couldn't afford to give the pitchers the outside corner. So I moved up closer to get the best possible look. Then I hung my head in there."

There have been times when Mrs. Robinson, who knew very little about baseball when she met her husband, couldn't stand to watch him at bat.

"At Cincinnati," she said, "the wives used to sit right behind home plate. Some days I would have to move. I can understand that the closer to the plate Frank stands the better he does, only I just couldn't take any more. Do you know that ball comes only *inches* away from Frank's head?"

In six years out of ten he was hit oftener than any other National Leaguer. Going into this season, he had been hit 118 times, and he was hit in his first at-bat as an American Leaguer. Three times he has been struck in the head and regained consciousness in the clubhouse or in the hospital. Still, he refuses to stand back from the plate. Late in the game, when the lines of the batter's box have been rubbed away, he seems to stand even closer.

When he was with Cincinnati, he once called a clubhouse meeting because too many Reds were being hit by the opposing pitchers. Robinson, standing in the middle of the room, delivered an ultimatum. The Cincinnati pitchers had to help out by brushing back the first batter they faced after one of the Reds was dropped.

What happened then is recalled by the Houston Astros's third baseman Gene Freese, who at the time was playing for Cincinnati. "One of our guys was hit the next game," Freese says, "but our pitcher forgot he was supposed to throw the brush-back ball. I looked over my shoulder and here comes Robinson. He's trotting in from right field to pop our pitcher right there on the mound.

"I hollered over, 'Here he comes! Here he comes!' The pitcher turned around, pretending to be rubbing up the ball, and waved Robinson back. He was nodding at Frank, 'OK, OK.'" As Freese remembers it, the very next pitch hit the batter under the ribs.

Robinson, as a new man on the Orioles, has called no clubhouse meetings. But he finds ways of being heard.

One night this spring, the team came home to Friendship Airport from a road trip to find 30 fans waiting, standing under umbrellas in a light rain. As their charter bus was filling up, a few players stood and signed autographs.

Second baseman Jerry Adair, hiding a can of beer in his raincoat, walked past this scene and from his seat at the rear of the bus began to ridicule.

"Look at those bush fans," he said. "Why don't they come out to the park and pay two-fifty? Damn, Baltimore is a bush town."

Despite the fact Adair holds four major-league fielding records, he was not playing. He had lost his job in spring training to Davey Johnson, a rookie, and he openly showed his unhappiness. Now he sipped his beer and looked around for someone to needle.

"Damn, Blefary got 20 hours' sleep and went 0-for-4," he said. "Me and my roomie got two hours' sleep and my roomie was 1-for-1."

"Hey, Robinson?" Adair said, meaning Frank, who was then hitting .400. "I'm going to work on you now. I got Blair shut up. He's down to .200. I want to catch your act in August, when you're only hitting .300."

"You may not be here in August," Robinson said, not even raising his voice. The line was well delivered and drew laughs. Suddenly the tension was gone out of the incident.

Jerry Adair quietly finished his beer then and rolled the can the length of the aisle. It was the way Robinson did it that was significant to the Orioles. He didn't cut Adair down hard. He didn't even demand the last word and, as he had guessed, the second baseman was traded to the White Sox in June.

Another speculation about Frank Robinson when he came to Baltimore was: How would he get along with Brooks Robinson, the gentle-mannered Arkansan who is the team's established star and its spokesman? The Orioles depend so heavily on Brooks that a bad press-box joke goes, "At 9:30 tonight, Brooks Robinson dropped dead at third base. At 9:45, manager Bauer decided to remove him from the lineup."

Frank has made no effort, other than that of his day-to-day performance, to challenge Brooks's position. And, except for the nine or more innings they are together on the field, they go their separate ways. But both are professional ballplayers beyond anything else, and each has a strong professional respect for the other.

"Frank got a lot of print when he came over," Brooks says, "and he deserved it. Looking at the records, he's the best ever to play for Baltimore. And he has taken over as team leader. I don't project the way he does. He can talk about hitting, and I can't. When he talks about hitting to the young players, they listen.

"But," Brooks adds quickly, so there is no misunderstanding, "I don't want to be second best, not even to Frank. As for which of us is No. 1, I think I am. We'll just have to see how it works out. All I know is that having Frank here is good for me because I try harder."

Frank is the higher-priced Robinson, earning about $62,000, $5000 more than Brooks, but Bauer will make no comparisons between his back-to-back batting stars. He knows only that the Orioles with two Robinsons are given their best chance to win a pennant since the moribund franchise of the St. Louis Browns was moved to Baltimore in 1954. In the 13 years since, the Orioles have challenged the league with 223 players, including the likes of Jehosie Heard, Frank Zupo and Angelo Dagres. But the '66 challengers, in addition to the Robinsons, are thoroughgoing major-leaguers—shortstop Luis Aparicio; Boog Powell, the 240-pound, freckle-faced first baseman; cocky Blefary; the rookie find, catcher Andy Etchebarren, and what Bauer calls "the best bullpen in baseball."

The Orioles's manager still wears his 1949 gold-and-diamond World Series ring. He also has eight other Series souvenirs from the years he played right field for the New York Yankees in much the same way that Frank Robinson now plays it for Baltimore.

"We had a saying on the Yankees," he remarked one day recently. "When someone didn't run going down to first or eased up in some way, one of us would get on him. 'Stop fouling up our Series money,' we'd tell him.

"Well, most of my guys are kind of quiet out there. But Frank, he has the same idea we had on the Yankees. He speaks up. He's not afraid. He's after that Series check."

18

Jackie Robinson

I know how difficult it can be to concentrate on baseball when you have added pressures from outside the game. In 1969, the Vietnam War Moritorium came right in the middle of our World Series with Baltimore. Since I had made known my views against the war—I believe an athlete has as much right to do that as an insurance salesman or a politician—I was asked to wear a black armband that day. I had to say no. I wasn't going to do anything that would disrupt my concentration on the game, especially in the World Series. I felt I owed that to myself and my team-mates.

So I can imagine what kind of ballplayer Jackie Robinson must have been, to enter the game in a storm of controversy, to carry the burden of being the first black in modern base-ball, to take all the abuse he did, and still concentrate on the game enough to become one of its great stars. Not letting that kind of pressure disrupt your performance takes a strong man.

Robinson was also a player who could put pressure on others, especially pitchers. As a base runner, he was a master of psychology. He could not only steal bases, but he knew just how to disrupt a pitcher's concentration.

Lou Brock is that kind of base runner. He steals bases when his team needs them. He puts the pressure on late in the game. When I'm faced with a runner like Brock is or Robinson was, I draw an imaginary line off the base beyond which I won't let the runner go. When he's on first, I watch him out of the corner of my eye as he takes his lead until he comes to a stop. I won't let him have a walking lead; if he takes off for second, it's going to be from a standing start. If he takes his lead beyond that imaginary line, I'll throw to first. Even though I won't have much chance of picking him off, I'll still throw, and throw every time he reaches the line, until he cuts down his lead. It drains a base runner's energy to keep busting back into first, especially if I'm turning and throwing quick. Rather than tire himself out, the runner usually will cut back on his lead.

Base running was just one of Robinson's skills. He was a great hitter and fielder, too. But most important, he delivered in clutch situations, as a ballplayer and as a man.

The Ten Years of Jackie Robinson
•

Roger Kahn

When the Brooklyn Dodgers are at home, Jackie Robinson may visit the United Nations on a Monday afternoon and discuss sociology with a delegate. "There is still a little prejudice in baseball," he will remark, "but we have reached the point where any Negro with major-league ability can play in the major leagues." That Monday night, Robinson may travel to Ebbets Field and discuss beanballs with an opposing pitcher. "Listen, you gutless obscenity," he is apt to suggest, "throw that obscene baseball at my head again and I'm gonna cut your obscene legs in half." If Jackie Robinson is an enigma, the reason may be here. He can converse with Eleanor Roosevelt and curse at Sal Maglie with equal intensity and skill.

As Robinson approaches the end of his tenth and possibly final season in organized baseball, he is known in many ways by many people.

Because in the beginning, Robinson endured outrage and vituperation with an almost magic mixture of humility and pride, there are those who know him as a saint.

Because today, Robinson fights mudslinging with mudslinging, and sometimes even slings mud first, there are those who know him as a troublemaker.

Because Robinson destroyed baseball's shameful racial barrier, there are those who know him as a hero.

Because in the ten seasons Robinson has turned not one shade lighter in color, there are those who know him as a villain.

Although Jackie Robinson is, perhaps, no longer baseball's most exciting player, he is still its most controversial one. The world of baseball is essentially simple. The men in the light uniforms—the home team—are the good guys. They may beat little old ladies for sport, they may turn down requests to visit children in hospitals, but on the field, just so long as their uniforms are white, they are the good guys. The fellows in the dark uniforms are bad. They may defend the little old ladies and spend half their time with the sick, but as soon as they put on gray traveling uniforms, they become the bad guys.

The one modern player who does not fit the traditional pattern is Robinson. He has been booed while wearing his white uniform at Ebbets Field. He has been cheered as a visiting player in Crosley Field, Cincinnati, or Busch Stadium, St. Louis. Robinson is not "of the Dodgers," in the sense that the description fits Pee Wee Reese or Duke Snider. First, Jackie is the Negro who opened the major leagues to his race. Second—but only second—he has been one of the Dodgers's most spectacularly effective stars.

As a ballplayer, Robinson has created one overwhelming impression. "He comes to win." Leo Durocher sums it up. "He beats you."

It is not as a Dodger star but rather as a man that Jackie arouses controversy. Ask 100 people about Robinson as an individual, and you are likely to get 100 different impressions.

"They told me when I went to Brooklyn that Robinson would be tough to handle," said Chuck Dressen, who managed the Dodgers from 1951 through 1953. "I don't know. There never was an easier guy for me to manage and there never was nothing I asked that he didn't do. Hit-and-run. Bunt. Anything. He was the greatest player I ever managed."

Walter O'Malley, who replaced Branch Rickey as Dodger president in 1951 but did not replace Rickey as Robinson's personal hero, has a different view. "Robinson," he insisted in an off-guard moment last May, "is always conscious of publicity and is always seeking publicity. Maybe it's a speech he's about to make, or a sale at his store, but when Robinson gets his name in the headlines, you can be sure there's a reason. Why, that business with Walter Alston in spring training, it was ridiculous. It was just another case of Robinson's publicity-seeking."

"I'll say this for Jack," Duke Snider declared, "when he believes something is right, he'll fight for it hard as anybody I ever saw."

"I'm just about fed up with Robinson fights and Robinson incidents and Robinson explanations," admitted a widely syndicated columnist. "He's boring. I'm going to heave a great big sigh of relief when he gets out of baseball. Then I won't have to bother with him any more."

"When I first came up, I was pretty scared by the big leagues," Carl Erskine recalled. "I remember how friendly Jackie was. I was just a kid. It's something you appreciate a whole lot."

"He's the loudest man around," an umpire said. "No, maybe Durocher is just as bad. But Robinson's gotta second guess every call and keep his big mouth going all the time."

"I've got to admire him," Ralph Kiner said. "He had a tough time when he was younger and he was a pretty rough character. That's no secret out on the Coast. But he's gotten over that now. You have to hand it to Robinson. He has come a long way and he's taken a hell of a lot but he's never stopped coming."

On the 1955 Brooklyn Dodgers, Jackie holds a peculiar position. In point of years he is an elder statesman, and in point of spirit he is a club leader. Yet he has no truly close friends among either white or Negro Dodgers.

Jackie is an inveterate card player and when the Dodgers travel, this passion seems to bring him near players with whom he cannot have much else in common. Frequently he plays with Billy Loes, a pitcher who walked out of the blackboard jungle and into the major leagues. Loes is interested in girls and, to a lesser degree, in baseball; he is interested in little else. Jackie's conversations with him occasionally run two sentences long.

"Boy, am I havin' lousy luck," Loes may offer.

"Your deal, Billy," is a typical Robinson reply.

Jackie rooms with Jim Gilliam, the young second baseman who usually has less to say than any other Dodger. Even when he might have roomed with Joe Black who, like himself, is a fluent and fairly sophisticated college man, he roomed with Gilliam. Robinson and Gilliam, in a sense, are business associates rather than friends, but Gilliam, during a recent burst of conversation, was able to cast a great deal of light on Robinson's relationship with other Negroes both in and out of baseball. "Some of my friends, when they hear I room with Jack, they say 'Boy, you room with him? Ain't he stuck up?' " Gilliam reported, "I tell them the truth. He's been wonderful to me. He told me about the pitchers and stuff like that, and how much I should tip and where I should eat and all that. He ain't been stuck up at all."

Inside the Brooklyn clubhouse, Robinson's position is more of what one would expect. He is a dominant figure. His locker is next to that of Gil Hodges. Next to Hodges's locker is a space occupied by a small gas heater, and on the other side of that sits Pee Wee Reese. As captain, Reese is assigned the only locker in the entire clubhouse that has a door.

Duke Snider is nearby and Reese's locker is one of the gathering points in the clubhouse. (The television set is another and that isn't far from Robinson's locker, either.) During clubhouse conversations, Jackie, like Reese and Erskine, is a club leader.

In many ways Jackie, after ten years, is the natural captain of the Dodgers. He is the team's most aggressive ballplayer and it has been suggested that had Robinson been white he would be captain now. Reese is the most respected of all Brooklyn players, but he doesn't have Robinson's fire.

To this day, a few Dodgers make occasional remarks about color. "Don't you think they're gonna take over baseball in ten years?" a player challenged a newspaperman earlier this year after a long and obviously fruitless conversation. "They can run faster; they'll run us white guys right out of the game." The player spoke sincerely. He has been happy to have Robinson on his side, but he is afraid that Robinson represents a threat. This ambivalent feeling is not uncommon on the Dodgers.

"The players were the easiest part of all," Jackie himself

insisted once when reviewing his struggle. "The press and fans made things a whole lot tougher." Robinson tends to say what he wishes were true and offer his wish as truth. The resentment of players obviously was among the most difficult obstacles he had to surmount. Robinson's introduction into the major leagues prompted Dixie Walker to ask that he be traded, and brought the St. Louis Cardinals to the verge of a player strike. A great deal of player resentment still remains, and in some cases Jackie's success has made it even stronger. Naturally, players who resent Robinson do not tell him so. Public proclamations of bigotry have virtually ended in baseball. Yet Jackie's subconscious awareness of resentment, plus the fact that resentment remains, are significant parts of any evaluation of his place on the Dodgers today. There has been integration. It has not been complete.

Jackie Roosevelt Robinson today is grayer, fatter, richer, and far more assured than he was ten years ago. He has built a handsome home set among three acres of rolling Connecticut woodland, but he has developed a nervous stomach. He has acquired considerable presence before a microphone; he is a good speaker.

We talked most recently one morning on a bumpy bus that carried the Dodgers from the Chase Hotel in St. Louis to the city's airport. Robinson is permitted to stay at the Chase and has been for the last two years. It is interesting to note that when the hotel management first suggested to the club that it was time the Negro players checked in at the Chase along with the rest of the Dodgers, certain qualifications were laid down. "They'll have to eat in their rooms," the hotel official said, "and they'll have to agree not to hang around the lobbies and the other public rooms." Told about the offer, Roy Campanella said he would pass it up. Roy wasn't going to stay anywhere he wasn't wanted. Don Newcombe, Jim Gilliam and Joe Black agreed. But

Jackie Robinson said he guessed the terms were all right with him, he would stay at the Chase. It was a wedge, anyway. So he did, and within an amazingly short time the hotel lifted all the bars and quietly passed the word that Jackie should consider himself just another guest and go where he pleased in the hotel and eat where everybody else ate. So now, because Jackie, eight years after he hit the big leagues, long after the "pioneering" days were supposed to be ended, was still willing to humble himself in order to advance the larger cause, all Negro ballplayers are welcome at the Chase—and another barrier has come down. Whereever Jackie goes, he encounters reminders of barriers that no longer exist because of himself.

"We feel," he began, "that . . ."

"Who is we?"

"Rachel and me," Robinson explained. Rachel, his wife, has played a tremendous role in the ten years of Jackie Robinson.

"Anyway," he said, "we feel that those barriers haven't been knocked down because of just us. We've had help. It isn't even right to say I broke a color line. Mr. Rickey did. I played ball. Mr. Rickey made it possible for me to play."

Of all the men Robinson has met in baseball, he considers Rickey "the finest, in a class by himself." Before the 1952 World Series, Jackie made a point of specifying that he wanted to win the Series for two people: "Rae and Mr. Rickey." Rickey was then general manager of the Pittsburgh Pirates and O'Malley had succeeded him as Dodger president. "But I wanted to let Mr. Rickey know where he stood in my book," Jackie explained.

"Aside from Mr. Rickey I haven't made any what you call real close friends in baseball," Jackie said. "I mean, I got a lot of respect for fellows. Pee Wee Reese."

I was taking notes on a bouncy bus. "Shall I write Durocher's name here, too?" I asked.

"No," Robinson said. "Don't write down Durocher. But I mean fellows like Gil Hodges. One of my biggest kicks was when I heard Ben Wade talking about me being a team man. It indicated to me a lot of guys have that feeling. I felt pretty happy about it."

"Are you pretty happy about most things?"

Robinson was carrying two large packages on his lap, juggling them as the bus swayed. "I don't think I can be any more contented than I am now," he said. "I've been awfully lucky. I think we've been blessed." He nodded toward the packages. "These are for Rae. Presents. We're very close. Probably it's because of the importance of what I've had to do. We've just gotten closer and closer. A problem comes up for me, I ask Rae. A problem for her, she asks me."

"What does she say about all the fights you get into?"

Jackie grinned. This had come up before. "Whenever I get in a real bad argument, I don't care about O'Malley or anything like that. I'm kinda worried about coming home. What's Rae gonna say? My real judge of anything is my family relations. That's the most important. The house, you know, it wasn't so important to me. Rae, it's something she always wanted for the kids. It's no real mansion. I mean there's only four bedrooms."

"Do *you* think you get involved in too many incidents?"

"If I stayed in a shell," Robinson said, "personally I could be maybe 50 percent better off in the minds of the little people. You know, the people that feel I should mind my place. But people that I know who aren't little, you know, people who are big in their minds, I've lost nothing by being aggressive. I mean that's the way I am, and am I supposed to try to act different because I'm Negro? I've lost nothing being myself. Here in St. Louis, you know how much progress in human relations we've made? Aggressiveness hasn't hurt."

"Suppose, Jack, you were to start in again. Would you be less aggressive? Would you act differently?"

Around Robinson on the bus, his teammates chattered among themselves. None bothered to eavesdrop. "I'll tell you one thing that would be different," Jackie said. "I sort of had a chip in the beginning. I was looking for things. Maybe in the early years I kept to myself more than I should have because of that chip. I think maybe I'd be more —what's the word?—outgoing. Yeah. I know that. I'd try and make friends quicker."

Jackie looked at his shoes, then glanced out the bus window. It was a factory neighborhood. The airport was still 20 minutes away. "I wouldn't be different about aggressiveness if I was doing it over again," he said. "I guess I'm an aggressive guy." Robinson stopped as if he were waiting for a refutation. "Funny thing," he said when none was offered, "about this whole business. A lot of times you meet white fellows from the South who never had a chance to mix. You find them more friendly than a lot of Northerners. It's the Northerners sometimes who make the fuss about aggressiveness."

Over the years, Jackie has been asked about retirement frequently. In 1952 he said difficulty with umpires was making him think of quitting. Since then he has repeatedly mentioned the thought of retirement from baseball, but only recently has he secured a high-paying job which is to start when his playing career ends. Robinson says he is now financially independent of baseball. He is playing only because he feels he owes the game a debt which he must repay by remaining in it as long as he can play well.

"I don't know about next year," he said. "It depends on the ball club: how much I can help the ball club. I'll be able to tell easy how much I can help, soon as I see the contract they offer me."

The bus pulled onto a concrete highway and, quite suddenly, the bouncing stopped. The sun had risen higher and heat was beginning to settle on St. Louis. It was going to be good to escape. There was only one other question I wanted to ask Jackie. His answer was not really satisfactory.

"The toughest stretch since I came into baseball?" he said. "I guess it was that Williams thing. I ran into Davey Williams at first base and there I was right in the middle of a big obscene mess again and I figured when I get home Rachel's gonna be sore and what the hell am I doing this for? I don't need it. I don't need the money. What for?" Jackie sometimes gets excited when he recalls something that is important to him and he seemed about to get angry all over again. Sal Maglie had thrown at a few Brooklyn hitters one game in May, and Robinson bunted to get Maglie within spiking distance. Maglie stayed at the mound and, instead, Davey Williams covered first after Whitey Lockman fielded the bunt. Jackie was out easily but he bowled over Williams as he crossed the base. Thereafter Maglie threw no more beanballs, and the Dodgers won the game, but Robinson, praised by some and damned by others, was a storm center again. As he thought of it, his anger rose.

"Wasn't it tougher in the early years?" I asked quickly.

"No," Jackie said. "In the early years I never thought of quitting. There was too much to fight for. With that Williams thing, I was fighting for nothing except to win. That was the toughest stretch I ever had to go through. I mean it."

If Robinson's evaluation of the Williams affair was valid, then he is the recipient of a lot of misplaced credit. Actually, his evaluation was wrong. The hardest thing Robinson ever had to do in baseball was the first thing he had to do—just be the first Negro in modern history to play organized ball. Almost willingly, he seems to have forgotten a great deal of his difficult past. Rarely now is there talk in baseball of the enormously courageous thing which Jackie accomplished.

On a train between Milwaukee and Chicago, Rube Walker, a reserve Dodger catcher from Lenoir, North Carolina, was talking about beanballs. "I don't like 'em no-how," he said.

"But what we see isn't so bad," said Dixie Howell, the Dodgers's No. 3 catcher, who lives in Louisville. "I was at Montreal when Robinson first broke in. Man, you never saw nothin' like that. Ev-y time he come up, he'd go down. Man, did they throw at him."

"Worst you ever saw?" asked Walker.

"By a long shot," Howell said.

Ballplayers are not demonstrative and Walker did not react further. This was in a dining car and his next words were merely "pass the salt, please." But he and Howell felt a matter-of-fact professional admiration for one of Jackie Robinson's many talents—his ability to get up from a knock-down pitch unfrightened.

To make a major point of a North Carolinian and a Ken-tuckian sharing admiration for a Negro would be wrong. After Jackie Robinson's ten years, Walker and Howell are not unique. The point is that after the ten years, Howell still regards the beanballs directed at Robinson by Inter-national League pitchers during the 1946 season as the most vicious he has ever seen. Jackie himself never mentions this. He cannot have forgotten it, nor is it likely that he has thrust the memory into his subconscious. But he would like to for-get it.

It is no small part of the ten years of Jackie Robinson that nobody any longer bothers to count the number of Negro players who appear on the field in a big-league game. There once was much discussion of what John Lardner called "the 50-percent color line." Branch Rickey described it as "the saturation point." When a major-league club first attempted to field a team of five Negroes and four white players, it was whispered, there would be trouble. There seemed to be an enormous risk in attempting to topple white numerical supremacy on a major-league diamond. Today the Dodgers can start Don Newcombe, Roy Campanella, Sandy Amoros, Jim Gilliam and Robinson without so much as a passing comment.

In October, 1945, William O'Dwyer was mayor of New York City, and Harry Truman was a rookie president. Dwight D. Eisenhower was wondering what new field he should try, because World War II had been over for two months. On the 23rd day of the month, Branch Rickey announced that the Brooklyn Dodgers had signed a 26-year-old Negro named Jackie Robinson and had assigned him to play for their Montreal farm team.

On the 24th day of October, the late William G. Bramham, commissioner of minor-league baseball, had a statement to make. "Father Divine will have to look to his laurels," Bramham told a reporter, "for we can expect Rickey Temple to be in the course of construction in Harlem soon." Exercising iron self-control, Bramham called Rickey no name worse than a carpetbagger. "Nothing to the contrary appearing in the rules that I know of," Bramham said with open anger, "Robinson's contract must be promulgated just as any other."

The day he announced the signing, Rickey arranged for Jackie to meet the press. "Just be yourself," he told him. "Simply say that you are going to do the best you can and let it go at that." Since more than 25 newspapermen flocked to the press conference, Robinson could not let it go at that.

"He answered a dozen questions," wrote Al Parsley in the Montreal *Herald*, "with easy confidence but no cocksureness. His was no easy chore . . . he was a lone black man entering a room where the gathering, if not frankly hostile, was at least belligerently indifferent." Robinson handled his chore splendidly; press reaction was generally favorable, although frank hostility was evident throughout much of baseball and in some newspaper columns.

Alvin Garner, the president of the Texas League, announced: "I'm positive you'll never see any Negro players on any teams in the South as long as the Jim Crow laws are in force."

Happy Chandler, commissioner of baseball, refused to comment.

Clark Griffith, president of the Washington Senators, who had long ignored clamor urging him to hire a Negro, suddenly accused Rickey of attempting to become "dictator of Negroes in baseball!"

Jimmy Powers, sports editor of the New York *Daily News*, a tabloid with the largest circulation of any newspaper in America, predicted: "Robinson will not make the grade in the big league this year or next. . . . Robinson is a 1000–1 shot."

Red Smith, writing in the now dead Philadelphia *Record*, summarized: "It has become apparent that not everybody who prattles of tolerance and racial equality has precisely the same understanding of the terms."

There was precious little prattling about tolerance in Florida that winter. In late February, Robinson flew from his California home to Daytona Beach, where the Montreal Royals were to train after a week of early drills at Sanford, a smaller town 20 miles distant. Jackie was cheerfully received by newspapermen, Dodger officials and Clay Hopper, the Mississippi-born manager of the Royals, but he was received in the established Southern tradition by the white citizens of Sanford. After two days of practice at Sanford, Robinson was forced to return to Daytona Beach. Before running him out of town, Sanford civic groups explained: "We don't want no *Nigras* mixing with no whites here."

At Daytona Beach, Jackie lived with a Negro family and encountered only isolated resistance. When the Royals traveled to Deland for an exhibition game with Indianapolis some weeks later, he was given another taste of democracy as it was practiced in Florida during mid-March of 1946.

As Robinson slid across home plate in the first inning of the game, a local policeman bolted onto the field.

"Get off the field right now," he ordered Robinson, "or I'm putting you in jail!"

Robinson claims that his first reaction was to laugh, so ludicrous did the situation seem. But he did not laugh. Then, as always in the South, Robinson had attracted a huge crowd, and as he faced the policeman, the crowd rose to its feet. The Indianapolis players, in the field, stood stark still, watching. Then Jackie turned and walked toward the dugout, and Clay Hopper emerged from it.

"What's wrong?" Hopper asked.

"We ain't havin' *Nigras* mix with white boys in this town," the policeman said. "You can't change our way of livin'. *Nigras* and white, they can't sit together and they can't play together and you know damn well they can't get married together."

Hopper did not answer.

"Tell that Nigra I said to git," the policeman said. And Jackie left.

Spring training ended on April 14, and when it did, the burden of living in the South was lifted from Jackie's shoulders. He had made the team, and when the 1946 International League season began, his job was pretty much limited to the field. Jackie had played shortstop for the Kansas City Monarchs when Clyde Sukeforth scouted him for Rickey in 1945, and he had tried out for the Royals as a shortstop. But the Royals owned a capable shortstop named Stan Breard and that, coupled with some questions about the strength of Robinson's arm, prompted a switch. As the 1946 season opened, Jackie Robinson was a second-baseman.

This was the season of the beanballs Dixie Howell remembers. It was the season in which a Syracuse player held up a black cat and shouted: "Hey, Robinson! Here's one of your relatives!" It was the season in which Baltimore players greeted Jackie with vile names and profanity.

But it was also the season in which beanballs so affected Robinson that he batted .349. And rather than answer the Syracuse player with words, Robinson replied with a double that enabled him to score the winning run. Rather than match names with the Baltimore players, he stole home one night and drew an ovation from the Baltimore fans. Probably 1946 was baseball's finest year, for in 1946 it was proved that democracy can work in baseball when it is given a chance.

At times during the 1946 season, Branch Rickey would travel from Brooklyn to Montreal for talks with Robinson. "Always," Rickey once said, "for as long as you are in baseball, you must conduct yourself as you are doing now. Always you will be on trial. That is the cross you must bear."

"I remember the meeting when Rickey said that," a man in the Dodger organization said. "Jackie agreed, too." The man chuckled. "I guess Jack's sort of changed his mind over the years." But it wasn't until the place of Negroes in baseball was assured that Robinson's conduct changed.

Late in the 1946 season, the Dodgers found themselves involved in a close race with the St. Louis Cardinals, and there was pressure applied to Rickey to promote Robinson in August and September. For a while Rickey held his peace, but finally he announced: "Robinson is the property of Montreal and that is where he will stay. Montreal is going to be involved in a playoff and we owe it to our Montreal fans to keep Robinson there." Montreal, with Robinson, won the Little World Series. The Dodgers, without him, lost a pennant playoff to the Cardinals in two consecutive games.

There was little connection between the reason Rickey gave for not promoting Robinson and the reasons that actually existed. As far as he could, Rickey wanted to make Robinson's task easy. To do that he needed time. All through the winter of 1946–47 Rickey met with leaders of the American Negro community. Just as Robinson would be on trial as a major-leaguer, he explained, so would Negroes be as major-league fans. Working directly with Negro groups and indirectly through Negro leaders, Rickey worked to make sure there would be as little friction in the grandstand as possible. While barring Negroes from play, the owners had not refused to allow them to buy tickets, of course, and the idea of Negroes in big-league stadiums was nothing new. Yet, with Robinson on the Dodgers, a whole new set of circumstances applied to the old idea. Rickey's caution was rewarded in 1947 and in Robinson's first major-league season there was not one grandstand incident worthy of note.

In another foresighted move, Rickey shifted the Dodger and Montreal training camps to Havana, where the air was free of the fierce racial tensions that throbbed in America's South. Finally, Rickey did not place Robinson on the Dodger roster before spring training started. He wanted the Dodgers first to see Jackie and to recognize what a fine ball-player he was. Then, Rickey hoped, there would be a sort of mass demand from Dodger players: "Promote Robinson." This just was not to be. Leo Durocher, who was then managing the Dodgers, is a man totally devoid of racial prejudice, but some of Durocher's athletes thought differently.

Dixie Walker wanted to be traded and wanted other Dodgers to join with him in protest against Robinson. Eddie Stanky wasn't sure. Happily, Walker found few recruits, and his evil influence was countered by that of Pee Wee Reese, a Kentucky gentleman. "The first time I heard Robinson had been signed," Reese said, "I thought, what position does he play? Then I found out he was a shortstop and I figured, damn it, there are nine positions on the field and this guy has got to be a shortstop like me. Then I figured some more. Maybe there'd be room for both of us on the team. What then? What would the people down around home say about me playing with a colored boy? I figured maybe they wouldn't like it, and then I figured something else. The hell with anyone that didn't like it. I didn't know Robinson, but I knew he deserved a chance, same as anybody else. It just didn't make any difference what anybody else had to say. He deserved a chance."

While the Dodgers trained in the city of Havana, Montreal drilled at Havana Military Academy, 15 miles away. The team was quartered at the school dormitory, but Robinson, who had been accompanied by a Negro pitcher named John Wright during 1946 and now was one of four Negroes in the Brooklyn organization, was booked into a Havana hotel. This meant 30 miles of travel daily and Robinson, unable to understand the reason for a Jim Crow pattern in Cuba, asked Rickey about it. "I can't afford to take a chance and have a single incident occur," Rickey answered. "This training session must be perfectly smooth."

For two weeks Montreal played exhibitions with a Dodger "B" squad and then the Royals and the Dodger regulars flew to Panama for a series of exhibitions. Shortly before the trip, Mel Jones, then business manager of the Royals, handed Robinson a first-baseman's mitt. "Listen," Robinson said, "I want to play second base. Didn't I do all right there last year?" Jones said he was sorry. "Just passing an order down from the boss," he said. "Mr. Rickey wants you at first base." Robinson did not do badly at first base in the Panama series, and in the seven games he batted .625 and stole seven bases. This was the demonstration Rickey had awaited. Unprejudiced Dodgers said they were impressed. Prejudiced Dodgers insisted that they were not. "I've seen hot-hittin' bushers before," one said. After the series the teams flew back to Cuba, and late one night Rickey passed along word to Robinson that on April 10 he was to become a Dodger. Eddie Stanky was the Dodger second-baseman. Robinson would have to play first.

Happy Chandler's suspension of Leo Durocher had taken the spotlight away from Robinson by the time April 10 arrived, and in retrospect Jackie insists he was just as glad to have a respite from publicity. The Dodgers had not asked for his promotion and as a whole their reception was cool. Robinson in turn remained aloof.

Jack has dark memories of 1947. He was reading in the club car of a train once while several other Dodgers played poker. Hugh Casey, the pitcher, was having a hard time winning a pot, and finally he got up from the table and walked over to Robinson. Without a word Casey rubbed Robinson's head, then turned and went back to his card game.

In 1947, Burt Shotton, who replaced Durocher, put Robinson second in the Brooklyn batting order. On several occasions Dixie Walker hit home runs with Robinson on base, but at no time did Jackie follow baseball custom and shake Walker's hand at home plate. "I wasn't sure if he'd take my hand," Robinson said, "and I didn't want to provoke anything."

In 1947 the Philadelphia Phillies, under Ben Chapman, rode Robinson so hard that Commissioner Chandler interceded.

But there are other memories of 1947 for Robinson; more pleasant ones. Jeep Handley, a Philadelphia infielder, apologized for Chapman's name-calling. Clyde Sukeforth, a coach under Shotton, never once left Robinson's corner. Hank Greenberg told him: "Let's have a talk. There are a few things I've learned down through the years that can help make it easier for you."

One player on the Chicago Cubs attempted to organize a strike against Robinson, but was unsuccessful. The situation on the St. Louis Cardinals was more serious. Only splendid work by Stanley Woodward, a magnificent newspaperman who at the time was sports editor of the New York *Herald-Tribune*, brought the story to light. Only forthright work by Ford Frick, the president of the National League who has since become baseball commissioner, killed the Cardinal strike aborning.

The original Cardinal plan, as exposed by Woodward, called for a strike on May 6, date of the team's first game against the Dodgers. "Subsequently," Woodward wrote, "the St. Louis players conceived the idea of a general strike within the National League on a certain date." An uncompromising mandate from Frick to the players who were threatening to strike went like this: "If you do this, you will be suspended from the league. You will find that the friends you think you have in the press box will not support you, that you will be outcasts. I do not care if half the league strikes. All will be suspended. . . . This is the United States of America and one citizen has as much right to play as any other."

If, in all the ten years of Jackie Robinson, there was a single moment when the success of his mission became assured, then it was the instant Frick issued this directive. It is impossible to order people to be tolerant, but once the price of intolerance becomes too high, the ranks of the bigots tend to grow slim.

For Robinson, 1947 was very much like 1946. He never argued with an umpire. When Lenny Merullo, a Chicago infielder, kneed him, Jackie checked the punch he wanted to throw. When Ewell Blackwell stopped pitching long enough to call him a long series of names, Robinson said only: "Come on. Throw the ball." Then he singled.

But gradually the web of tension in which Robinson performed began to loosen. In the spring of 1948, the Ku Klux Klan futilely warned him not to play in Atlanta. But by the summer of '48, Robinson had relaxed enough to argue with an umpire. This was in Pittsburgh, and he was joined by Clyde Sukeforth. The two argued so violently that they were ejected.

Robinson became a major-league second baseman in 1948,

but, except for an appearance before the House Committee on Un-American Activities, it was not a notable year for him. Called to Congress to refute Paul Robeson's statement that American Negroes would never fight against the Soviet Union, Robinson delivered an eloquent speech. Rickey and Lester Granger, head of the Urban League, a National Negro organization, helped him write it and applause came from all sides. On the field, however, Robinson slumped. He had grown fat over the winter and not until 1949 was Robinson to regain top form.

The Dodgers finished third in 1948 but in 1949, when Robinson won the batting championship and a Most Valuable Player award, they won the pennant. By '49 Robinson felt free to criticize umpires whenever the spirit moved him; by '50 he was feuding with umpires and Leo Durocher and by '51 he was just about as controversial as he is today.

Currently Robinson will call a newspaperman down when he feels the reporter has been biased or inaccurate. Two seasons ago he had his most interesting argument with a reporter. Dick Young, of the *Daily News*, had written somewhat sharply about Robinson and then made a customary visit to the dugout before a Dodger game in Philadelphia. A few minutes before game time nearly all the Dodgers were seated in the dugout and Young was standing nearby talking. "If you can't write the truth, you shouldn't write," Robinson shouted quite suddenly from his seat.

Unaware that Robinson was shouting at him, Young continued talking. "Yeah, you, Young," Robinson hollered. "You didn't write the truth."

George Shuba, the Dodger sitting next to Robinson, was studying the floor. Other Dodgers were staring at left field. None was saying anything.

"Ever since you went to Washington, Robinson," Young screamed as he attempted to seize the offensive, "your head has been too big."

"If the shoe fits," Robinson shouted, "wear it."

"Your head is big," Young screamed.

"If the shoe fits wear it," Robinson shouted.

The screaming and shouting continued until game time, when Young left for the press box and Robinson devoted his attention to his job. "I couldn't let him get away with yelling at me in front of the whole team," Young said later. Relations between the two were cool for a while but time has healed the rift.

This season Robinson called down Francis Stann, a Washington columnist, before an exhibition game in Griffith Stadium. Stann had quoted an anonymous third party as saying that Robinson was about through and Robinson lashed him mercilessly and profanely.

"What good can that possibly do?" someone asked Robinson. "You'll only make an enemy."

"I can't help it," Robinson said. "I get so mad I don't know what I'm saying."

Why get so angry at newspapermen, who as a class are not more bigoted or biased than lawyers, congressmen or physicians? Well, newspapermen have hurt Robinson and in his lifetime Robinson has been hurt more than any man should be.

When a Dodger kicked in the door to the umpires' dressing room at Braves Field in 1951, a Boston reporter blamed Robinson for the kicking. "I'm sorry, Jackie," the reporter said when he was told the truth. "It was right on the deadline and I didn't have time to check."

Another newspaperman once stole Robinson's name to use as a byline on a story consisting of lies and opinions with which Robinson did not agree. This was during a period of racial tension on the Dodgers and the reporter's piracy put Robinson in the position of lying about the most important cause in his life. No one could take this in stride, of course, but Robinson took it particularly badly.

The rantings at reporters are well-known in the newspaper

business and possibly because they have made him a formidable target for all but the most bull-voiced of critics, Robinson has almost reveled in his notoriety. But he gets along with most reporters most of the time and he occasionally makes an effort to help one.

Three springs ago during the period when Robinson was associated with a magazine, he fell to chatting in Miami with a newspaperman whose newspaper had just died. They talked vaguely of baseball for ten minutes before the newspaperman without portfolio ambled off in the general direction of a martini.

"He didn't take any notes," Robinson mused aloud. "I guess I didn't give him a story."

A bystander pointed out that the man's paper had folded. "Well, what's he doing down here?" Robinson asked.

"Looking for a job in baseball, maybe."

"Is he in a bad way?" Robinson said bluntly.

"He's not in a good way."

"Well, look," Robinson said. "He can write, can't he?"

"Sure."

"Well, look," Robinson repeated. "Tell him to go see the fellows at the magazine when he's in New York. I'll let them know he's coming and they'll give him some stories to write."

Robinson and the unemployed newspaperman had never been close. When a different sort of misfortune befell a sportswriter with whom he had been friendly, Robinson's reaction was even more direct and more swift. Telephoning about a luncheon, Robinson asked how things were and the sportswriter mentioned the death of a child.

"Oh, no," Robinson exclaimed. Instantly, he added: "How is your wife?"

"Not too bad."

"Is she home now?" Robinson asked.

"Yes."

"I'm going to call her," Robinson said and, without another word he hung up.

Later, the sportwriter's wife was explaining how much the call had moved her. "It wasn't just that Jackie called," she said. "It was the way he called. The first thing he said was: 'I hope my bringing this up doesn't upset you, but I just want you to know that I'm sorry.' That was a particularly sensitive thing to say. It was a lovely way to say something that I know must have been very hard for him to say at all."

There are assorted targets for Robinson's current wrath. He is a harsh bench-jockey, and his needling is sharper than it ought to be. Even when he is not angry, he is so intent upon speaking his mind, regardless of whom he may hurt, that he is often indiscreet.

Jackie Robinson will speak his mind. This American Negro born in Georgia, bred in California, loved and hated everywhere, will not sit in the back of a bus or call all white men "Mister." He does not drawl his words and he isn't afraid of ghosts and he isn't ashamed of his skin and he never ever says: "Yowsah, boss." This American Negro, this dark symbol of enlightenment, is proud and educated and sensitive and indiscreet and hot-tempered and warm-hearted.

Those who do not know Robinson will call him "troublemaker." Those who do not understand him will call him "pop-off guy." Perhaps both terms are right. Robinson has made trouble for bigots, more trouble than they could handle.

Branch Rickey, who supposedly is the finest scout in baseball history, chose Robinson with wisdom, that borders upon clairvoyance, to right a single wrong. Robinson had the playing ability to become a superstar, plus the intelligence to understand the significance of his role. He had the fighting temperament to wring the most from his ability and he had the self-control to keep his temper in check. Why has he let himself go?

One excuse might be that he has been called "nigger" a thousand times in ten baseball seasons; another is that he was scarred in his crusade. But, really Jackie Robinson doesn't need any excuse. If the man rugged enough to break baseball's color line turns out to be a thoroughly rugged man, no one has any license to be surprised.

19

Honus Wagner

Honus Wagner has always been a special favorite of mine among the old-time ballplayers. Perhaps it was because he seemed to be such a likable, genial person, a quality which shows through in this article by him, published in 1937.

I always think of old Honus with a slight smile on his face, helping out some young ballplayer. He was quite a contrast with his contemporary, Ty Cobb, who I think of with a frown on his face, being ornery to an opponent or a teammate. After they retired, Cobb was always belittling modern ballplayers, while Wagner happily conceded that the game was continuing to improve. That's another reason I like Wagner.

In the pre-Babe Ruth days, the argument over who was the greatest player in baseball always came down to Cobb vs. Wagner. Honus ranks fourth on the all-time list in total hits and in stolen bases; Cobb is first in both categories as well as in career batting average. But Wagner was much better in the field. While Cobb rated as only an average outfielder, Wagner was the greatest shortstop of his era. John McGraw called him the nearest approach to baseball perfection he'd ever seen.

Cobb and Wagner played in different leagues, but they did meet head-on once, when Cobb's Tigers faced Wagner's Pirates in the 1909 World Series. Cobb, a five-year veteran then, was only 22 years old; Wagner was 35. Cobb hit .231 and stole two bases, while Wagner batted .333 and stole six, and the Pirates won in seven games. It probably grated on young Cobb no end to be bested by the smiling Dutchman. But when the comparison in stolen bases was mentioned to Wagner, he merely said, "You can't steal bases unless you get on. And I just got on more times than Cobb."

Even back in the hard-nosed old days of baseball, Wagner showed that you could be a tough competitor and still be a gentleman.

I Never Got Tired of Playing
●

Honus Wagner

People always ask me how present-day baseball compares with the baseball of my time and often they don't believe me when I say it's better now. There were great players in the old days and men like Ty Cobb and Ed Delehanty and King Kelly would be as great now as they were then, but the general level is higher. The play is faster, the players are more businesslike and the pitching has to be stronger.

I got my start in the big leagues with Louisville in the old National League. That was a 12-club circuit and I went along to Pittsburgh when the transfer was made several years later and stayed there until I finished my career. Tommy Leach and I went to Louisville together and broke into the lineup right away but that didn't mean we were taken into the club. We were on the team all right but we didn't get a chance in batting practice. I tried to get in for a lick the first day and somebody looked at me and said: "Get out of there, kid, before I brain you with this bat." That was how things went in the old days. Tommy and I shagged flies while the other fellows hit.

After a week of that the manager said: "Why ain't you taking your licks?" and I said, "They won't let me," and he said, "Who won't let you?" and I said, "The other players," and he said, "You go up there and take your licks or *I'll* brain you with a bat." So I went up and pushed my way in and made a suggestive motion with my bat at the first man who tried to stop me and after that we had batting practice with the others.

Nowadays the club does everything for the new men but send out their laundry, and I think it's a better system. When I broke in, a newcomer literally had to fight his way into a job. The old-timers ganged together and hung onto their jobs and made it tough on the kids. You've probably heard about Cobb fighting everybody on the Detroit club before they would accept him; that is a true story. It happened on all the clubs. The first college man I ever met in baseball was Wills at Louisville. They tried to kill him. They'd come up close and throw the ball at him with all their might and then bawl him out if he didn't hold it. They didn't want sissies in the game and it was years before the college men were treated as anything but freaks.

I can give you an idea of the difference between present times and the old days by telling how we used to meet in the clubhouse before a game. The manager would say: "We lost to those bums yesterday. What are we going to do today? What are you going to do, Jake?" And Jake would say, "I'm going to bump that first baseman out into right field the first time I hit one. If I get on I'm going to cut that blankety blank at short from the ankle to the eyebrows when I go down." "Fine!" says the manager. And then it's decided that the outfielders should do most of the bumping

and spiking because they aren't covering the bases themselves and the other guys can't go out and get to them in
return. About this time the pitcher speaks up. "I guess I can
do a little something, too," he says, referring to dusting the
opponents off. And that was the old times. You've heard
tales about the players sharpening their spikes with a file, and
they are true.

Nowadays the club meets and discusses the other team.
What to pitch to Mel Ott, how to play for Babe Herman,
whether it's good policy to give Chuck Klein a low curve on
the outside. The game is much more scientific. The players
make it a business and they have the advantage of all the
experience gathered from 40 years of baseball.

In general I think the old-timers were crazier about the
sport. Jack Dots Miller, our second baseman on the Pirates,
was so nutty about the game that on rainy days he used to
go under the stands and play catch. I can never remember
getting tired of playing. I never went stale and I was as keen
at the end of the season as in spring training.

The most vital change in the game is the pitching. They
talk about the lively ball and I suppose it is better made than
it used to be, but what makes the difference in hitting is
the elimination of the spitball, the emery ball, the shiner.
The only way you could meet that type of pitching was to
choke the bat, watch every dip of the pitch and take only a
short swing. If they had grabbed the bat at the end and
taken the roundhouse wallop they use now, most of the
batters would still be trying to get their first hit. I don't
think I'd be able to hit at all with the long swing, lively ball
or not. The short swing was my style.

The best catch I ever saw was made by Jack "Red" Murray of the Giants. It was the ninth inning of a game in Pittsburgh, the Giants were one run ahead, there were two out
and I was on first base. As we had come to bat, the rain had
started. It was an electrical storm, with lots of thunder and

lightning and the Giants were stalling to get the game called and we were trying to hurry it. The pitcher finally threw one and the batter hit it on a line toward right field. By that time it was almost impossible to see the players through the rain and dusk, but that didn't seem to bother Murray. He started when the ball was hit, turned his back to the plate and pedaled toward the fence. Suddenly there was a flash of lightning and what the crowd saw was Murray jumping about a mile in the air and spearing that ball with his bare hand! There wasn't any doubt that he had caught it, for the whole field lighted up for that instant.

As I was saying before, the pitching has to be much better now. Trick deliveries have been ruled out, the half balk which held runners on base is barred, the quick pitch is no more. Men like Carl Hubbell and Dizzy Dean and Lon Warneke have to be magical with that ball to keep from being murdered. They have nothing but that ball and a glove and they have to put the apple past hitters who have taken a toe hold and know that there are no mechanical miracles coming from the mound.

The craziest play I ever took part in was the result of the quick pitch. There were three on and none out when I came up one day in Chicago with Three-Finger Brown pitching. I stepped into the box and before I had a chance to look up, Brown had slipped a quick pitch over the outside. Johnny Kling took it and slammed it down to second, catching the runner between bases. He started for third, the man on third started home and the fun waxed hot, with every player on the Cubs getting into it. The first result was that our men got back safely to third and second. The man on first, however, had wandered away in the excitement and Tinker banged the ball over to Chance, who had the runner trapped but muffed the ball, which rolled away a few feet. That started it all over again. The man from third dashed for home, Chance went back and got the ball and banged

it home—and it ended up after a wild chase with three men
out and me still standing there helplessly with the bat in my
hand!

When they make jokes about Brooklyn teams these days,
I never say a word. If you look into it you'll find that every
team has made a monkey of itself that way.

There was no fraternizing in the old days. I never talked
with an opposing player for three years after I broke in with
Louisville but one day when the Giants were playing us,
Gore, the left fielder, hit home runs the first two times up.
I was playing left field for Louisville and when I passed him
on the way in when the inning was ended, I said in a kindly
spirit:

"Nice hits there, Gore."

He turned around and gave me one of the hardest looks
I've ever had and growled: "Go to hell."

I stopped being friendly after that.

I've thought over an All-Time All-Star team for many
years, after playing with most of the old-timers and watching the newer stars. I suppose not many people will agree
with my full selection but I haven't done it lightly and I
feel that the men I have selected are the best by every test
which establishes the worth of a ballplayer. I never played
out of the National League and therefore confine myself to
that circuit. The only time I saw the American Leaguers
was in spring training and in an occasional World Series,
which doesn't make me an expert on the subject. My All-
Time All-Star National League team is:

Christy Mathewson	
Grover Cleveland Alexander	
Rube Waddell	Pitchers
Roger Bresnahan	
Johnny Kling	Catchers

Bill Terry	First Base
Rogers Hornsby	Second Base
Joe Tinker	Shortstop
Pie Traynor	Third Base
Fred Clarke	Left Field
Clarence Beaumont	Center Field
Willie Keeler	Right Field

People are generally surprised at the selection of Beaumont, but he was one of the best players who ever lived. I saw him beat out six infield hits in one game, which will give some idea of his speed.

As pinch-hitters on that team, I would pick either Moose McCormick or Sammy Strang of the New York Giants or Ham Hyatt of the Pirates. Good pinch-hitters are really a miracle. I don't know how they can hit at all, going in there cold; I know I never could do it.

I suppose I'm prejudiced in favor of the Pirates but the best thrower I ever knew was Chief Wilson, who could throw strikes to the bases from anywhere in right field. Red Murray was great, Chick Hafey was great and I hear that this DiMaggio is wonderful, but I never saw Wilson's equal. Lots of funny things happen in baseball but the most hilarious one to me was about the two rookies we once had on the Pirates. We were about nine runs behind one day and Fred Clarke decided to give them a chance to hit. The first boy was a fresh kid named Riggs and when the umpire asked him what his name was and who he was batting for, the kid yelled:

"My name is Riggs and I'm batting for myself!"

The ump was so dumbfounded he let him get away with it, but he was boiling with wrath. His temper wasn't made any better by the fact that Riggs slammed the first pitch for a single.

Clarke then sent the next kid up. He was a modest, retiring little fellow who never spoke unless spoken to, but he was a pretty good ballplayer. When he came up the umpire stuck his chin out and bellowed: "What's *your* name and who are you batting for?"

And the little kid drew his head in and looked scared and said in a tiny little voice: "Boo!"

With which the ump leaped about three feet in the air and began waving his arms and shouting: "Get out of the game! Get out of the park! Get out of my sight before I murder you!"

It took ten minutes' argument by Clarke to convince the ump that the boy's name really was Boo—Everett Boo, and in that period of time we almost laughed ourselves to death.

But baseball is always baseball. The game is even better now, as I say, and I have never worried about its future. I played 21 years in the National League with Louisville and Pittsburgh and had a few years of good ball still left when I quit. Barney Dreyfuss owned the club and he thought I was still as good as most shortstops but I was getting thrown out by a step or two on plays I used to make easily and I decided it was time to get out. After that I managed my own traveling semipro team for 11 years and had a lot of fun at it. Now I'm back as coach with the Pirates and the game means as much to me as it ever did. I'm 62 years old but my eyes are still so good (they've improved remarkably in the last few years) that I can trap pop flies at short and still hit the ball at the plate.

Individually, players don't vary much from year to year. The Waners would have been good ballplayers any time and Babe Ruth would have been a star with any kind of a team. John McGraw would have been smart no matter what sort of ball was being played.

We used to have a signal whereby I dropped my glove a bit lower an my knee when I wanted a throw from the catcher to trap a man off second. McGraw got wise to it one day and when I gave that signal the runner broke for third as soon as the throw started and made it standing up. I knew what had happened but didn't say anything, but in New York, on the next trip, I gave that same signal, the runner started and the catcher threw him out at third by a mile. McGraw was on the coaching lines at first and when the inning was over he looked at me with a sour look and said:

"You're pretty damned smart for a Dutchman at that."

Which I always thought was the best testimonial I ever had.

20

Ted Williams

Ted Williams claimed that hitting a baseball was the most difficult thing to do in all of sports, and I agree. So he did with hitting what I try to do with pitching—he reduced it to as exact a science as possible.

In a series of articles written after he had retired, Williams described his personal chart of the strike zone, in which he had figured out his average on pitches thrown in each section of the zone. He had his "happy zone"—waist high down the middle of the plate—where he figured he could hit .400. Against pitches on the very lower outside corner of the plate, though, he figured he could hit only .230.

If I pitched to Williams enough, I might be able to compile my own chart of his strike zone that would be almost as detailed as his.

Williams's first principal at the plate was to get a good ball to hit. He felt that a batter who swings at bad pitches will get nothing but bad ones from pitchers (whom he considered, as a breed, "dumb and hardheaded"). Williams calculated that by swinging at pitches just two inches outside the strike zone on every side, a batter increases the pitcher's target by 37 percent.

Everything Williams tried consciously to do when he was at the plate, I try consciously to break down. He knew his timing as a hitter to the millisecond; I try to know a hitter's timing so I can disrupt it. He knew just what his balance should be when swinging his bat; I try to throw a hitter off his normal balance.

If I were pitching to Williams I would do my best to make him violate his rule against swinging at pitches outside the strike zone. I would throw him breaking pitches that would start in the strike zone, but wouldn't end up there. If he didn't go for them, I guess I'd have to settle for that .230 area of his on the low outside corner.

That outside corner was his weakest area because Williams was emphatically a pull-hitter, probably the greatest ever. He was often criticized for trying to pull his hits to right field even when the defenses were stacked against him in the "Williams shift"—the center fielder playing in right-center, the left fielder in left-center, the shortstop behind second, etc. But if I were Ted Williams, I would do the same thing. What the "Williams shift" tried to do was make him hit away from his strength, and a great batter couldn't allow that. Willie Stargell, another great pull-hitter who faces the same kind of defense, once explained, "They can't catch it if I hit it over their heads."

Williams's studious attitude toward hitting a baseball helped him immensely as a ballplayer, I know, but I doubt it helped him much as a manager. He was such a perfectionist he probably couldn't understand why the players he tried to teach were so slow to learn. That might be why he doesn't seem anxious to take another managerial job.

Williams always went his own way. As John Updike writes in this article, no player ever had as dramatic an exit from baseball as Williams. His last game would have been a nice time for him to bury the hatchet with the Boston sportswriters, but he didn't. His final home run would have been a fine time for him to tip his hat to the fans, but he wouldn't. He wasn't going to let leaving his profession change his attitude. I have to confess a sneaking admiration for his consistency.

Hub Fans Bid Kid Adieu

•

John Updike

Fenway Park, in Boston, is a lyric little bandbox of a ball park. Everything is painted green and seems in curiously sharp focus, like the inside of an old-fashioned peeping-type Easter egg. It was built in 1912 and rebuilt in 1934, and offers, as do most Boston artifacts, a compromise between Man's Euclidean determinations and Nature's beguiling irregularities. Its right field is one of the deepest in the American League, while its left field is the shortest; the high left-field wall, 315 feet from home plate along the foul line, virtually thrusts its surface at right-handed hitters. On the afternoon of Wednesday, September 28, as I took a seat behind third base, a uniformed groundkeeper was treading the top of this wall, picking batting-practice home runs out of the screen, like a mushroom gatherer seen in Wordsworthian perspective on the verge of a cliff. The day was overcast, chill and uninspirational. The Boston team was the worst in 27 seasons. A jangling medley of incompetent youth and aging competence, the Red Sox were finishing in seventh place only because the Kansas City Athletics had locked them out of the cellar. They were scheduled to play the Baltimore Orioles, a much nimbler blend of May and December, who had been dumped from pennant contention a week before by the insatiable Yankees. I, and 10,453

others, had shown up primarily because this was the Red
Sox's last home game of the season, and therefore the last
time in all eternity that their regular left fielder, known to
the headlines as TED, KID, SPLINTER, THUMPER, TW, and,
most cloyingly, MISTER WONDERFUL, would play in Boston.
"WHAT WILL WE DO WITHOUT TED? HUB FANS ASK" ran the
headline on a newspaper being read by a bulb-nosed cigar
smoker a few rows away. Williams's retirement had been
announced, doubted (he had been threatening retirement
for years), confirmed by Tom Yawkey, the Red Sox owner,
and at last widely accepted as the sad but probable truth.
He was 42 and had redeemed his abysmal season of 1959
with a—considering his advanced age—fine one. He had
been giving away his gloves and bats and had grudgingly
consented to a sentimental ceremony today. This was not
necessarily his last game; the Red Sox were scheduled to
travel to New York and wind up the season with three
games there.

I arrived early. The Orioles were hitting fungoes on the
field. The day before, they had spitefully smothered the
Red Sox, 17–4, and neither their faces nor their drab gray
visiting-team uniforms seemed very gracious. I wondered
who had invited them to the party. Between our heads and
the lowering clouds a frenzied organ was thundering
through, with an appositeness perhaps accidental, "You
maaaade me love you, I didn't wanna do it, I didn't wanna
do it. . . ."

The affair between Boston and Ted Williams has been
no mere summer romance; it has been a marriage, composed
of spats, mutual disappointments and, toward the end, a mel-
lowing hoard of shared memories. It falls into three stages,
which may be termed Youth, Maturity, and Age; or Thesis,
Antithesis, and Synthesis; or Jason, Achilles, and Nestor.

First, there was the by now legendary epoch when the
young bridegroom came out of the West, announced, "All

I want out of life is that when I walk down the street folks
will say, 'There goes the greatest hitter who ever lived.'"
The dowagers of local journalism attempted to give elementary deportment lessons to this child who spake as a god,
and to their horror were themselves rebuked. Thus began
the long exchange of backbiting, bat-flipping, booing and
spitting that has distinguished Williams's public relations.
The spitting incidents of 1957 and 1958 and the similar dock-
side courtesies that Williams has now and then extended to
the grandstand should be judged against this background:
The left-field stands at Fenway for 20 years have held a
large number of customers who have bought their way in
primarily for the privilege of showering abuse on Williams.
Greatness necessarily attracts debunkers, but in Williams's
case the hostility has been systematic and unappeasable. His
basic offense against the fans has been to wish that they
weren't there. Seeking a perfectionist's vacuum, he has
quixotically desired to sever the game from the ground of
paid spectatorship and publicity that supports it. Hence his
refusal to tip his cap to the crowd or turn the other cheek
to newsmen. It has been a costly theory—it has probably
cost him, among other evidences of good will, two Most
Valuable Player awards, which are voted by reporters—but
he has held to it from his rookie year on. While his critics,
oral and literary, remained beyond the reach of his discipline, the opposing pitchers were accessible, and he spanked
them to the tune of .406 in 1941. He slumped to .356 in
1942 and went off to war.

In 1946 Williams returned from three years as a marine
pilot to the second of his baseball avatars, that of Achilles,
the hero of incomparable prowess and beauty who nevertheless was to be found sulking in his tent while the Trojans
(mostly Yankees) fought through to the ships. Yawkey, a
timber and mining maharajah, had surrounded his central
jewel with many gems of slightly lesser water, such as

Bobby Doerr, Dom DiMaggio, Rudy York, Birdie Tebbetts
and Johnny Pesky. Throughout the late '40s, the Red Sox
were the best paper team in baseball, yet they had little
three-dimensional to show for it, and if this was a tragedy,
Williams was Hamlet. A succinct review of the indictment
—and a fair sample of appreciative sports-page prose—appeared the very day of Williams's valedictory, in a column
by Huck Finnegan in the Boston *American* (no sentimenta-
list, Huck):

> Williams's career, in contrast [to Babe Ruth's], has
> been a series of failures except for his averages. He
> flopped in the only World Series he ever played in
> (1946) when he batted only .200. He flopped in the
> playoff game with Cleveland in 1948. He flopped in
> the final game of the 1949 season with the pennant
> hinging on the outcome (Yanks 5, Sox 3). He flopped
> in 1950 when he returned to the lineup after a two-
> month absence and ruined the morale of a club that
> seemed pennant-bound under Steve O'Neill. It has al-
> ways been Williams's records first, the team second,
> and the Sox non-winning record is proof enough of
> that.

There are answers to all this, of course. The fatal weakness of the great Sox slugging teams was not-quite-good-
enough pitching rather than Williams's failure to hit a
home run every time he came to bat. Again, Williams's de-
pressing effect on his teammates has never been proved. Despite ample coaching to the contrary, most insisted that they
liked him. He has been generous with advice to any player
who asked for it. In an increasingly combative baseball atmosphere, he continued to duck beanballs docilely. With
umpires he was gracious to a fault. This courtesy itself an-
noyed his critics, whom there was no pleasing. And against
the ten crucial games (the seven World Series games with

the St. Louis Cardinals, the 1948 playoff with the Cleveland Indians, and the two-game series with the Yankees at the end of the 1949 season, winning either one of which would have given the Red Sox the pennant) that make up the Achilles heel of Williams's record, a mass of statistics can be set showing that day in and day out he was no slouch in the clutch. The correspondence columns of the Boston papers now and then suffer a sharp flurry of arithmetic on this score; indeed, for Williams to have distributed all his hits so they did nobody else any good would constitute a feat of placement unparalleled in the annals of selfishness.

Whatever residue of truth remains of the Finnegan charge those of us who love Williams must transmute as best we can, in our own personal crucibles. My personal memories of Williams begin when I was a boy in Pennsylvania, with two last-place teams in Philadelphia to keep me company. For me, "W'ms, lf" was a figment of the box scores who always seemed to be going 3-for-5. He radiated, from afar, the hard blue glow of high purpose. I remember listening over the radio to the All-Star Game of 1946, in which Williams hit two singles and two home runs, the second one off a Rip Sewell "blooper" pitch; it was like hitting a balloon out of the park. I remember watching one of his home runs from the bleachers of Shibe Park; it went over the first baseman's head and rose meticulously along a straight line and was still rising when it cleared the fence. The trajectory seemed qualitatively different from anything anyone else might hit. For me, Williams is the classic ballplayer of the game on a hot August weekday, before a small crowd, when the only thing at stake is the tissue-thin difference between a thing done well and a thing done ill. Baseball is a game of the long season, of relentless and gradual averaging-out. Irrelevance—since the reference point of most individual games is remote and statistical—always threatens its interest, which can be maintained not by the occasional heroics that sportswriters feed upon but by players who always *care*; who care, that is to say, about themselves and their art. Insofar as the clutch hitter is not a sportswriter's myth, he is a vulgarity, like a writer who writes only for money. It may be that, compared to managers' dreams such as Joe DiMaggio and the always helpful Stan Musial, Williams is an icy star. But of all team sports, baseball, with its graceful intermittences of action, its immense and tranquil field sparsely settled with poised men in white, its dispassionate mathematics, seems to me best suited to accommodate, and be ornamented by, a loner. It is an essentially lonely game. No other player visible to my generation has concentrated within himself so much of the sport's poignance, has so assiduously refined his natural skills, has so constantly brought to the plate that intensity of competence that crowds the throat with joy.

By he time I went to college, near Boston, the lesser stars Yawkey had assembled around Williams had faded, and his craftsmanship, his rigorous pride, had become itself a kind of heroism. This brittle and temperamental player developed an unexpected quality of persistence. He was always coming back—back from Korea, back from a broken collarbone, a shattered elbow, a bruised heel, back from drastic bouts of flu and ptomaine poisoning. Hardly a season went by without some enfeebling mishap, yet he always came back, and always looked like himself. The delicate mechanism of timing and power seemed locked, shockproof, in some case outside his body. In addition to injuries, there were a heavily publicized divorce, and the usual storms with the press, and the Willaims Shift—the maneuver, custom-built by Lou Boudreau, of the Cleveland Indians, whereby three infielders were concentrated on the right side of the infield, where a left-handed pull hitter like Williams generally hits the ball. Williams could easily have learned to punch singles through the vacancy on his left and fattened his average hugely. This was what Ty Cobb, the Einstein of average, told him to do. But the game had changed since Cobb; Williams believed that his value to the club and to the game was as a slugger, so he went on pulling the ball, trying to blast it through three men, and paid the price of perhaps 15 points of lifetime average. Like Ruth before him, he bought the occasional home run at the cost of many directed singles—a calculated sacrifice certainly not, in the case of a hitter as average-minded as Williams, entirely selfish.

After a prime so harassed and hobbled, Williams was granted by the relenting fates a golden twilight. He became at the end of his career perhaps the best *old* hitter of the century. The dividing line came between the 1956 and the 1957 seasons. In September of the first year, he and Mickey Mantle were contending for the batting championship. Both were hitting around .350, and there was no one else near them. The season ended with a three-game series between the Yankees and the Sox, and, living in New York then, I went up to the Stadium. Williams was slightly shy of the 400 at-bats needed to qualify; the fear was expressed that the Yankee pitchers would walk him to protect Mantle. Instead, they pitched to him—a wise decision. He looked terrible at the plate, tired and discouraged and unconvincing. He never looked very good to me in the Stadium. (Last week, in *Life*, Williams, a sportswriter himself now, wrote gloomily of the stadium, "There's the bigness of it. There are those high stands and all those people smoking—and, of course, the shadows. . . . It takes at least one Series to get accustomed to the stadium and even then you're not sure.") The final outcome in 1956 was Mantle .353, Williams .345.

The next year, I moved from New York to New England, and it made all the difference. For in September of 1957, in the same situation, the story was reversed. Mantle finally hit .365; it was the best season of his career. But Williams, though sick and old, had run away from him. A bout of flu had laid him low in September. He emerged from his cave in the Hotel Somerset haggard but irresistible; he hit four successive pinch-hit home runs. "I feel terrible," he confessed, "but every time I take a swing at the ball it goes out of the park." He ended the season with 38 home runs and an average of .388, the highest in either league since his own .406, and, coming from a decrepit man of 39, an even more supernal figure. With eight or so of the "leg hits" that a younger man would have beaten out, it would have been .400. And the next year, Williams, who in 1949 and 1953 had lost batting championships by decimal whiskers to George Kell and Mickey Vernon, sneaked in behind his teammate Pete Runnels and filched his sixth title, a bargain at .328.

In 1959, it seemed all over. The dinosaur thrashed around in the .200 swamp for the first half of the season, and was even benched ("rested," manager Mike Higgins tactfully said). Old foes like the late Bill Cunningham began to offer batting tips. Cunningham thought Williams was jiggling his elbows; in truth, Williams's neck was so stiff he could hardly turn his head to look at the pitcher. When he swung, it looked like a Calder mobile with one thread cut; it reminded you that since 1953 Williams's shoulders had been wired together. A solicitous pall settled over the sports pages. In the two decades since Williams had come to Boston, his status had imperceptibly shifted from that of a naughty prodigy to that of a municipal monument. As his shadow in the record books lengthened, the Red Sox teams around him declined, and the entire American League seemed to be losing life and color to the National. The inconsistency of the new superstars—Mantle, Colavito, and Kaline—served to make Williams appear all the more singular. And off the field, his private philanthropy—in particular, his zealous chairmanship

of the Jimmy Fund, a charity for children with cancer—
gave him a civic presence somewhat like that of Richard
Cardinal Cushing. In religion, Williams appears to be a hu-
manist, and a selective one at that, but he and the cardinal,
when their good works intersect and they appear in the
public eye together, make a handsome and heartening pair.

Humiliated by his '59 season, Williams determined, once
more, to come back. I, as a specimen Williams partisan, was
both glad and fearful. All baseball fans believe in miracles;
the question is, how *many* do you believe in? He looked like
a ghost in spring training. Manager Jurges warned us ahead
of time that if Williams didn't come through he would be
benched, just like anybody else. As it turned out, it was
Jurges who was benched. Williams entered the 1960 season
needing eight home runs to have a lifetime total of 500; after
one time at bat in Washington, he needed seven. For a
stretch, he was hitting a home run every second game that
he played. He passed Lou Gehrig's lifetime total, then the
number 500, then Mel Ott's total, and finished with 521,
13 behind Jimmy Foxx, who alone stands between Williams
and Babe Ruth's unapproachable 714. The summer was a
statistician's picnic. His 2000th walk came and went, his
1800th run batted in, his 16th All-Star Game. At one point,
he hit a home run off a pitcher, Don Lee, off whose father,
Thornton Lee, he had hit a home run a generation before.
The only comparable season for a 42-year-old man was Ty
Cobb's in 1928. Cobb batted .323 and hit one homer. Williams batted .316 but hit 29 homers.

In sum, though generally conceded to be the greatest hitter of his era, he did not establish himself as "the greatest
hitter who ever lived." Cobb, for average, and Ruth, for
power, remain supreme. Cobb, Rogers Hornsby, Joe Jackson and Lefty O'Doul, among players since 1900, have
higher lifetime averages than Williams's .344. Unlike Foxx,
Gehrig, Hack Wilson, Hank Greenberg, and Ralph Kiner,

Williams never came close to matching Babe Ruth's season home-run total of 60. In the list of major-league batting records, not one is held by Williams. He is second in walks drawn, third in home runs, fifth in lifetime averages, sixth in runs batted in, eighth in runs scored and in total bases, 14th in doubles and 13th in hits. But if we allow him merely average seasons for the four-plus seasons he lost to two wars, and add another season for the months he lost to injuries, we get a man who in all the power totals would be second, and not a very distant second, to Ruth. And if we further allow that these years would have been not merely average but prime years, if we allow for all the months when Willaims was playing in sub-par condition, if we permit his early and later years in baseball to be some sort of index of what the middle years could have been, if we give him a right-field fence that is not, like Fenway's, one of the most distant in the league, and if—the least excusable "if"—we imagine him condescending to outsmart the Williams Shift, we can defensibly assemble, like a colossus induced from the sizable fragments that do remain, a statistical figure not incommensurate with his grandiose ambition. From the statistics that are on the books, a good case can be made that in the *combination* of power and average Williams is first; nobody else ranks so high in both categories. Finally, there is the witness of the eyes; men whose memories go back to Shoeless Joe Jackson—another unlucky natural—rank him and Williams together as the best-looking hitters they have seen. It was for our last look that 10,000 of us had come.

Two girls, one of them with pert buckteeth and eyes as black as vest buttons, the other with white skin and flesh-colored hair, like an underdeveloped photograph of a redhead, came and sat on my right. On my other side was one of those frowning, chestless young-old men who can frequently be seen, often wearing sailor hats, attending ball-games alone. He did not once open his program but instead tapped it, rolled up, on his knee as he gave the game his disconsolate attention. A young lady, with freckles and a depressed, dainty nose that by an optical illusion seemed to thrust her lips forward for a kiss, sauntered down into the box seats and with striking aplomb took a seat right behind the roof of the Oriole dugout. She wore a blue coat with a Northeastern University emblem sewed to it. The girls beside me took it into their heads that this was Williams's daughter. She looked too old to me, and why would she be sitting behind the visitors' dugout? On the other hand, from the way she sat there, staring at the sky and French-inhaling, she clearly was *some*body. Other fans came and eclipsed her from view. The crowd looked less like a weekday ball-park crowd than like the folks you might find in Yellowstone National Park, or emerging from automobiles at the top of scenic Mount Mansfield. There were a lot of competitively well-dressed couples of tourist age, and not a few babes in arms. A row of five seats in front of me was abruptly filled with a woman and four children, the youngest of them two years old, if that. Someday, presumably, he could tell his grandchildren that he saw Williams play. Along with these tots and second-honeymooners, there were Harvard freshmen, giving off that peculiar nervous glow created when a quantity of insouciance is saturated with insecurity; thick-necked army officers with brass on their shoulders and lead in their voices; pepperings of priests; perfumed bouquets of Roxbury Fabian fans; shiny salesmen from Albany and Fall River; and those gray, hoarse men—taxi drivers, slaughterers, and bartenders—who will continue to click through the turnstiles long after everyone else has deserted to television and tramporamas. Behind me, two young male voices blossomed, cracking a joke about God's five proofs that Thomas Aquinas exists—typical Boston College levity.

The batting cage was trundled away. The Orioles flut-

tered to the sidelines. Diagonally across the field, by the Red
Sox dugout, a cluster of men in overcoats were festering like
maggots. I could see a splinter of white uniform, and Williams's head, held at a self-deprecating and evasive tilt. Williams's conversational stance is that of a six-foot-three-inch
man under a six-foot ceiling. He moved away to the patter
of flash bulbs, and began playing catch with a young Negro
outfielder named Willie Tasby. His arm, never very powerful, had grown lax with the years, and his throwing motion
was a kind of muscular drawl. To catch the ball, he flicked
his glove onto his left shoulder (he batted left but threw
right, as every schoolboy ought to know) and let the ball
plop into it comically. This catch session with Tasby was
the only time all afternoon I saw him grin.

A tight little flock of human sparrows who, from the lam-
bent and pampered pink of their faces, could only have been
Boston politicians moved toward the plate. The loudspeakers
mammothly coughed as someone huffed on the microphone.
The ceremonies began. Curt Gowdy, the Red Sox radio and
television announcer, who sounds like everybody's brother-
in-law, delivered a brief sermon, taking the two words
"pride" and "champion" as his text. It began, "Twenty-one
years ago, a skinny kid from San Diego, California . . ." and
ended, "I don't think we'll ever see another like him."
Robert Tibolt, chairman of the board of the Greater Boston
Chamber of Commerce, presented Williams with a big Paul
Revere silver bowl. Harry Carlson, a member of the sports
committee of the Boston Chamber, gave him a plaque, whose
inscription he did not read in its entirety, out of deference
to Williams's distaste for this sort of fuss. Mayor Collins
presented the Jimmy Fund with a thousand-dollar check.

Then the occasion himself stooped to the microphone,
and his voice sounded, after the others, very Californian; it
seemed to be coming, excellently amplified, from a great
distance, adolescently young and as smooth as a butternut.

His thanks for the gifts had not died from our ears before he glided, as if helplessly, into "In spite of all the terrible things that have been said about me by the maestros of the keyboard up there. . . ." He glanced up at the press rows suspended above home plate. (All the Boston reporters, incidentally, reported the phrase as "knights of the keyboard," but I heard it as "maestros" and prefer it that way.) The crowd tittered, appalled. A frightful vision flashed upon me, of the press gallery pelting Williams with erasers, of Williams clambering up the foul screen to slug journalists, of a riot, of Mayor Collins being crushed. ". . . And they *were* terrible things," Williams insisted, with level melancholy, into the mike. "I'd like to forget them, but I can't." He paused, swallowed his memories, and went on, "I want to say that my years in Boston have been the greatest thing in my life." The crowd, like an immense sail going limp in a change of wind, sighed with relief. Taking all the parts himself, Williams then acted out a vivacious little morality drama in which an imaginary tempter came to him at the beginning of his career and said, "Ted, you can play anywhere you like." Leaping nimbly into the role of his younger self (who in biographical actuality had yearned to be a Yankee), Williams gallantly chose Boston over all the other cities, and told us that Tom Yawkey was the greatest owner in baseball and we were the greatest fans. We applauded ourselves heartily. The umpire came out and dusted the plate. The voice of doom announced over the loudspeakers that after Williams's retirement his uniform number, 9, would be permanently retired—the first time the Red Sox had so honored a player. We cheered. The national anthem was played. We cheered. The game began.

Williams was third in the batting order, so he came up in the bottom of the first inning, and Steve Barber, a young pitcher who was not yet born when Williams began playing for the Red Sox, offered him four pitches, at all of which he disdained to swing, since none of them were within the strike zone. This demonstrated simultaneously that Williams's eyes were razor-sharp and that Barber's control wasn't. Shortly, the bases were full, with Williams on second. "Oh, I hope he gets held up at third! That would be wonderful," the girl beside me moaned, and, sure enough, the man at bat walked and Williams was delivered into our foreground. He struck the pose of Donatello's David, the third-base bag being Goliath's head. Fiddling with his cap, swapping small talk with the Oriole third baseman (who seemed delighted to have him drop in), swinging his arms with a sort of prancing nervousness, he looked fine—flexible, hard and not unbecomingly substantial through the middle. The long neck, the small head, the knickers whose cuffs were worn down near his ankles—all these points, often observed by caricaturists, were visible in the flesh.

One of the collegiate voices behind me said, "He looks old, doesn't he, old; big deep wrinkles in his face. . . ."

"Yeah," the other voice said, "but he looks like an old hawk, doesn't he?"

With each pitch, Williams danced down the base line, waving his arms and stirring dust, ponderous but menacing, like an attacking goose. It occurred to about a dozen humorists at once to shout, "Steal home! Go, go!" Williams's speed afoot was never legendary. Lou Clinton, a young Sox outfielder, hit a fairly deep fly to center field. Williams tagged up and ran home. As he slid across the plate, the ball, thrown with unusual heft by Jackie Brandt, the Oriole center fielder, hit him on the back.

"Boy, he was really loafing, wasn't he?" one of the boys behind me said.

"It's cold," the other explained. "He doesn't play well when it's cold. He likes heat. He's a hedonist."

The run that Williams scored was the second and last of the inning. Gus Triandos, of the Orioles, quickly evened the score by plunking a home run over the handy left-field wall. Williams, who had had this wall at his back for 20 years, played the ball flawlessly. He didn't budge. He just stood there, in the center of the little patch of grass that his patient footsteps had worn brown, and, limp with lack of interest, watched the ball pass overhead. It was not a very interesting game. Mike Higgins, the Red Sox manager, with nothing to lose, had restricted his major-league players to the left-field line—along with Williams, Frank Malzone, a first-rate third baseman, played the game—and had peopled the rest of the terrain with unpredictable youngsters fresh, or not so fresh, off the farms. Other than Williams's recurrent appearances at the plate, the *maladresse* of the Sox infield was the sole focus of suspense; the second baseman turned every grounder into a juggling act, while the shortstop did a breathtaking impersonation of an open window. With this sort of assistance, the Orioles wheedled their way into a 4–2 lead. They had early replaced Barber with another young pitcher, Jack Fisher. Fortunately (as it turned out), Fisher is no cutie; he is willing to burn the ball through the strike zone, and inning after inning this tactic punctured Higgins's string of test balloons.

Whenever Williams appeared at the plate—pounding the dirt from his cleats, gouging a pit in the batter's box with his left foot, wringing resin out of the bat handle with his vehement grip, switching the stick at the pitcher with an electric ferocity—it was like having a familiar Leonardo appear in a shuffle of *Saturday Evening Post* covers. This man, you realized—and here, perhaps, was the difference, greater than the difference in gifts—really intended to hit the ball. In the third inning, he hoisted a high fly to deep center. In the fifth, we thought he had it; he smacked the ball hard and high into the heart of his power zone, but the deep right field in Fenway and the heavy air and a casual east wind defeated him. The ball died. Al Pilarcik leaned his back against the big "380" painted on the right-field wall and caught it. On another day, in another park, it would have been gone. (After the game, Williams said, "I didn't think I could hit one any harder than that. The conditions weren't good.")

The afternoon grew so glowering that in the sixth inning the arc lights were turned on—always a wan sight in the daytime, like the burning headlights of a funeral procession. Aided by the gloom, Fisher was slicing through the Sox rookies, and Williams did not come to bat in the seventh. He was second up in the eighth. This was almost certainly his last time to come to the plate in Fenway Park, and instead of merely cheering, as we had at his three previous appearances, we stood, all of us—stood and applauded. Have you ever heard applause in a ball park? Just applause—no calling, no whistling, just an ocean of handclaps, minute after minute, burst after burst, crowding and running together in continuous succession like the pushes of surf at the edge of the sand. It was a somber and considered tumult. There was not a boo in it. It seemed to renew itself out of a shifting set of memories as the kid, the marine, the veteran of feuds and failures and injuries, the friend of children, and the enduring old pro evolved down the bright tunnel of 21 summers toward this moment. At last, the umpire signaled for Fisher to pitch; with the other players, he had been frozen in position. Only Williams had moved during the ovation, switching his bat impatiently, ignoring everything except his cherished task. Fisher wound up, and the applause sank into a hush.

Understand that we were a crowd of rational people. We knew that a home run cannot be produced at will; the right pitch must be perfectly met and luck must ride with the ball. Three innings before, we had seen a brave effort fail. The air was soggy; the season was exhausted. Nevertheless, there will always lurk, around a corner in a pocket of our knowledge of the odds, an indefensible hope, and this was one of the times, which you now and then find in sports, when a density of expectation hangs in the air and plucks an event out of the future.

Fisher, after his unsettling wait, was wide with the first pitch. He put the second one over, and Williams swung mightily and missed. The crowd grunted, seeing that classic swing, so long and smooth and quick, exposed, naked in its failure. Fisher threw the third time. Williams swung again, and there it was. The ball climbed on a diagonal line into the vast volume of air over center field. From my angle, behind third base, the ball seemed less an object in flight than the tip of a towering, motionless construct, like the Eiffel Tower or the Tappan Zee Bridge. It was in the books while it was still in the sky. Brandt ran back to the deepest corner of the outfield grass; the ball descended beyond his reach and struck in the crotch where the bullpen met the wall, bounced chunkily, and, as far as I could see, vanished.

Like a feather caught in a vortex, Williams ran around the square of bases at the center of our beseeching screaming. He ran as he always ran out home runs—hurriedly, unsmilingly, head down, as if our praise were a storm of rain to get out of. He didn't tip his cap. Though we thumped, wept and chanted, "We want Ted," for minutes after he hid in the dugout, he did not come back. Our noise for some seconds passed beyond excitement into a kind of immense open anguish, a wailing, a cry to be saved. But immortality is nontransferable. The papers said that the other players, and even the umpires on the field, begged him to come out and acknowledge us in some way, but he never had and did not now. Gods do not answer letters.

Every true story has an anticlimax. The men on the field refused to disappear, as would have seemed decent, in the smoke of Williams's miracle. Fisher continued to pitch, and escaped further harm. At the end of the inning, Higgins sent Williams out to his left-field position, then instantly replaced him with Carrol Hardy, so we had a long last look at Williams as he ran out there and then back, his uniform jogging, his eyes steadfast on the ground. It was nice, and we were grateful, but it left a funny taste.

One of the scholasticists behind me said, "Let's go. We've seen everything. I don't want to spoil it." This seemed a sound aesthetic decision. Williams's last word had been so exquisitely chosen, such a perfect fusion of expectation, intention, and execution, that already it felt a little unreal in my head, and I wanted to get out before the castle collapsed. But the game, though played by clumsy midgets under the feeble glow of the arc lights, began to tug at my attention, and I loitered in the runway until it was over. Williams's homer had, quite incidentally, made the score 4–3. In the bottom of the ninth inning, with one out, Marlin Coughtry, the second-base juggler, singled. Vic Wertz, pinch-hitting, doubled off the left-field wall, Coughtry advancing to third. Pumpsie Green walked to load the bases. Willie Tasby hit a double-play ball to the third baseman, but in making the pivot throw Billy Klaus, an ex-Red Sox infielder, reverted to form and threw the ball past the first baseman and into the Red Sox dugout. The Sox won, 5–4. On the car radio as I drove home I heard that Williams had decided not to accompany the team to New York. So he knew how to do even that, the hardest thing. Quit.

DATE DUE

JUN 2 '83

MAR '84
MAY